100 GREATEST AMERICAN STAMPS

Janet Klug and Donald J. Sundman

Foreword by William H. Gross

Whitman Publishing, LLC
PUBLISHING SINCE 1934

Whitman Publishing, LLC
Atlanta, GA

100 GREATEST AMERICAN STAMPS

© 2007 Whitman Publishing, LLC

3101 Clairmont Road • Suite C • Atlanta GA 30329

The 100 Greatest colophon is a registered trademark of Whitman Publishing, LLC.

Correspondence concerning this book may be directed to the publisher,
Attn: 100 Greatest American Stamps, at the address above.

ISBN: 0-7948-2248-7

Printed in China

For a complete catalog of numismatic and philatelic reference books, supplies, and storage products, visit Whitman Publishing online at www.whitman**books**.com

CONTENTS

The story of how I became a stamp collector is like many others': I was introduced to the hobby by my mother when I was a kid growing up in Ohio. At that time I was fascinated by the beauty and intrigue of stamps from countries I had barely even heard of. Any stamp added to my collection at that time could have easily made my list of the 100 Greatest, as any one stamp that I did not already have was a "great" addition to my burgeoning collection. Back then I never even dreamed of ever owning stamps that now would be considered among the 100 Greatest American Stamps by serious philatelists.

But like almost all other collectors, as a teenager my attentions were naturally focused on other interests, followed by college, military service, starting a family, and building a business career. Stamps took a "back seat" to all of life's other priorities—but the thrill and excitement of collecting was still there, waiting for a time when I could go back to the hobby that gave me so much pleasure.

In the early 1990s I was drawn back to stamps—first in a modest way, but soon I was attracted to stamps that in my childhood years I could have never dreamed of owning. What really was an incentive was seeing old auction catalogs and philatelic handbooks that described and pictured stamps that were considered rare or desirable in some way. Seeing and reading about stamps that are among the elite of all collectible stamps was inspiring, even if I did not, or could not, own them. That is what makes the publication of *this* book so special to me. It pictures and describes stamps that are coveted by collectors at all levels. Whether or not one is privileged to own them is not as important as having the knowledge of their existence and learning more about their storied histories.

Over the past 15 years I have been very fortunate to acquire examples of many of what are here presented as the 100 Greatest American Stamps. I strongly feel that my obligation as a collector is to act as a "caretaker" for these fascinating stamps, until such time as they are once again placed back into the marketplace, in the custody of future caretakers. These collectors of the future will hopefully be inspired by the stamps described and pictured in this book. While it may be only a dream for some to own them, there will be those who will be fortunate enough to actually acquire them and call them their own!

William H. Gross
Laguna Beach, California

William H. Gross is a lifelong philatelic hobbyist, and the author of numerous articles and books on the bond market. He attended Duke University, graduating with a bachelor's degree in psychology; served as a naval officer off the coast of Vietnam; and earned an MBA from UCLA. His collection of United States classic stamps of 1847 to 1869 has won numerous prestigious philatelic awards and ultimately the Grand Prix National in Washington, 2006. In November 2005, Gross became the only philatelist to form a complete collection of 19th-century United States postage stamps, having traded his unique Inverted Jenny plate block for the only privately available 1868 1¢ Z Grill stamp. He and his family live in Laguna Beach, California.

Welcome to *100 Greatest American Stamps.* I'm writing this surrounded by millions of United States stamps, some rare and others not rare. I love them all for different reasons. Perhaps the most significant of all is that the great unfolding story of America is on our stamps.

Donald J. Sundman

We had great fun creating this book as we spoke with collectors from around the country about their personal favorites for the greatest American stamps. We hope you enjoy reading about their choices as much as we enjoyed putting this book together for you.

As we've spoken with collectors the most common question is, "Which stamp is #1?" Many made their selection based on rarity. In the end, we would not have been surprised if the Inverted Jenny, Scott #C3a, was selected as the greatest stamp based on its beauty, fame, value, and emotional connection with collectors and non-collectors around the world. One of the great news stories of 2006 involved the supposed use of an inverted Jenny to mail an absentee ballot to the election board in south Florida. The idea that someone might have used a stamp worth hundreds of thousands of dollars to mail a letter captured popular imagination.

We expected to see rarities in the 100 Greatest, and there are. Every collector knows of these remarkable rarities and dreams of owning them, so the voting was very close for the top 10 greatest stamps. For example, a single vote separated No. 5 from No. 6. Both stamps, rare and valuable, are highly prized by collectors.

Other collectors made their choices based on historical significance. America's first stamp, showing America's first postmaster general of the united colonies, seemed likely to garner the top spot. What could be more fitting than having the first U.S. stamp selected as No. 1 by collectors?

Less expected but particularly pleasing are the 20th-century definitives and modern commemoratives that were honored among the 100 Greatest American Stamps. These choices show that a collector of modest means can have as much fun with stamps as the wealthy royals who gave stamp collecting the name "hobby of kings."

In fact, many of the choices for the 100 Greatest American Stamps can be purchased for a few dollars or less. That's part of the romance of stamp collecting. As collectors, we can hold stamps that actually carried news of the 1857 Indian Rebellion, legal papers involved in the Supreme Court's Dred Scott decision, or the zany proclamations of Joshua Norton, the self-appointed "Emperor of These United States."

Stamp collectors are naturally curious, and we've included lots of fun and informative tales to satisfy that passion for knowledge. As you leaf through the following pages, you'll find interesting behind-the-scenes stamp stories, technical information, and neat trivia. Historic market value for each stamp is included to help you identify trends, compare stamp values, and understand the various elements that affect catalog values.

For your enjoyment, full-color pictures of some of the world's most famous philatelic items accompany our choices of the great American stamps. The famous Ice House Cover, the Tre Skilling yellow error stamp, and the controversial 24¢ Continental Banknote stamp are an important part of stamp collecting's rich lore and enhance the story of the 100 Greatest American Stamps.

We hope you enjoy reading *100 Greatest American Stamps,* and return to it often for information, advice, and inspiration. We also hope this book becomes a treasured family heirloom, one that introduces future generations to the world's greatest hobby!

Donald Sundman
Camden, New York

Donald Sundman is the president of Mystic Stamp Company, located in Camden, New York. He serves on the Philatelic Foundation's Board of Trustees and is actively involved with the American Philatelic Society. He has sponsored more than 4,900 collectors for membership—a record number in the history of the APS. Don serves as chairman of the National Postal Museum's Council of Philatelists and co-sponsors its Maynard Sundman Philatelic Lecture series.

The problem with selecting only 100 "greatest" American stamps is that thousands of terrific postage stamps, revenues, locals, and special-service stamps are not going to make the list. Only a hundred?

Janet Klug

Many of my personal favorites did not make the cut. The 4¢ U.S.–Japan Treaty stamp issued in 1960 is a good example. This lovely stamp features the Washington Monument with a branch from a cherry-blossom tree in the foreground. The stamp honors a treaty of friendship and commerce signed by Japan and the United States in 1960. Remarkably, the U.S. issued this stamp, an enduring icon of friendship between nations, a mere 15 years after the end of World War II, when the two countries were bitter enemies.

My favorite airmail stamp, Scott #C46, is an 80¢ denomination that illustrates an airplane flying over Diamond Head on the island of Oahu, Hawaii. Hawaii was a territory and not a state when this stamp was issued in 1952, but what about that 80¢ denomination at a time when it cost 6¢ to send an airmail letter? A clue is the color of the stamp. Maybe you would call it "orchid." The stamp was created to mail one-pound parcels of live orchids and flower leis from Hawaii to the mainland United States.

I am partial to the block of four 6¢ botanical stamps released on August 23, 1969, the day before the 11th International Botanical Congress commenced in Seattle, Washington. The day of issue also happened to be my wedding day. I would have used those stamps on my wedding invitations had they been released a couple of months earlier. Instead I used the July 16, 1969, California Settlement 6¢ stamp that showed the bells within a California mission belfry. It was the closest thing I could find to "wedding bells." Now we have Love stamps for brides to use on their wedding invitations. Stamps touch lives every day.

The 3¢ Fort Bliss centennial stamp released in 1948 (Scott #976) is a cool stamp. There is so much going on with it that you need a magnifying glass to see everything. A rocket blasts off within a central triangle, making this the first U.S. stamp to illustrate such a missile. Marching within the border that surrounds the central triangle is a parade of incongruous animals and objects. Look closely and you will see a camel that harkens back to the days when these animals transported mails in the southwestern U.S.; cavalry horses; and even a military tank in recognition of the Army's armored division based at Fort Bliss.

My all-time favorite U.S. stamp actually did make the top 100. It is the 1869 3¢ locomotive (Scott #114), finishing at No. 18 in the poll. This was the first individual stamp I ever purchased from a stamp dealer. I was eight years old and wanted a stamp that would go on the first page of my stamp album. I honestly did not have many choices that fit within my budget, but when I saw the

3¢ locomotive that was the one I wanted. I still have the stamp I purchased many, many years ago. I hope you enjoy reading the story about this great stamp and all the rest in the 1869 series.

Every stamp has a story. Stamps portray famous people, historic events, favorite animals, and scenic wonders. Stamp collectors form personal attachments to certain stamps. Some collectors even specialize in one stamp and learn everything they can about it, looking for printing varieties and seeking them used on envelopes in interesting, intriguing ways.

Only a hundred greatest? Consider it a starting place for thousands more great stamps and fascinating stories.

Janet Klug
Pleasant Plain, Ohio

Janet Klug began collecting stamps as a child and has been involved to varying degrees ever since. She writes regular columns in Linn's *and* Scott Stamp Monthly. *Janet has held a variety of offices in a number of philatelic organizations. She is past president of the American Philatelic Society, and was formerly chairman of the APS Committee on the Accreditation of National Exhibitions and Judges. She lives near Cincinnati, Ohio, with her husband.*

The authors would like to thank the following individuals and organizations for their contributions to this book. The **American Philatelic Society** contributed an image. **Harvey Bennett** of Matthew Bennett, Inc., contributed several images. **Charles Berg** provided several images. **Q. David Bowers** reviewed the book's galleys. The **British Library, Tapling Collection,** shared several images. **Edward A. and Joanne Dauer** contributed a currency note image. **Elvis Presley Enterprises** shared permission to reproduce the Elvis stamp. **David Feldman** contributed several images. **H.E. Harris & Co.** provided several images. **Bernard Heller** contributed several images. **Ken Lawrence** contributed an image. **Littleton Coin Company** contributed images of various coins and currency notes. **Yossi Malamud** of Inter-Governmental Philatelic Corporation helped with image permissions. The staff of **Mystic Stamp Company** assisted with images and research. **NASA** provided the image of John Glenn and John F. Kennedy for No. 29. The **National Postal Museum** contributed various historical and philatelic images. **Shreves Philatelic Galleries, Inc.,** contributed several images. **Siegel Auction Galleries** contributed several images. **United States Postal Service** stamp images © 2007 United States Postal Service; All Rights Reserved; Used With Permission.

Special thanks to **Terry Christmas** for her energy, effort, and enthusiasm for turning the concept into reality.

The following are among the philatelists—collectors, dealers, historians, and researchers—who participated in the voting for the *100 Greatest American Stamps:*

Michael E. Aldrich	Ken Lawrence
Michael Baadke	Joann Lenz
William H. Bauer	Thomas Lera
Daniel A. Brouillette	Ron Lesher
Cora B. Collins	Mike Milam
Leroy Collins	Charles Peterson
Allison Cusick	Paul Phillips
Richard Drews	Steven J. Rod
J.A. Farrington	Stephen L. Suffet
Tom Fortunato	Ross A. Towle
Ken Grant	Steve Walske
Barth Healey	Alan Warren
Eric Jackson	Kent M. Wilson
Jim Kotanchik	Wayne Youngblood

In 1840, Sir Rowland Hill revolutionized Great Britain's postal system. His innovations changed communication by lowering prices, simplifying the rate structure, and creating a postage stamp as a simple way to pay for a mailing a letter.

Prior to the changes, it cost 8 pence to send a one-page letter 50 miles and 12 pence for 150 miles. After the restructuring, a one-ounce letter cost just one penny, delivered anywhere in England.

In the 20th century, air travel would become common after the deregulation of the airline industry brought lower prices. In the 19th century, England's postage rates were similarly lowered, and mail volume increased. Lower prices encouraged people to write frequent letters to their friends and relatives and promoted a boon in communication. Mail volume more than doubled in the year following the issue of England's Penny Black, and increased after that. In 20 short years, more than 70 countries had joined the party by issuing their own postage stamps. It was a revolution in communication that quickly spread around the world.

The Penny Black.

The United States' First Postage Stamps

The United States issued its first national postage stamps on July 1, 1847. Copying Britain's plan, the nation implemented a uniform rate structure with lower fees. Five cents paid for a typical letter to travel up to 300 miles; 10¢ for destinations greater than 300 miles; and 40¢ from the East to the Pacific coast. As in England, the lower prices led to more mail being sent and more communication between Americans.

Two national icons grace the first United States stamps: George Washington, our first president, on the 10¢; and Ben Franklin, our first postmaster general, on the 5¢. The original specifications called for bi-color stamps with a red overprint, to thwart counterfeiters. Officials determined that the price was prohibitive, and the first U.S. adhesive stamps were issued in shades of brown and black.

Perforations hadn't been invented yet so the first stamps

1847 10¢ Washington.

1847 5¢ Franklin.

were issued imperforate, and postmasters were required to cut individual stamps from large sheets. Precise records of the number of stamps issued weren't kept, but estimates place the number of 5¢ stamps distributed at approximately 3.6 million, and the 10¢ at 864,000. The figures are interesting in light of the 1850 census, which reported more than 23 million people living in the United States.

Lower Rates With the Introduction of Mandatory Prepayment

In spite of the reforms, most letters sent in 1847 were sent stampless. Perhaps one in 50 letters mailed in the inaugural year bore a postage stamp. In 1851, when U.S. postal rates dropped to 3¢ to mail a letter anywhere in the country, prepayment of postal fees became mandatory. Mail volume continued to grow. Now families left back East wrote to their husbands and sons who were mining, hoping to strike gold in the hills of California, for just 3¢. For a few pennies, tales of the ice jam that stopped the flow of water over the mighty Niagara Falls traveled around the world, and the announcement of the birth of an infant named Thomas Edison was carried to friends and relatives who lived hundreds of miles away.

Timbromania Sweeps the Globe

Almost immediately, U.S. stamps captured imaginations, and collectors responded by saving them from destruction. Their early efforts preserved many great rarities for modern collectors.

The first collectors tended to be children and teenagers. Parents approved of the hobby, which proved to be a valuable way to learn history, economics, geography, and an awareness of global events. The hobby, known at the time as *timbromania* or *stamp madness*, (and today as *philately*), swept throughout Europe. One young woman in Paris reportedly wallpapered her bedroom with sheets of 100 French stamps.

By the late 1800s, many of the earliest collectors reached adulthood and began the systematic study of worldwide stamps. Stamp albums, catalogs, and stamp dealers all helped collectors enjoy their hobby. During the early 1900s, the increased number of stamp collectors drove prices upward and attracted the attention of postal administrations worldwide. Many stamps were issued recognizing that collectors were an important market.

The Hobby of Kings

Early in the 20th century stamp collecting became known as the "hobby of kings," as royalty and wealthy collectors pursued the world's greatest rarities. Remarkable amounts were paid for the treasures, and entertaining stories were added to the rich lore that is associated with stamp collecting.

An early story involved the legendary Mauritius two-pence blue and its 1904 sale. Over breakfast, a courtier asked the Duke of York if he had seen that "some damned fool" had paid 1,400 pounds for a single stamp. The prince replied, "I was that damned fool." It is said the future King George V spent three hours a day studying his stamps.

In the United States, a 1918 headline chided a purchase made by flamboyant multi-millionaire Colonel Edward H.R. Green: "E.H.R. Green Pays $20,000 For Hundred Spoiled Stamps." The colonel had the last laugh. Today the surviving Jenny Invert stamps have a combined estimated value in excess of $30 million!

In 1937, King Carol II of Romania paid 5,000 British pounds for the rare Swedish Tre Skilling yellow error stamp. Carol fled in a hail of gunfire three years later, taking his stamp collection as he left his kingdom to live in exile. Today the Tre Skilling yellow is one of the world's most desired and valuable stamps.

America's 32nd president, Franklin D. Roosevelt, began collecting stamps as a child. His collection included detailed notes about the various countries, the history of the stamps, and personal comments. Stricken with polio as a young adult, Roosevelt credited his hobby with helping him through the lengthy recuperation period.

Roosevelt was a passionate collector who shared his enthusiasm with others. During World War II, he appointed Joseph Kennedy to be the ambassador to Britain. In 1940, Kennedy's young son Robert wrote FDR to express his appreciation for the gift of stamps and an album:

> Dear Mr. President, I liked the stamps you sent me very much and the little book is very useful. I am just starting my collection and it would be great fun to see yours which mother says you have had for a long time. . . . Daddy, Mother, and all my brothers and sisters want to be remembered to you.
>
> *Bobby Kennedy*

Roosevelt's passion for stamps carried over into his terms in office. He was intimately involved in the design and subject of each of the 200 stamps released during his presidency. He also amended laws that prevented publishers from printing pictures of U.S. stamps in catalogs and album pages.

Roosevelt's personal collection included gifts from the celebrities of the day, particularly in the relatively new field of flight. Upon his death, the firm H.R. Harmer's auctioned off Roosevelt's collection, authenticating each piece with a rubber stamp indicating the item's provenance. A collector today can own a piece of history whose provenance can be traced directly to a president!

Collecting Gets Organized

As the hobby of stamp collecting spread from kings to commoners, the need for information led to a growth in organizations devoted to philately. The American Philatelic Society was founded in 1886. Today, it is the largest nonprofit stamp organization in the world, with more than 44,000 members in 110-plus countries. Formed in 1896, the Collectors Club of New York and Collectors Club of Chicago serve as meeting places for interested collectors to exchange information, share stories, and trade stamps.

Specialist stamp publications flourished, with *Linn's Stamp News* and *Meekel's* disseminating the latest information to the collecting community. Expertizing services that allow collectors to buy and sell stamps with confidence were founded. The Philatelic Foundation, chartered in 1945, maintains one of the largest philatelic libraries in the world.

Companies such as Scott and H.E. Harris developed album pages, designed specifically for mounting stamps. The *Scott Catalogue* developed a uniform numbering system, widely adopted, to help collectors and stamp dealers identify and describe their stamps. Dealers introduced approval services—a convenience that delivers stamps directly by mail, allowing collectors to examine stamps in the comfort of their home and make informed decisions.

A Mature Hobby

Interest in stamp collecting grew steadily through the post–World War II years, as the booming economy left people with increased leisure time and disposable income. A speculative boom

King George V (shown here on a Canadian 2¢ stamp) paid 1,400 pounds for a Mauritius two-pence blue. Of the 12 known today, only one example is in private hands. The used Mauritius two-pence blue is valued at $675,000.

Another royal collector, King Carol II of Romania (shown here on a silver 250-lei coin of 1939), paid 5,000 pounds for a rare Tre Skilling stamp in 1937.

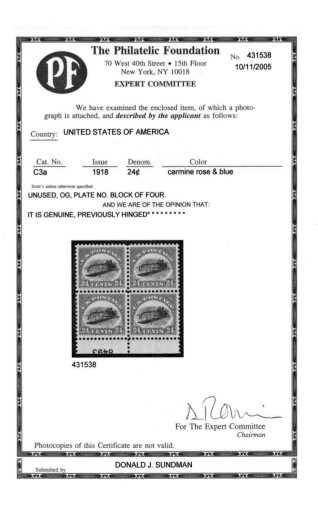

Benjamin and Joseph Adamowicz are believed to have been the first amateur pilots to make a trans-Atlantic flight. This cover, flown aboard their historic 1934 flight from New York City to Poland, was presented to President Franklin Roosevelt. The authentication stamp from H.R. Harmer's can be seen in the close-up below.

began in the late 1970s and peaked in the early 1980s, before the price of rare stamps declined and eventually stabilized to a level of healthy growth.

Recent events have captured America's attention and focused positive attention on stamp collecting. Public voting in the design selection for the Elvis Presley commemorative stamp (see No. 81) and in the content selection of the Celebrate the Century series introduced non-collectors to the wealth of stamp subjects.

The discovery of the CIA Invert mystery in 1987 (No. 66), the release of the Legends of the West sheet with the wrong image of Bill Pickett (see appendix B), the trade of the Jenny Invert Plate-Number Block for the 1868 1¢ Z Grill, and the ongoing discovery of unissued yellow "H" Hat stamps all keep stamp collecting in the news.

Grading Stamps

A few years ago Professional Stamp Experts (PSE) introduced numerical grading to the stamp hobby, emulating successful systems used for coins and sports cards. Third-party coin grading expanded the size of the numismatic market because collector-investors had confidence a particular coin would grade the same when they sold it as when they bought it. Before third-party grading, it was common for some coin dealers to grade a coin conservatively when buying and much more liberally when selling (buying at the Mint State–63 price, for example, and selling at the Mint State–65 price). The Philatelic Foundation (PF) quickly joined PSE by grading stamps on a 5–100 scale.

For years collectors have described stamps using *words* (Average, Fine, Very Fine, Superb, Never Hinged, etc.) to reflect their eye appeal. Many prefer this traditional system of grading stamps and bristle at the numerical system. The numerical system does have flaws but is easy to understand: 80 is higher, and thus "better," than 50. Numerical grading for highest-quality stamps (graded 90–100) is gaining traction with a new class of collectors who pay large premiums for very high grades.

Market observers predict numerical grading is here to stay and will exist side-by-side with the thriving trade in traditionally described stamps. Huge premiums paid for high-grade but common post-1935 stamps may be unsustainable; the attractive prices encourage dealers and collectors to submit additional well-centered stamps for grading, thereby increasing the supply.

Numerical Grade	Stamp Grade
100	Gem: • Four equal and large margins can be seen visibly. Difficult or impossible to find one margin smaller than the remaining three, even after close examination.
98	Superb: • Perfect in all respects—the finest quality. • A rare grade.
95	XF–Superb: • Very well centered design with at least one normal-sized margin.
90	Extremely Fine or Extra-Fine (XF): • Nearly perfect. • Well-centered design. Even margins all around. Perforations do not infringe into the design. Imperforates feature even margins that are wider than usual for the particular issue. • Light, neat cancels. • Mint stamps have original gum. • Rich, bright color. Clean, with perforations intact and no faults.
85	VF–XF: • Slightly off center in one or more directions, but with better centering than most examples. • Full, ample margins.
80	Very Fine (VF) • Design is well centered and balanced, with ample margins. • Imperforate stamps have three normal-sized margins. • Cancels are light and neat. • Mint stamps have original gum. • Rich, bright color. Clean, with perforations intact and no faults. • This is the grade typically used for catalog values.

Encapsulated Stamps

At first, PSE-graded stamps were sealed in hard plastic cases designed to protect the stamp and keep the stamp and its grade together, preventing anyone from pairing a lower-grade stamp with a high-grade certificate. Officially called "encapsulated" stamps, the widely used slang term "slabbed" became much more common.

Initially, traditional collectors treated encapsulated stamps with disdain because the bulky holders could not be mounted in albums or exhibits at stamp shows. A collection of encapsulated stamps was stored in a box where viewers flipped through the stamps, reminiscent of CD displays at Wal-Mart. After a few years, PSE modified the traditional "standalone" certificates collectors knew and loved to include a numerical grade, when the grade was requested. This new certificate has proven popular.

Philately Today

Today the hobby of kings is also the king of hobbies. Although the rarest stamps are owned by those with great wealth, collectors saving stamps from their own mail and trading duplicates with fellow collectors enjoy their hobby every bit as much as the multimillionaires. An estimated 25 million collectors across the United States continue the fine tradition of preserving these national treasures for future generations.

Stamp collecting is remarkably free of rules and encumbrances. Most people build a personalized collection by adding those stamps that appeal to their interests, be it for design, history, personal connection, or other reasons. This freedom invites diversity, which makes it difficult to define the "greatest stamps." In the following pages, we'll explore some of the most beloved American stamps. You'll discover extremely rare stamps and contemporary favorites as you fall in love with collecting for the first time, or all over again.

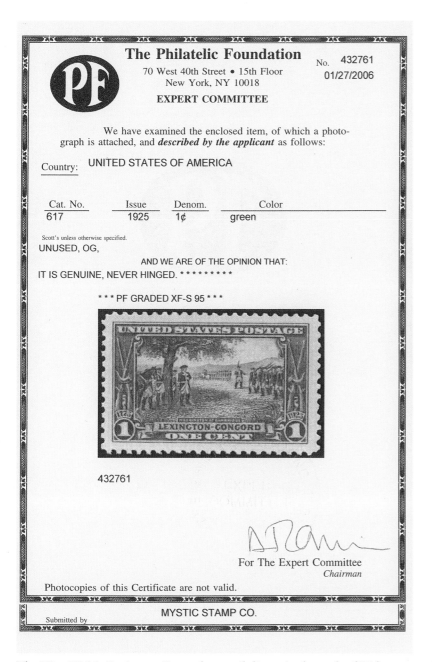

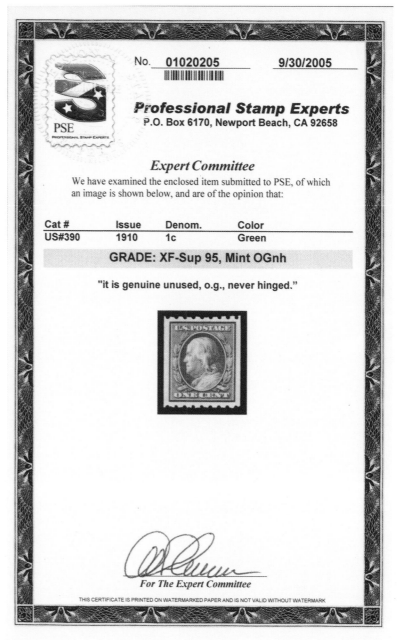

The Mint 1925 1¢ Lexington-Concord stamp (left) received a grade of 95 from the Philatelic Foundation. Notice the even centering, large margins, clean perforations, and fresh color. The Professional Stamp Experts assigned the 1910 1¢ Franklin (Scott #390, right) a grade of XF-Sup 95, which means that it is Extra Fine to Superb. Both stamps feature original gum and have never been hinged. More information on the Philatelic Foundation may be found on their web site at www.philatelicfoundation.org. The Professional Stamp Experts web site is www.psestamp.com.

In Mint, never-hinged condition, Scott #332 has a catalog value of $14. The same stamp with a grade of 100J (gem with jumbo margins) sold for $6,000 in August 2007.

Stamps do more than let us communicate through letters; they make a statement about who we are as Americans. They are symbols of our struggles and our strengths, of victory in war, progress in peace, and our faith in the future. Like little mirrors, United States stamps also reflect our cultural heritage, the important events that shaped our history, individuals of distinction, and the values we hold dear. Stamps chart the course of history, and, on occasion, change it. They reveal the fabric of life that makes Americans unique—our passionate pursuit of liberty, our dedication to the rights of every individual, and our quest to reach higher, understand more, and explore the unknown.

1492: Columbus Discovers the New World

The United States' first commemorative stamps were issued in conjunction with the 1893 Columbian Exposition, a celebration of the 400th anniversary of the discovery of the New World. The series of 16 commemorative stamps chronicle that event and are among the most desirable of all U.S. stamps. The 1¢ Columbian pictures Columbus sighting land on his first voyage, which he made in 1492. Convinced he had found the route to Asia, Columbus is credited today with introducing a new era in exploration and discovery.

Scott #230 commemorates the 400th anniversary of Columbus's voyage.

1587: Virginia Dare is Born

President Franklin D. Roosevelt personally designed the commemorative stamp honoring Virginia Dare, the first child of English descent to be born in America. The Virginia Dare stamp is the first truly square U.S. stamp, as well as the first printed in pale-blue ink. Virginia's parents and grandfather were members of a group of English colonists who settled on Roanoke Island in 1587. Her grandfather returned to England for supplies nine days after Virginia was born. Upon his return in 1590, he discovered that the entire colony of 116 people had disappeared without a clue.

This 1937 commemorative honors the 350th anniversary of Virginia Dare's birth.

1773: The Boston Tea Party Sparks a Revolution

In 1976, the U.S. issued a se-tenant depicting the Boston Tea Party as part of its Bicentennial celebration. The Boston Tea Party was a protest by England's American colonists against excessive taxation. On the night of December 16, 1773, the Sons of Liberty crept aboard three ships anchored in Boston Harbor and dumped more than 45 tons of tea from the ships' holds into the water. In response, Britain passed the "Intolerable Acts"—oppressive measures that helped fuel unrest throughout the colonies and led to the American Revolution.

1925 Lexington-Concord issue.

1789: The United States Elects Its First President

The 150th anniversary of George Washington's inauguration was commemorated in 1939. Washington led the Continental Army to victory in the American Revolution, and was chosen to be the nation's first president. The Electoral College vote was unanimous, as it would be again in 1792, a situation that has never been duplicated in American history. Insisting that lofty royal titles be abandoned in favor of democratic address, Washington rejected "His Highness" for "Mr. President." He served two four-year terms in office before retiring to Mount Vernon.

1939 Washington Inauguration 150th-anniversary commemorative.

1803: The Louisiana Purchase Fuels Westward Expansion

1903 10¢ Louisiana Purchase Centennial commemorative.

Fearful that French concessions allowing U.S. interests to operate in the Port of New Orleans would be revoked, President Thomas Jefferson sent a delegation to Paris to negotiate the purchase of the city. To their surprise, Napoleon Bonaparte authorized the sale of the port and 530,000,000 acres west of the Mississippi River for approximately 3¢ per acre, nearly doubling the size of the United States. Three commemorative stamps were issued in 1903 in conjunction with the Louisiana Purchase Exhibition, celebrating the centennial anniversary of the historic event.

The 150th anniversary of the purchase was celebrated in 1953.

1848: Gold is Discovered at Sutter's Mill

Series of 1851–1857 3¢ Washington.

Two 1851 3¢ Washington stamps satisfied the postal rate for letters sent from coast to coast, bringing news of the California Gold Rush and the "forty-niners." More than 300,000 people moved to California following the discovery of gold at Sutter's Mill on January 24, 1848. The population of San Francisco swelled from 1,000 to more than 25,000 in just two years as prospectors and the agencies needed to support them flooded into California. The rapid expansion created several "boomtowns," and helped pave the way for California statehood in 1850.

1948 Gold Rush centennial commemorative.

1858: The Lincoln–Douglas Debates Enthrall a Divided Nation

Scott #222.

One hundred years after they were held, the Lincoln-Douglas debates were remembered for the eloquence of both candidates. Republican hopeful Abraham Lincoln challenged Democrat incumbent Stephen A. Douglas for the Illinois U.S. Senate seat in 1858. The candidates met for a series of seven debates that focused on slavery, a topic that was dividing the country. Although Lincoln was defeated in the election, his stand on slavery was widely reported in the national newspapers, which earned him the 1860 presidential nomination.

1958 Lincoln–Douglas debate centennial commemorative.

1860: The Pony Express Delivers Election News in Record Time

Pony Express garter stamp.

The Pony Express began in 1860, carrying vital documents and news to Western outposts and the California coast in record time. Eight days after the 1860 elections, Californians learned that Lincoln had won the presidency, threatening to plunge the nation into Civil War. An early secession crisis was diverted when news of a high-ranking officer's treachery was carried by Pony Express from California to President Lincoln. Throughout the buildup to the war, the Pony Express carried military communications, news, and calls for volunteers.

1940 Pony Express commemorative.

1861: Shots Are Fired at Fort Sumter

The 1961 Fort Sumter commemorative stamp chronicles the opening volleys of the American Civil War. Fort Sumter in Charleston Bay (South Carolina) remained under the control of the Union after the state seceded on December 20, 1860. Shots rang out at Fort Sumter on April 12, 1861, as the Confederates took control of the stronghold. President Abraham Lincoln immediately called for militias to retake the property, beginning the first military campaigns of the devastating American Civil War.

At the outbreak of the Civil War, the Series of 1861–1862 replaced the demonetized Series of 1858–1861.

4¢ stamp of the Civil War centennial series.

1863: The Civil War Rages

The Union issued the 3¢ Washington.

Postal service between the Union and the Confederate States of America was suspended effective June 1, 1861. Existing federal postage stamps were demonetized (rendered invalid) to prevent their use in the South, and new stamps were issued. In spite of limited resources, the Confederacy produced its own postage stamps. Letters sent to loved ones from Northern prisoner-of-war camps required a U.S. stamp to prepay postal rates in the North and a Confederate stamp to prepay the Southern rate.

The Confederate States of America issued the 2¢ Jackson.

1865: The Civil War Ends

Milestones and heroes of the American Civil War are popular U.S. stamp subjects. The war ended with General Robert E. Lee's surrender to Ulysses S. Grant at Appomattox Courthouse on April 9, 1865. Five days later, the Stars and Stripes was ceremoniously raised over Fort Sumter, the site of the opening shots of the Civil War. Later that evening, President Lincoln was assassinated by John Wilkes Booth in a plot to overthrow the federal government. Grant was elected president in 1869, while Lee served as president of Washington College.

1867: Seward's Folly is Purchased

The 1909 Alaska–Yukon commemorative stamp honors Secretary of State William Seward, who negotiated the purchase of six million acres of frozen tundra from Russia for $7.2 million in 1867. The purchase was widely criticized in newspapers, and Congress delayed the appropriation of money for more than a year. Seward was vindicated in 1896, when the great Klondike gold rush began, and again during World War II when Alaska proved to be a strategic military location. Alaska became a territory in 1912, and was granted statehood in 1959.

Secretary of State William Seward was responsible for the purchase of Alaska.

1869: The Transcontinental Railroad is Completed

The 3¢ Locomotive pictorial stamp was issued in 1869, the same year the transcontinental railroad was completed. The railroad, which linked the East and West coasts, was one of the greatest technological feats of the 19th century. Prior to its completion, the journey could only be made by wagon across the plains or by ship around South America—each was a four-month journey. The transcontinental railroad was completed on May 10, 1869, at Promontory, Utah. Travel time from coast to coast was reduced to less than one week, which helped boost the economy of the American West.

The transcontinental railroad linked the East and West coasts.

1908: The Model T Revolutionizes American Industry

Henry Ford's contributions to the way America lives, works, and travels was recognized in the Prominent Americans series. Ford's 1908 Model T was the first affordable automobile, largely due to his innovative production procedures. Ford discarded individual handcrafting in favor of an assembly line, which slashed the amount of time required to produce a vehicle. Workers at the Ford Motor Company were also paid substantial wages, which provided an instant market for the Model T. Ford's business and production models were adopted by many major corporations worldwide.

Henry Ford was honored in the 1965–1981 Prominent Americans series.

1914: Mothers are Honored With a National Holiday

In 1934, President Franklin D. Roosevelt authorized a Mother's Day commemorative stamp based on James McNeill Whistler's acclaimed painting of his mother, Anna. President Woodrow Wilson had proclaimed the second Sunday in May as a national holiday in honor of mothers in 1914. His action followed years of lobbying, first by Julia Ward Howe, who wanted a day for mothers dedicated to peace, and later by Anna M. Jarvis, a Philadelphia schoolteacher.

In 1940, J.A. McNeill Whistler was commemorated in the Famous Americans series.

1917: The World is Embroiled in War

The sinking of several American merchant ships prompted the U.S. to enter the Great War on April 6, 1917. The American Expeditionary Force began mobilizing to France in June, with 10,000 "doughboys" arriving each day until the force was one million strong. Special booklet panes of 30 1917 1¢ and 2¢ Washington stamps were produced for the forces to use while overseas. The stamps were only in use for a few months during unfavorable conditions, and the stamps were not widely collected at the time. Fewer than 200 of the 2¢ panes are estimated to survive today.

1918: Communication is Revolutionized

The first scheduled airmail service was introduced on May 15, 1918. Although World War I limited the resources of the Bureau of Engraving and Printing, a special 24¢ bi-color stamp was ordered. The design pictured a Curtiss JN-4 airplane in patriotic red, white, and blue. Although the day was marked by the discovery of inverted stamps, empty gas tanks, and a pilot who flew in the wrong direction, a new era in communication had begun. Within a few months, the service was deemed a success and the cost of mailing a first-class letter decreased to 6¢.

Although it was the first U.S. airmail stamp, the 1918 24¢ Jenny was assigned *Scott Catalogue* #C3.

1918: The Allies Achieve Victory in Europe

As Europe struggled to recover from the devastation caused by World War I, America extended its hope for peace with a commemorative stamp issued on March 3, 1919. Entitled "Victory," the commemorative pictures the allegorical figure of the Goddess of Liberty Victorious holding a sword and the scales of justice. In recognition of America's allies, the flags of Great Britain, Belgium, and Italy appear in the background next to the U.S. flag. The 3¢ stamp paid the postage for a first-class letter, a rate that was reduced to the pre-war amount in June of 1919.

General John J. Pershing led the American Expeditionary Force to victory in World War I, mentoring a generation of soldiers who would be among the most famous generals of World War II.

1919: Relief Supplies are Sent to War-Torn Europe

As all of Europe tried to rebuild in the wake of World War I, Russia faced the dual plagues of revolution and famine. Over time, Europe required 34 million metric tons of food to feed 83 million men, women, and children at an estimated cost equal to $50 trillion in today's wages. Average Americans provided much of the humanitarian relief by mailing packages containing food, clothing, and medical supplies franked with the $2 Madison and $5 Marshall stamps of the Series of 1916–1917.

1927: Lindbergh Flies Solo

Like the flight it commemorates, the 1927 10¢ Spirit of St. Louis air-mail stamp is historic. It was the first stamp honoring a living person to include the honoree's name in the inscription, and the first airmail stamp to be produced in booklet form. Within one week of Charles Lindbergh's daring solo non-stop flight from New York to Paris, officials were overwhelmed with requests for a tribute stamp. Sales were brisk, and the Spirit of St. Louis proved to be the most popular U.S. airmail stamp to date.

Spirit of St. Louis

1929: The Stock Market Crashes

Issued in 1928, the 2¢ Washington stamp was current when the stock-market crash ended the euphoria of the Roaring Twenties. Vast fortunes were lost overnight, and the nation was plunged into the Great Depression. America's financial hardships affected every industrial nation around the world, causing a global depression that lasted nearly 10 years. In 1932, presidential candidate Franklin D. Roosevelt campaigned on a platform that promised a "new deal" and hope to the American people. Roosevelt was elected, and aggressive programs designed to improve the economy were implemented.

FDR is credited with steering the nation out of the Great Depression.

1932: A Stamp Collector Wins the Presidential Election

President Roosevelt began his first term in office in 1933. A life-long stamp collector, he was actively involved in the subject selection and design of every stamp issued during his three terms in office. Roosevelt frequently sketched his ideas on paper, and many of the hand-drawn models survive today. Among his successes are the Presidential Series ("Prexies") and the National Parks Issue. Roosevelt is also credited for his effective use of design and message during World War II, when the symbolism of U.S. commemorative stamps brought hope to a war-weary world.

FDR was personally involved in the design of every U.S. stamp issued during his administration.

1941: "A Date Which Will Live in Infamy. . ."

Japan's surprise attack on U.S. naval forces in Pearl Harbor pushed America into World War II. Americans gathered around radio sets on May 7, 1941, as news of the attack and the deaths of more than 2,400 military personnel and civilians reached the mainland. President Franklin D. Roosevelt addressed Congress the following day, describing the attack as "a date which will live in infamy." Congress passed a declaration of war against Japan on the same date. Throughout the prolonged war, the 1/2¢ Franklin stamp paid various make-up rates for third-class mail.

The 1/2¢ Franklin was current at the time of the attack on Pearl Harbor.

1941–1945: World War II Rages

The simple yet powerful "Win the War" stamp was issued to show America's resolve during the global conflict. With more than 20 billion issued, Win the War was the predominant stamp of its era and a welcome sight on letters to servicemen stationed overseas. The Win the War stamp featuring an American eagle was issued on Independence Day, 1942. Singapore and the Philippines had fallen to the Japanese Empire, but the U.S. had just delivered a stunning defeat at the Battle of Midway. In spite of the victory, it was clear that the world was embroiled in a protracted war on many fronts.

More than 100 million servicemen from 61 nations fought in World War II.

1954: A Supreme Court Decision Ushers in the Civil Rights Movement

In 1954, news of a landmark Supreme Court case was carried around the world. The court case reversed an earlier decision, one in which it had ruled that segregated schools could provide equal educational opportunities to black and white students. In *Brown v. Board of Education of Topeka*, the Supreme Court declared that separate public schools based on race were inherently unequal. The decision paved the way for the integration of public facilities and was an important milestone in the Civil Rights movement.

1954 "Eagle in Flight" Airmail.

1963: One Brief, Shining Moment That Was Known as Camelot

The 1964 Kennedy memorial stamp was issued to a nation that was still in mourning for its fallen leader. The 5¢ stamp pictures the charismatic president and the eternal flame that burns next to his grave together with a line from his inaugural speech. Kennedy's assassination marked the end of 1950s innocence, and helped set the stage for the disillusionment of the turbulent '60s. In the years that followed, the Vietnam War, civil rights, and the assassinations of Martin Luther King Jr. and Robert Kennedy cast a shadow on our nation.

The Eternal Flame.

1969: One Giant Step for Mankind

President John F. Kennedy's dream of landing a man on the Moon and safely returning him to Earth was realized on July 20, 1969. With an estimated 500–700 million television viewers watching, astronaut Neil Armstrong became the first man to walk on the Moon. The historic event was a clear victory for the United States, which had been embroiled in a race to demonstrate its technological superiority over the Soviet Union. The U.S. successfully completed five additional manned lunar landings—the only nation to do so.

A record number of people watched the televised 1969 lunar landing.

1989: The Berlin Wall Falls

Once an icon of oppression and Cold War hostilities, the infamous Berlin Wall fell in November 1989. Built in the aftermath of World War II, the wall had separated West Berlin from East Berlin for 28 years. The wall was built by the Communist government of East Germany to separate its citizens from democratic West Germany. The heavily guarded barrier divided the once-united nation, and prevented East Germans from crossing into the west to pursue lucrative employment and freedom from the oppressive Communist regime. Following months of unrest, the Soviet government announced it would allow border crossings on November 9. In a peaceful revolution, thousands of Germans from both sides of the Berlin Wall swarmed the barrier and reunited. Within months, the Soviet Union collapsed. United States president Ronald Reagan, who once challenged Soviet leader Mikhail Gorbachev to "tear down this wall," is credited with helping to bring about its fall.

The fall of the Berlin Wall was one of the defining moments of the Reagan presidency.

1997: *Pathfinder* Explores the Surface of Mars

Following a seven-month voyage, *Mars Pathfinder* reached the surface of the red planet on July 4, 1997. A stationary lander and a remote-controlled vehicle named *Sojourner* descended to the surface of Mars. *Pathfinder* sent 16,000 images from the lander and 550 images from the rover back to Earth. In addition to providing pictures taken on Mars, the mission took 15 soil samples from the planet's surface, conducted experiments, and gathered weather data. In honor of the achievement, the U.S. issued a $3 Priority Mail stamp with a reproduction of one of the first images taken during the mission. The stamp is the biggest ever issued for regular U.S. postage. Only the newspaper and periodical stamps of 1865 are larger.

The Mars Pathfinder commemorative measures 3" by 1-1/2".

2001: September 11 Changes the Nation

Heroes of 2001 semi-postal stamp.

On a crystal-clear autumn morning, America suffered a series of devastating attacks. Two hijacked airplanes struck New York City's Twin Towers, the heart of U.S. commerce. Another struck the Pentagon, while passengers aboard a fourth prevented it from reaching the nation's capital. In the hours that followed, ordinary Americans proved themselves to be heroes. More than 400 firefighters, police officers, and Port Authority personnel died attempting to rescue victims. As the nation struggled to grasp the meaning behind the attack and the tremendous loss of nearly 3,000 innocent people, a simple photograph captured the spirit of the heroes of September 11. At the base of the Twin Towers, in the area known as "Ground Zero," weary rescue personnel raised an American flag. Although it was later revealed that the flag had been appropriated from a nearby yacht without the owner's knowledge, the photograph has become an icon of this fateful event in American history. The U.S. Postal Service based the design of the second U.S. semi-postal stamp on the image, and dedicated the funds to the families of the heroes of 9/11.

Several dozen respected stamp collectors, dealers, historians, curators, designers, and other philatelists contributed to the selection of the 100 Greatest American Stamps. The discussion involved was often spirited and sometimes passionate. With thousands of noteworthy issues to choose from, this lively debate over which stamps are truly the greatest reflects the very reasons stamp collecting is the world's greatest hobby.

Every collector dreams of owning truly rare stamps, and these gems of philately were selected for the 100 Greatest American Stamps. However, many of the great American issues are remarkable for other reasons—and in that fact lies stamp collecting's unique appeal.

Stamps are history—direct ties to past events that shaped America. And these precious souvenirs of the past can be surprisingly affordable. For less than $10, a collector can own a 150-year-old stamp, one that could actually have carried news of a young upstart lawyer named Lincoln who was creating a stir in Illinois debating the issue of slavery!

American stamps are miniature works of art. The earliest stamps preserve the craftsmanship of yesterday's finest engravers. Migratory Bird (Duck) stamps feature the work of the most talented wildlife artists in the United States. Throughout the years, U.S. stamps have showcased the work of renowned artists such as Norman Rockwell, Georgia O'Keeffe, Peter Max, Winslow Homer, and Frederic Remington. Placing these masterpieces in an album creates a miniature art gallery, one that can be enjoyed any time in the comfort of home.

Stamps are a form of transportation, a way to travel across the globe,

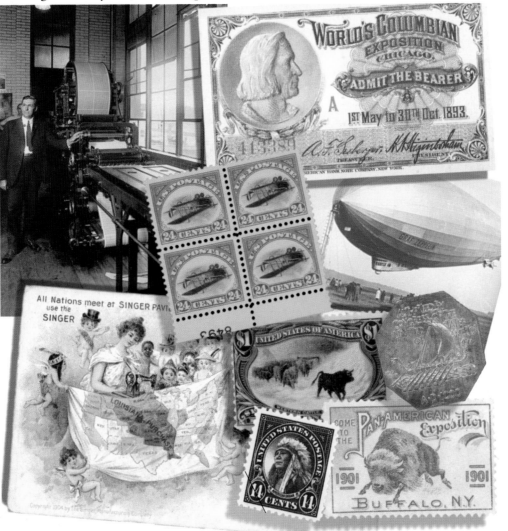

beneath the oceans, and into the universe. United States stamps capture the tentative first steps into space, the frigid ice fields of Antarctica, and the wonderful diversity of the American landscape.

Stamp collectors continue a fine tradition that is now more than 150 years old. Like the forward-thinking men and women of the Victorian age, modern stamp collectors gently preserve our nation's philatelic treasures for future generations.

Stamp collecting is a special corner of the world, a haven from the hectic pace of everyday life. It's a time to relax and escape to another time and place.

Stamp collecting is freedom, with hobby hours spent in control of one's own destiny, unburdened by rules. Collectors are able to sort and arrange their collections any way they like, learn the intriguing stories behind the stamps, explore the fascinating world of watermarks, secret marks, errors, and perforations, and experience the thrill of the chase as they pursue those special stamps that capture their imaginations.

So what should *you* collect? It's your call! Stamp collecting is remarkably free of rules, so you're in charge of collecting the stamps that appeal to you the most.

Some of the world's greatest collectors began with the stamps that arrived on their own mail. Others selected topics that interested them, such as the American Revolution, animals, or airmail stamps, and focused entire collections around those special areas. We hope you choose the course that will bring you the greatest amount of satisfaction; you'll find lots of inspiration in *100 Greatest American Stamps*.

Post offices are frequently closed before the business hours of merchants are over; and there are at present no conveniences for the prepayment of postage after the offices are closed. Stamps for single and double letters, could be prepared with a trifling expense; and would secure the pre-payment of many thousand letters which otherwise w'd not be prepaid, in consequence of the inconvenience (in large cities particularly) of making payment in advance by the present method.

J. Smith Homan, in a letter written to Postmaster General Cave Johnson, April 7, 1845

Postmaster General Johnson must have received many such pleas from businessmen seeking more convenience and efficiency for their correspondence. In the 1840s, the United States was a rapidly developing nation increasingly dependent on good transportation and a reliable communications network.

In the late 1830s, Great Britain led the world in postal reforms, brought about largely by the recommendations put forward by educator and tax reformer Rowland Hill. In his 1837 pamphlet, *Post Office Reform: Its Importance and Practicability*, he demonstrated that lower postal fees and operating costs would create greater volume and greater revenue. He suggested a uniform postal rate structure to replace rates figured by distance and weight (which were collected from the recipient instead of the sender). All of that handling added significant costs to the business of delivering a letter. Hill also suggested postal fees could be paid by the sender by affixing to the letter "a bit of paper just large enough to bear the stamp, and covered at the back with a glutinous wash. . . ." With that phrase, Hill invented the postage stamp.

Great Britain implemented Hill's reforms and, in May of 1840, issued the world's first postage stamp.

Other nations observed the forward progress of Britain's postal reforms, but the postage stamp was slow to catch on. Between 1840, when Britain issued the first stamp, and 1847, when the United States issued her own, only Brazil and two Swiss cantons (Zurich and Geneva) had released postage stamps.

The United States adopted new, reduced postal rates in 1845. The first postage stamps were issued on July 1, 1847: a 5¢ denomination with a portrait of Benjamin Franklin, first postmaster general of the United States, and a 10¢ value depicting George Washington, the nation's first president.

Franklin very nearly lost out to Andrew Jackson for the honor of being on the first stamp, according to a letter from security printers Rawdon, Wright, Hatch & Edson, dated March 20, 1847, to the assistant postmaster general. It states:

We beg to submit for your approval, the enclosed design, which we have prepared for the new stamps for the Post Office Department. In accordance with your suggestion, we have substituted the Head of Franklin for that of Genl. Jackson, which our Mr. Rawdon was requested to use by the Post Master General; should the P.M.G. still desire the head of Jackson, it can be used.

Rawdon, Wright, Hatch & Edson got the contract to produce the stamps. The 5¢ stamp was printed in red brown, but many collectible shades exist. Collectors also have a host of printing varieties to seek, as well as folded letters or envelopes, referred to as "on cover" by stamp collectors.

An early use of Scott #1: two stamps on cover, sent from Charleston, South Carolina, to Philadelphia.

	MARKET VALUES									
	1920	1930	1940	1950	1960	1970	1980	1990	2000	2007
MINT	$15.00	$35.00	$40.00	$63.00	$90.00	$285.00	$3,000.00	$4,000.00	$5,250.00	$6,500.00
USED	$3.00	$8.00	$9.00	$28.00	$38.00	$60.00	$550.00	$500.00	$600.00	$650.00

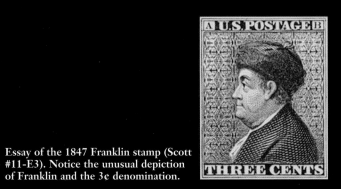

Essay of the 1847 Franklin stamp (Scott #11-E3). Notice the unusual depiction of Franklin and the 3¢ denomination.

A pane of 100 specimen stamps.

A NEW ERA IN U.S. MAIL SERVICE
1847 10¢ GEORGE WASHINGTON

Scott #2 • Quantity Known: 863,800

The 1847 10¢ George Washington shares the spotlight with the 5¢ Benjamin Franklin as one of the first stamps of the United States. Both were released on July 1, 1847. The two portraits established a pattern of Franklin and Washington appearing on regular-issue postage stamps that went unbroken until the 1870s, when objects more frequently replaced these Founding Fathers as stamp subjects.

The 5¢ Franklin prepaid the postal fees for single letters being delivered less than 300 miles, and the 10¢ Washington covered fees for single letters sent more than 300 miles (or double-weight letters under 300 miles). Compare this to the previously enacted postal rate of 25¢ for single letters over 400 miles.

The U.S. Post Office Department slowly phased in the postal reforms that began in 1845. The use of stamps to pre-pay postal fees was not compulsory. Postal customers could still send letters unpaid, as had been the custom, with the Post Office collecting postal fees from the recipient upon delivery. If letters went unclaimed, the Post Office did not recover the costs of delivery.

The 10¢ Washington stamp experienced a problem first seen in Great Britain seven years earlier. Printers Rawdon, Wright, Hatch and Edson printed the stamps in black, just as had been the world's first stamp (which came to be known as the Penny Black). Marking the stamps to render them invalid for further use was difficult. In Great Britain, postmasters used red ink applied to canceling devices, but soon the British Post Office changed the stamp's color to red to preserve their revenue. Black cancels on red stamps were easier to see, and more difficult to remove, than red cancels on black stamps.

The 10¢ Washington brought the same kind of complaints from postmasters. "There has [sic] been several stamps received that the cross upon them to distinguish they had been in use were so lightly done that a person could not have discovered it without a close examination and it is the opinion of many in this place that they could extract the ink and place them again," wrote the postmaster of Williamsport, Pennsylvania, to John Marron, third assistant postmaster general, on January 4, 1848.

Nevertheless, the 10¢ Washington remained in service until July 1851, when new stamps and new, cheaper rates went into effect.

Like its partner, the 5¢ Franklin, the 10¢ Washington has much to offer stamp collectors. There are shades—yes, even black ink can have shade varieties—as well as plate varieties and usages that require much searching and study. There have been official reprints and reproductions. Most recently, modified designs of the 5¢ and 10¢ 1847 stamps were used for stamps released in 1997 for the 150th anniversary of the United States' first stamps. Earlier, in 1947, variations of the designs had been used on a souvenir sheet released to commemorate the 100th anniversary.

MARKET VALUES										
	1920	1930	1940	1950	1960	1970	1980	1990	2000	2007
MINT	$75.00	$150.00	$150.00	$175.00	$275.00	$1,300.00	$15,000.00	$17,500.00	$26,000.00	$32,500.00
USED	$15.00	$35.00	$33.00	$80.00	$110.00	$190.00	$1,650.00	$1,400.00	$1,400.00	$1,500.00

Scott #2 on cover. America's first adhesive postage stamps were issued on July 1, 1847. Prepayment of postal fees was optional until 1855, and stamps were not mandatory until 1856.

THE WORLD'S MOST FAMOUS STAMP
1918 24¢ JENNY INVERT
Scott #C3a • Quantity Issued: 100

Known to collectors and non-collectors alike, the Jenny Inverts are the most-recognized stamps in the world. In addition to their rarity, many remarkable stories add to the rich lore of the legendary "upside-down airplane" stamps.

In the midst of World War I, the Bureau of Engraving and Printing was given less than two weeks to produce a new bi-colored airmail stamp to satisfy the 24¢ airmail rate. The overworked staff accidentally fed a few sheets of stamps through the printing press backwards, creating sheets of 100 stamps with inverted center designs. One complete sheet of 100 inverted stamps slipped by inspectors and was distributed to a post office in Washington, DC.

On the morning prior to the inaugural flight in 1918, William Robey withdrew $30.00 (a figure equal to more than $1,300 in today's wages) from his bank account to purchase a full sheet of the new stamps. Although he was an avid stamp collector, Robey's "heart stood still" when the postal clerk handed him the full sheet of 100 24¢ airmail stamps with inverted centers. Other error sheets were discovered and destroyed, making Robey's error sheet the only one to slip by the bureau's inspectors.

Dealer Eugene Klein purchased the entire sheet from Robey for $15,000 and sold it intact to multi-millionaire Colonel Edward H.R. Green. Acting on Green's behalf, Klein lightly numbered each stamp and separated the sheet into single stamps and blocks. This simple act has allowed collectors to trace the provenance of the beloved Jenny Invert stamps through the years.

Over the course of time, the Jenny Inverts have been owned by some of the most famous stamp collectors. The philatelic elite has set and reset record U.S. stamp sale prices in their quest to own what is known universally as "a Jenny." In 1989, the unique Jenny Invert Plate-Number Block was purchased by an anonymous collector for a record-setting $1.1 million.

After years in relative seclusion, the Jenny Invert Plate-Number Block was auctioned for $2.97 million in 2005, setting a record for the highest amount paid for a United States philatelic item. Days later, the rarity made news again when it was traded to Mystic Stamp Company in a one-to-one exchange for the unique 1868 1¢ Z Grill stamp (see No. 15). The trade prompted a flurry of media coverage and focused positive attention on stamp collecting.

Blockbuster Stamp Swap Worth Millions
– ABC News

Stamp Collectors Make Blockbuster NY Trade
Pakistan Times

2 Collectors Set to Swap Rare Stamps
The New York Times

Stamp Sale Lands $3m "Holy Grail"
– BBC NEWS

Philatelists Make $3 Million Trade
–National Public Radio

A multi-millionaire with a passion for collecting, Colonel Edward H.R. Green's goal was to "spend one day's income in one day." Green purchased the entire sheet of 100 inverted stamps for $20,000.

News of the one-for-one trade of America's greatest stamp rarities was carried by major news organizations around the world.

		MARKET VALUES								
	1920	1930	1940	1950	1960	1970	1980	1990	2000	2007
MINT	N/A	$2,000.00	$4,500.00	$4,000.00	$6,000.00	$25,000.00	$115,000.00	$135,000.00	$150,000.00	$450,000.00
USED	N/A	N/A	N/A	N/A	N/A	N/A	N/A	N/A	N/A	N/A

A cover flown on May 15, 1918, aboard the first U.S. airmail flight. Addressed to the Scott Stamp and Coin Company, the cover bears a non-error 24¢ Jenny stamp.

"In fourteen hundred and ninety two, Columbus sailed the ocean blue." Most schoolchildren learn that little rhyme during their first American History class, but the United States stamps released to mark the 400th anniversary of the voyages of Christopher Columbus did not arrive until January 2, 1893. That was good timing to publicize the World's Columbian Exposition opening later that year on May 1 in Chicago.

The $5 denomination is the highest value in a set of 16 stamps that illustrate Columbus's voyages to the New World. The set of stamps had a total face value of $16.34. According to an Oregon State University inflation conversion chart, that equates to nearly $350 in 2007 dollars.

The $5 black Columbian features a central portrait of Columbus within a coin-like circle. That could have been the first United States "coin-on-stamp" topical, except that the Christopher Columbus image on the stamp faces left and the image of Columbus on the half-dollar coin (a commemorative that was minted at the same time) faces right. The two surrounding images are allegorical figures. On the left of Columbus is Liberty and to Columbus's right is America. Two engravers worked on this stamp—Alfred Jones and Charles Skinner. The stamps were printed by the American Bank Note Company.

The Columbians were the first commemorative stamps of the United States, and as such were not without their critics. Businesses complained about their large size, claiming they were difficult to separate from one another. Stamp collectors lamented the cost of purchasing them. Indeed, even 20 years later, they had not appreciated in value to any great degree. Although the engraving and colors selected for the stamps were beautiful, the paper, printing, and perforating were not of matching quality. The stamps are prone to scuffs and creases. Today's collectors who seek perfect centering and condition for the $5 Columbians are required to pay a significant premium over catalog value when such a stamp may be found.

The United States Mint coined a special commemorative half dollar to celebrate the World's Columbian Exposition (shown enlarged).

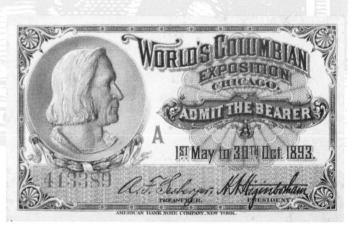

A ticket to the exposition.

	MARKET VALUES									
	1920	1930	1940	1950	1960	1970	1980	1990	2000	2007
MINT	$9.00	$20.00	$65.00	$90.00	$125.00	$450.00	$3,100.00	$3,000.00	$3,750.00	$3,500.00
USED	$9.00	$20.00	$45.00	$80.00	$110.00	$300.00	$1,000.00	$1,300.00	$1,600.00	$1,800.00

Watercolor from "World Columbian Exposition,"
a rare limited-edition multi-volume collection
featuring highlights of the World's Fair.

Exposition exhibitors received
a richly engraved certificate.
These are collectible today.

1869 PICTORIAL ISSUE
90¢ ABRAHAM LINCOLN

Scott #122 • Quantity Issued: 55,500

By 1869, the United States of America had been issuing and using postage stamps for 18 years. The nation was struggling to reunite after the Civil War and heal the residual physical and emotional devastation.

On April 14, four years earlier, President Abraham Lincoln had been shot by an assassin's handgun. This was only five days after Confederate general Robert E. Lee surrendered to Union general Ulysses S. Grant at Appomattox, Virginia. Vice President Andrew Johnson took the oath of office, and just two years later, in 1867, ran afoul of the Senate, which enacted bills to limit the president's authority. A year later, Johnson narrowly avoided impeachment because the Senate did not achieve a two-thirds majority vote. Grant, the hero of the Civil War, was elected the 18th president of the United States.

The U.S. Post Office Department's launch of a new series of regular-issue stamps might have gone unnoticed in the midst of all this political change. Instead, the stamps came under attack for their radically different appearance. They were square rather than rectangular. Some of the values were printed in two colors, a first for the United States. Only three of the stamps bore portraits, which had been the mainstay of U.S. stamp design for the first 18 years. The remaining seven stamps were pictorial, and different, and therefore unpopular. To make matters worse, postal customers complained that the gum was not sticking properly.

The highest denomination in the series was the 90¢ stamp bearing the portrait of Abraham Lincoln. It was printed in two colors (a "bi-color") with a carmine frame and a black portrait. Of the bi-color 1869 stamps, the 90¢ issue was the only denomination with no known genuine inverted centers. It was not the first stamp to show the recently deceased President Lincoln. (That honor belongs to a 15¢ stamp issued in 1866.) Lincoln's image on the 90¢ 1869 stamp was taken from a Mathew Brady photograph.

The 90¢ stamp, being of the highest value in the series, was printed in reduced quantities (estimated at just over 55,000). Only one cover believed to be genuine is known to exist: the now infamous "Ice House" cover sent from Boston to "Mr. James H. Bancroft, Ice House, Calcutta, East Indies." That cover was stolen from Indianapolis collector J. David Baker in 1967, and its where-abouts remained unknown until January 4, 2006, when the cover was brought to a Chicago-area stamp dealer by an elderly couple. At the present time, the recovered "Ice House" cover has been claimed by a number of individuals, and collectors wait as court hearings are held to decide the rightful owner.

MARKET VALUES										
	1920	1930	1940	1950	1960	1970	1980	1990	2000	2007
MINT	$50.00	$125.00	$175.00	$200.00	$225.00	$700.00	$4,250.00	$7,000.00	$7,500.00	$12,000.00
USED	$20.00	$50.00	$50.00	$95.00	$120.00	$235.00	$750.00	$1,200.00	$2,100.00	$2,250.00

1869 PICTORIAL ISSUE
90¢ ABRAHAM LINCOLN

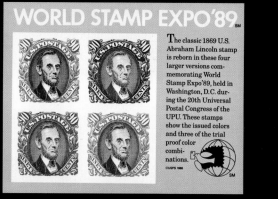

This is the only known genuine cover bearing an 1869 90¢ Lincoln stamp. Named the Ice House Cover because of the recipient's address, the rarity was stolen in Indianapolis in 1967 and recovered in 2006.

WORLD STAMP EXPO '89

The classic 1869 U.S. Abraham Lincoln stamp is reborn in these four larger versions commemorating World Stamp Expo '89, held in Washington, D.C. during the 20th Universal Postal Congress of the UPU. These stamps show the issued colors and three of the trial proof color combinations.

To commemorate World Stamp Expo '89, the USPS produced a special souvenir sheet featuring reprints of Scott #122 as it was issued and three of the trial proof color combinations.

The 1898 "Western Cattle in Storm" stamp is widely considered to be one of the most beautiful ever issued. That the stamp is often noted for its visual appeal is significant, given the fact that it is also scarce.

Held in Omaha, Nebraska, the Trans-Mississippi Exposition opened on June 1, 1898, and ran for four months. More than 4,000 exhibits showcased social, economic, and industrial resources of the American West. Although the event was not considered a financial success overall, it is credited with revitalizing a community hit hard by drought and depression.

More than 2,600,000 visitors attended the Trans-Mississippi Exposition. One of the most popular events was the Indian Congress, the largest Native-American gathering of its kind. More than 500 members of 28 tribes camped on the grounds and introduced Americans from the East to their way of life. Daily reenactments of the explosion of the battleship *Maine* also fueled patriotic fervor and support for the Spanish-American War, which was being fought while the expo was under way.

Unlike the World's Columbian Exposition commemoratives, the stamps of the Trans-Mississippi series didn't include the name or dates of the event. Instead, each stamp bears a caption with the name of the photograph or painting upon which its design was based.

Original proposals called for the Trans-Mississippi to be printed in bi-color. A red frame with a black vignette was planned for the $1 Western Cattle in Storm. However, the challenge of producing revenue stamps to fund the Spanish-American War had strained the resources of the Bureau of Engraving and Printing, and the 1898 stamp was printed in black only. A bi-color stamp bearing the original design would be produced 100 years later to mark the Trans-Mississippi series' centennial.

Postal officials described the stamp subject as "a herd of cattle, preceded by the leader, seeking safety from a gathering storm." Shortly after the stamp was issued, it was discovered that the scene was based on *The Vanguard*, a painting by artist J.A. MacWhirter, set in the highlands of Scotland.

Western Cattle in Storm was issued on June 17, 1898. Its high denomination hindered collectors who were trying to complete the still-current 1893 Columbian series. After only four months of sales, all unsold Trans-Mississippi stamps were destroyed. There are no records to confirm how many of the 56,900 Scott #292 stamps survive, but it is known that sales were poor and it is likely that a significant number were destroyed.

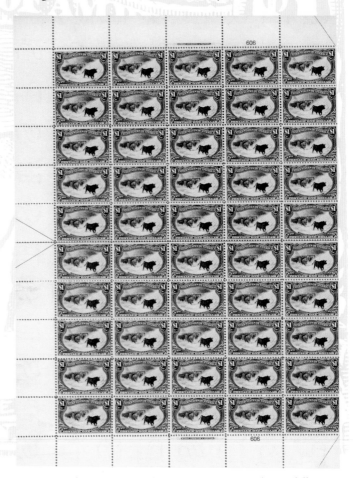

Half pane of $1 Western Cattle in Storm stamps. Only two full panes are thought to exist.

		MARKET VALUES								
	1920	1930	1940	1950	1960	1970	1980	1990	2000	2007
MINT	$3.00	$9.00	$35.00	$65.00	$90.00	$265.00	$1,400.00	$1,325.00	$1,250.00	$1,800.00
USED	$3.00	$9.00	$23.00	$48.00	$75.00	$170.00	$450.00	$475.00	$525.00	$600.00

1898 TRANS-MISSISSIPPI EXPOSITION
$1 WESTERN CATTLE IN STORM

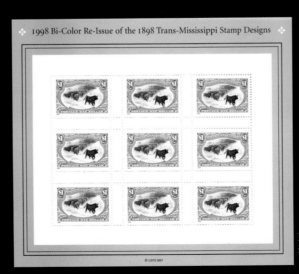

In 1998, bi-color reprints of the Western Cattle in Storm stamp were issued to commemorate the 100th anniversary of the beloved stamps.

The second-highest denomination in the ten-stamp 1869 series of regular issues is the 30¢ Shield, Eagle, and Flag. It probably is not appropriate to discuss this bi-color beauty without mentioning the 10¢ value as well. They share commonalities of design elements.

British-born engraver Douglas S. Ronaldson was responsible for the flags and lettering on the 30¢. The frame of flags was printed in blue and the shield in red, but the design was oddly created so that the red spelled-out denomination crossed over into the blue flag printing. The registration of colors on all of the bi-color 1869 Pictorials was not particularly accurate, and this was especially exaggerated on the 30¢ value. Lester Brookman, in his seminal work *The United States Postage Stamps of the 19th Century*, said this of the 30¢ value: "Were it not for the fact that the method of lettering in the denomination 'Thirty Cents' is most inartistic this stamp might lay claim to being a handsome stamp."

The 1869s exist both with and without grills (see No. 15, the 1868 1¢ Z Grill, for more information about grills). The grills added fuel to customer complaints about these stamps, which were unpopular in their day. Some complained that the procedure weakened the paper enough that stamps would tear when separating one from another along the perforations.

The 30¢ Shield, Eagle, and Flag, as well as the other nine values of the 1869 series, were reprinted by the U.S. Post Office Department in 1875.

According to a lecture given by Eustace B. Power in 1934, these "Special Printings" were made by the Post Office Department "in order that the Government might be able to show a complete set of the various issues at the Centennial" and "that the Government might be able to comply with the many requests for stamps that they have received from stamp collectors."

Power further described the 1869 Special Printings as having "colors. . . [that] are very brilliant, but it is almost impossible for me to distinguish them from the originals by description. Perhaps I might say that they appear fresher and that the colors are brighter and just a little bit deeper than the issued set and that the paper is white."

The Special Printings were valid for postage.

The eagle became the national emblem in 1782, when the Great Seal of the United States was adopted. It is said the eagle was chosen after an early-morning battle during the Revolution. The noise of the struggle awoke the sleeping eagles on the heights and they flew from their nests, circling over the heads of the fighting men, and shrieking shrilly as if cheering for freedom.

	1920	1930	1940	1950	1960	1970	1980	1990	2000	2007
MINT	$15.00	$40.00	$50.00	$88.00	$95.00	$300.00	$1,300.00	$2,250.00	$5,500.00	$8,000.00
USED	$4.00	$5.00	$9.00	$25.00	$25.00	$53.00	$160.00	$1,200.00	$550.00	$550.00

MARKET VALUES

The eagle and shield are traditional design elements of United States stamps and currency (such as the early gold and silver coins seen here, shown enlarged). This might have disappointed Benjamin Franklin, the nation's first postmaster general, who once said, "For my own part I wish the Bald Eagle had not been chosen the Representative of our Country. He is a Bird of bad moral Character." Franklin proposed the turkey as the national bird.

1898 TRANS-MISSISSIPPI EXPOSITION
$2 MISSISSIPPI RIVER BRIDGE

Scott #293 • Quantity Issued: 56,200

Issued in 1898, the Trans-Mississippi Exposition commemorative stamps represent the pinnacle of 19th-century craftsmanship. With an estimated 25,000 in existence, the $2 Mississippi River Bridge stamp is the rarest Trans-Mississippi stamp and the key to owning a complete set.

The Trans-Mississippi stamps were the first commemoratives produced by the Bureau of Engraving and Printing. Each depicts a scene intended to showcase the development of natural resources west of the Mississippi River, a theme paralleling that of the exposition. The $2 denomination pictures the Eads Bridge, an engineering marvel that forms a natural boundary between America's East and West. At the time of its 1874 construction, it was the longest arch bridge in the world, with an overall length of 6,442 feet. Although it was a major engineering feat, the bridge was a financial disaster.

The vignette was duplicated from guest tickets distributed for the 1896 Republican Convention held in St. Louis. The entire run was printed in a single day, and the stamps were sold for a limited time. An unknown quantity of unsold $2 Trans-Mississippi stamps was destroyed. Experts estimate that 25,000 $2 stamps made their way into the public's hands.

The high $2 denomination prevented many casual collectors from purchasing Scott #293. In addition to the cost, the earlier-printed 1893 Columbians were still current, and many collectors were struggling to complete that set. The $2 Trans-Mississippi stamp is scarce today as a result. The series is known for poor centering, and Fine used copies are hard to find.

❖ 1998 Bi-Color Re-Issue of the 1898 Trans-Mississippi Stamp Designs ❖

At the time the Trans-Mississippi series was designed, the 2¢ denomination depicted the Mississippi River Bridge and the $2 denomination bore a farming scene. A switch was made before the 1898 stamp was printed so that the farming scene could appear on the 2¢ stamp, the most commonly used in the series. The USPS commemorated the 100th anniversary of the Trans-Mississippi series with a souvenir sheet. Each stamp is bi-color, as originally intended.

Eads Bridge under construction.

	1920	1930	1940	1950	1960	1970	1980	1990	2000	2007
MARKET VALUES										
MINT	$6.00	$17.00	$50.00	$85.00	$115.00	$350.00	$2,250.00	$1,950.00	$2,100.00	$2,250.00
USED	$6.00	$17.00	$35.00	$60.00	$85.00	$200.00	$650.00	$725.00	$900.00	$1,000.00

As this essay shows, the Eads Bridge design was originally planned for the 2¢ denomination.

$5 AMERICA

Construction of the United States Capitol Building dome began in 1856 and was still incomplete when the Civil War began in 1861. Although resources on both sides of the conflict were strained, President Abraham Lincoln insisted that the work continue as a symbol of American unity.

As the Confederacy tore up rail lines to melt down to make cannons, nearly nine million pounds of ironwork was used to build the famous Capitol dome. On December 2, 1863, the *Statue of Freedom* was placed on top of the dome. Fanfare included a 35-gun salute, one gun for every state of the Union plus those that had seceded, and a return salute from 12 forts surrounding Washington, DC. The pageantry, and the crowning *Statue of Freedom*, was visible from nearby Virginia, the home state of Richmond, capital of the Confederate States of America.

The *Statue of Freedom*, also known as *Armed Freedom*, is a female allegorical figure sculpted by Thomas Crawford. Crawford was commissioned to design the sculpture in 1854, and executed the plaster model in his Rome, Italy, studio. The figure holds a sheathed sword in her right hand and a laurel victory wreath and the shield of the United States with 13 stripes in her left.

Crawford died in 1857 with the model still in his studio. It was later packed into six crates and endured a perilous ocean crossing to America. The statue was cast in five main sections at a Washington, DC, foundry, and hoisted by sections above the Capitol building.

Crawford's iconic statue had been selected to grace Newspaper and Periodical Revenue stamps in 1875 and 1895. When the Statue of Freedom was again selected for the new stamp series in 1922, the Bureau of Engraving and Printing had an existing engraving in its files. The engraving had been mistakenly labeled "America," and the incorrect name was inscribed on the $5 Series of 1922 stamp.

The 23 stamps of the Series of 1922 were issued over an extended period of time and frequently with limited distribution. The $5 America stamp was issued on March 20, 1923, in Washington, DC. The high-denomination stamp is the only bi-color issue in the Series of 1922, and is especially dramatic with deep shades of carmine and blue.

Erected atop the U.S. Capitol Building at the height of the Civil War, the *Statue of Freedom* can be seen from Virginia (once the home of the Confederate capital city).

Workers cleaning the statue in 1909.

MARKET VALUES										
	1920	1930	1940	1950	1960	1970	1980	1990	2000	2007
MINT	N/A	$8.00	$8.00	$10.00	$17.00	$32.00	$425.00	$200.00	$150.00	$150.00
USED	N/A	$2.00	$1.00	$1.00	$2.00	$4.00	$10.00	$13.00	$15.00	$15.00

A Mint block of four "America" stamps is worth more than $475.

The *Statue of Freedom* is also featured on the 1895 1¢ Newspaper and Periodical stamp.

1860 90¢ WASHINGTON

In June of 1860, the third assistant postmaster general issued specifications to Toppan, Carpenter, Casilear and Co., regarding a new 90¢ postage stamp. "With this stamp the Postmaster General desires the head of Washington and I need not suggest to you the importance of expending upon it all the talent you can command in respect to designing, engraving and coloring."

Toppan, Carpenter, Casilear and Co., the skilled printers who produced the 5¢ Franklin and 10¢ Washington stamps of 1847, heeded the recommendations. The result is Scott #39, with a design based on John Trumbull's painting of Washington in his dress uniform. Printed in a rich shade of blue ink, the 1860 90¢ Washington is widely considered to be one of the most beautiful of all United States stamps.

The 90¢ Washington stamp was needed to satisfy the rate of 20¢ per half ounce for letters and packages sent more than 2,500 miles to foreign countries. Issued late in 1860, it was the highest-denominated U.S. stamp to date. The denomination was the monetary equivalent of more than $140 today, so demand was projected to be low, and relatively few were produced. For the small number of stamp collectors in 1860, the stamp's high cost was also somewhat prohibitive.

The earliest-known use of Scott #39 was in the fall of 1860. Throughout the winter and spring of 1861, tension grew between the North and South over the issues of slavery and states' rights. Following the secession of several Southern states, the federal government announced that it would suspend postal service to the new Confederate States of America and demonetize (render worthless) existing U.S. stamps, including the 90¢ Washington stamp. Unsold inventories were returned to the U.S. Post Office Department and destroyed.

Due to their short period of use, genuine used examples of Scott #39 are much rarer than Mint stamps. Accordingly, used 1860 90¢ Washington stamps command a higher market price, frequently more than double the value of the same issue in Mint condition. Of the used Scott #39 stamps, those bearing a genuine stamped cancel are valued considerably higher than those canceled with a pen or manuscript.

Trumbull's painting depicts the scene in the Old Senate Chamber of the Maryland State House on December 23, 1783, when General George Washington resigned his commission as commander-in-chief of the Continental Army.

MARKET VALUES										
	1920	1930	1940	1950	1960	1970	1980	1990	2000	2007
MINT	$800.00	$1,000.00	$1,000.00	$80.00	$125.00	$300.00	$900.00	$1,250.00	$2,500.00	$3,500.00
USED	N/A	N/A	N/A	$125.00	$175.00	$800.00	$2,000.00	$3,500.00	$5,500.00	$9,000.00

GENERAL GEORGE WASHINGTON
1860 90¢ WASHINGTON

Valid for only a few months, the
1860 90¢ Washington is much
scarcer in postally used condition.

1860 90¢ Washington proof sheet.

ZEPPELIN PASSING GLOBE
1930 $2.60 GRAF ZEPPELIN
Scott #C15 • Quantity Issued: 61,296

Graf Zeppelins were issued to commemorate the dirigible's historic 1930 round-trip flight between Europe and the Americas. The stamps were on sale at a limited number of post offices for a mere five weeks and two days. Only 61,296 of the $2.60 Graf Zeppelins were sold, and remaining stamps were destroyed. Today, the high-value #C15 is key to owning a complete Graf Zeppelin set.

Their story began when the Luftschiffbau Zeppelin company was stripped of its three airships and left with an $800,000 war-reparations debt after Germany's World War I defeat. To capitalize on the demand for trans-Atlantic flight, Zeppelin offered to build an airship for the United States as payment for its war debt. The U.S. agreed, but with one stipulation: the dirigible had to be proven by a trans-Atlantic delivery.

Amid a flurry of media coverage, the dirigible completed its 77-hour flight on October 16, 1924. The *LZ-126* arrived in Lakehurst, New Jersey, carrying 55,714 pieces of mail.

After this triumph the company built an even larger airship. The 775-foot-long *LZ-127* featured 10 sleeping cabins and a dining room, and carried 20 passengers. One year later, the *Graf Zeppelin* became the first passenger aircraft to completely circumnavigate the globe.

Zeppelin scheduled a 1930 round-trip voyage between Europe and North and South America. As he had in the past, Zeppelin chief Dr. Hugo Eckener planned to transport mail aboard the flight to offset his expenses. Eckener requested U.S. stamps to frank mail carried aboard the historic Pan-American flight. Under the agreement, the Zeppelin company received $2.15 of the fee, the U.S. received 40¢, and the German government 5¢ for each flown cover.

The success of the 1930 Pan-American flight convinced the Zeppelin company to introduce the world's first regular trans-Atlantic airship line. Despite the Great Depression and the growing technology of fixed-wing aircraft, the *LZ-127* transported an increasing number of commercial passengers and mail across the ocean until 1937, when a fire aboard Zeppelin's *Hindenburg* dirigible killed 36 people. The event was widely broadcast in the media and the company was unable to rebound from the bad publicity.

Today, Scott #C15 is a historic link to the romance of the pioneering dirigible flights and is especially desirable to United States stamp collectors.

LZ-127, the *Graf Zeppelin* dirigible.

MARKET VALUES										
	1920	1930	1940	1950	1960	1970	1980	1990	2000	2007
Mint	N/A	N/A	$22.00	$63.00	$100.00	$300.00	$2,750.00	$1,050.00	$800.00	$775.00
Used	N/A	N/A	$22.00	$55.00	$80.00	$190.00	$1,000.00	$550.00	$575.00	$575.00

1845 POSTMASTER PROVISIONAL
20¢ ST. LOUIS BEARS

Scott #11X3 • Quantity Known: 137

Shrouded in secrecy for decades, the 20¢ St. Louis Postmaster Provisional is the rarest stamp of the group known collectively as the "St. Louis Bears."

Following the postal reforms of 1845, the St. Louis postmaster printed provisional stamps to indicate pre-payment of fees, as a courtesy for his customers. The St. Louis Postmaster Provisionals were engraved on a small copper plate in three rows of two stamps each. The plate bore one column of three 5¢ stamps and another of the 10¢ denomination. Only 500 sheets, of six stamps each, were printed on greenish-gray wove paper in the initial run.

The need for a 20¢ denomination became apparent immediately. To fill this void, the numeral on each of the 5¢ stamps on the original plate was replaced with the number 20. A few sheets of 10¢ and 20¢ denominations were printed on the greenish-gray wove paper. Of these, the 20¢ denomination is the rarest of all St. Louis Bears. The balance of the 500-sheet printing run, which included a 20¢ denomination, was completed on grayish-lilac paper.

Although they were intended as a convenience, the stamps were unpopular with the general public. Experts believe the unsold inventory of St. Louis Postmaster Provisionals was destroyed.

Articles about the legendary Bears appeared in philatelic journals as early as 1863. The first major find of the St. Louis Bears occurred in 1869. J.W. Scott (founder of the *Scott Catalogue*) purchased fifty 5¢, one hundred 10¢, and three 20¢ St. Louis Postmaster Provisionals.

Leading experts of the era doubted the authenticity of the 20¢ denomination until an 1895 discovery of 137 Bears. A porter in a Louisville hotel found the stamps while burning trash and gave them to his supervisors. The supervisors bought the porter a drink in gratitude and sold the stash for a reported $20,000. Included in the lot were sixteen 20¢ stamps.

The last major discovery occurred in 1942. A new law-firm partner sold an accumulation of old papers and letters to the Hemingway Paper Stock Co. Owner F.D. Hemingway recognized the rare Bear stamps and sold them for several thousand dollars. The sale prompted massive publicity and an unsuccessful lawsuit to recover the stamps.

The St. Louis Postmaster Provisional stamps were issued with denominations of 5¢, 10¢, and 20¢.

	MARKET VALUES									
	1920	1930	1940	1950	1960	1970	1980	1990	2000	2007
MINT	N/A	N/A	N/A	N/A	N/A	N/A	N/A	N/A	N/A	N/A
USED	N/A	N/A	$2,500.00	$2,500.00	$2,500.00	$11,000.00	$18,500.00	N/A	N/A	$85,000.00

THE FIRST U.S. POSTAGE STAMP
1845 5¢ NEW YORK POSTMASTER PROVISIONAL

Scott #9X1 • Quantity Known: 5,500

Three weeks after the 1775 battles of Lexington and Concord, the Second Continental Congress met to discuss vital services necessary to sustain the rebelling colonies during and after the War of Independence. On July 25, 1775, Benjamin Franklin was named America's first postmaster general. A complicated postal rate system based on weight and mileage remained in place for nearly 70 years. In addition, the tradition of the *recipient* paying the postage was continued, a practice that often led to letters being refused (leaving the postal service to bear the expense for services rendered).

In 1840, postal reforms in England led to uniform rates and the world's first adhesive postage stamps. The United States Congress passed the Act of March 3, 1845, which established uniform rates of 5¢ per half ounce for letters carried less than 300 miles and 10¢ for those of the same weight traveling more than 300 miles. The act allowed for the prepayment of postage rates; however, it didn't specifically provide for *stamps*. Individual postmasters were allowed to issue stamps valid only at their local post office.

Robert H. Morris was appointed New York City's postmaster on May 1, 1845. Eager to make a name for himself, Morris arranged to have adhesive 5¢ postage stamps printed by Rawdon, Wright and Hatch. Proofs exist in a range of colors and papers, an indication of Morris's meticulous attention.

The stamps were delivered on July 12, 1845, and placed on sale shortly thereafter. Morris immediately sent copies to postmasters in Philadelphia, Boston, Albany, and Washington, DC.

Within days, Morris decided that stamps needed to be initialed by postal clerks in order to be valid. #9X1 bears the initials "ACM" (for Alonzo Castle Monson). It is extremely rare with original gum.

Other major cities soon followed suit and issued their own Postmaster Provisional stamps. However, New York's stamps were the only Postmaster Provisionals to be used extensively on mail abroad. #9X1 is known to have franked mail to Canada, Mexico,

and Europe. It was also recognized as pre-payment of incoming mail to New York City.

The success of the New York City Postmaster Provisional led to the Congressional Act of March 3, 1847, which authorized the postmaster general to issue 5¢ and 10¢ stamps nationwide. Impressed with the quality of workmanship in #9X1, the federal government awarded Rawdon, Wright and Hatch the right to produce Scott #1 and #2 (Nos. 1 and 2 among the 100 Greatest) without competition.

Coins as well as stamps have commemorated George Washington over the years. This half dollar is from 1982. (shown enlarged)

	1920	1930	1940	1950	1960	1970	1980	1990	2000	2007
MINT	$50.00	N/A	$100.00	$100.00	$150.00	$225.00	$550.00	$800.00	$1,300.00	$1,500.00
USED	$30.00	N/A	$50.00	$55.00	$75.00	$110.00	$300.00	$325.00	$500.00	$525.00

MARKET VALUES

1869 PICTORIAL ISSUE
24¢ DECLARATION OF INDEPENDENCE
Scott #120 • Quantity Issued: 248,925

"When in the Course of human Events, it becomes necessary for one People to dissolve the Political Bands which have connected them with another, and to assume among the Powers of the Earth, the separate and equal Station to which the Laws of Nature and of Nature's God entitle them, a decent Respect to the Opinions of Mankind requires that they should declare the causes which impel them to the Separation."

And so began a document signed by representatives to the Continental Congress in Philadelphia on August 2, 1776, codifying adoption on July 4 of a vote for independence the Congress had taken two days earlier. This "declaration" advised King George III that the colonies were breaking their ties to Britain because "The History of the present King of Great-Britain is a History of repeated Injuries and Usurpations, all having in direct Object the Establishment of an absolute Tyranny over these States. To prove this, let Facts be submitted to a candid World." The document then detailed a litany of charges against the British government.

The Declaration's preamble enumerates the rights of the people, stated as "We hold These truths to be self-evident, that all Men are created equal, that they are endowed by their Creator with certain unalienable Rights, that among these are Life, Liberty, and the pursuit of Happiness." This oft-quoted passage, written by Thomas Jefferson, makes the parchment that has come to be known as the Declaration of Independence one of the most important documents of all time.

The 1869-series 24¢ stamp illustrates that moment in time when the Declaration was being presented to members of the Continental Congress by the drafting committee. (The source painting, created by John Trumbull in 1817 and 1818, is frequently mis-described as illustrating the signing of the Declaration of Independence.)

The stamp's green frame was engraved by Douglas Ronaldson. The violet vignette was engraved by James Smillie, who managed to capture the enormous detail of the original 12-feet-tall by 18-feet-wide painting in an area less than an inch wide and 3/8 of an inch high.

The 1869 24¢ reproduction was the first use on a postage stamp of Trumbull's famous painting, but it would not be the last. The Trumbull painting resurfaced in 1976 for the United States Bicentennial. A souvenir sheet containing five 18¢ stamps reproduced a portion of the painting, and a polyptych of four se-tenant 13¢ stamps showed a larger area of the painting.

John Trumbull's painting portrays the presentation of the Declaration of Independence in what is now known as Independence Hall, in Philadelphia. In it, Thomas Jefferson presents the document to Continental Congress President John Hancock as John Adams, Roger Sherman, and Benjamin Franklin look on.

	1920	1930	1940	1950	1960	1970	1980	1990	2000	2007
					MARKET VALUES					
MINT	$15.00	$30.00	$50.00	$78.00	$80.00	$250.00	$1,400.00	$2,500.00	$5,500.00	$9,500.00
USED	$7.00	$10.00	$15.00	$38.00	$38.00	$90.00	$375.00	$450.00	$700.00	$775.00

RAREST U.S. POSTAGE STAMP
1868 1¢ Z GRILL
Scott #85A • Quantity Known: 2

Only two 1868 1¢ Z Grills are known to exist, and one of them is permanently locked away in the New York Public Library's Benjamin Miller collection. The second is the only 1¢ Z Grill available to collectors, which makes it the rarest United States postage stamp.

Grills were an experimental security measure applied to U.S. stamps for a short period beginning in 1867. Officials were concerned with the cleansing and re-use of stamps, a crime that caused the loss of postal revenues because it required the agency to provide service without payment.

Charles F. Steel developed the concept of grilling. No example of the grilling apparatus survives, and no one knows what the device looked like that was used to produce the embossed grill patterns. A widely accepted theory is a metal roller was cut to form a waffle-like grid of tiny pyramid-shaped projections. Applied to the stamps under pressure, the device broke the paper fibers in a variety of patterns. When cancelled, grilled stamps absorbed the ink deeply, making it impossible to re-use the stamp.

William L. Stevenson devised a standard classification system for grills based on the pattern produced. The letters A through J and Z represent 11 grill types. Stevenson identified a stamp in his collection as possessing a Z-shaped grill. The unique feature of the Z Grill is the horizontal orientation of the points.

Stevenson later sold his stamp collection, and the 1¢ Z Grill was eventually acquired by Benjamin K. Miller. Miller donated his stamp collection to the New York Public Library. It remains there today, out of public view except on extremely rare occasions.

After selling several times for noteworthy prices, the single available 1868 1¢ Z Grill sold for a record-setting price in 1986. Robert Zoellner, who was assembling a complete U.S. collection, purchased the rarity from L.A. Lakers owner Dr. Jerry Buss for $418,000. Just 12 years later, 11-year-old Zachary Sundman, bidding on behalf of Mystic Stamp Company, purchased the 1868 1¢ Z Grill for the record-breaking price of $935,000.

In 2005, Mystic traded the 1¢ Z Grill to collector Bill Gross for the unique 1918 Jenny Invert Plate-Number Block (see No. 3) in a one-to-one exchange. The trade, which involved America's rarest stamp as well as the world's greatest stamp rarity, had a combined value of $6 million.

1¢ essay featuring a Bowlsby coupon, intended to prevent the reuse of postage stamps. A receipt is attached to a normal-sized stamp with a horizontal perforation through its center and gum on the lower half. The stamp was invalid without the coupon, which was to be removed by the postmaster.

The result of the grilling process can be seen in this essay for the 1868 1¢ stamp.

Steel developed the concept of grilling stamps to prevent reuse.

MARKET VALUES										
	1920	1930	1940	1950	1960	1970	1980	1990	2000	2007
MINT	N/A	N/A	N/A	N/A	N/A	N/A	N/A	N/A	N/A	N/A
USED	N/A	N/A	N/A	N/A	N/A	$20,000.00	$90,000.00	$418,000.00	$935,000.00	$3,000,000.00

AN INNOVATION IN COMMUNICATION
1861 $2 WELLS FARGO PONY EXPRESS
Scott #143L1 • Quantity Issued: Unknown

"Wanted! Young, skinny, wiry fellows. Not over 18. Must be expert riders. Willing to risk death daily. Orphans preferred. Wages $25 a week."

This advertisement was a call for horse riders for an innovative but dangerous business venture called the "Pony Express." Nothing conjures up images of the American Wild West faster than the Pony Express, arguably the most famous mail-delivery system of all time.

The Pony Express was operated by the Central Overland California and Pike's Peak Express Company. It was established to expedite the delivery of mail between St. Joseph, Missouri, and Sacramento, California. "Young, skinny, wiry" boys and men on fast horses carried letters in saddlebags called *mochilas*. Each rider would change horses at stations spaced about 10 miles apart, established along a 2,000-mile route.

The intrepid riders, of whom William "Buffalo Bill" Cody was the most famous, faced many hazards. They were paid well for the time because they were not able to carry firearms to protect themselves from marauders or hostile Indians. Guns added too much weight and slowed their travel. The riders traversed challenging terrain and had to travel regardless of inclement weather conditions.

The Pony Express began in April 1860 and ended as a financial failure only 18 months later, in October 1861. An estimated 35,000 letters were carried by the Pony Express, a service that reduced the time it took to send a letter across country from eight weeks down to 10 days.

Initially the postage for a half-ounce letter was $5, an exorbitant amount of money for the time. Three months later, a quarter-ounce rate of $2.50 was implemented. In April 1861, Wells, Fargo & Co. became agents for the Pony Express, and the price of a half-ounce letter was reduced to $2. In July 1861, that rate dropped to $1. The lower rates did not generate greater demand for the service because by this time the first transcontinental telegraph line was nearing completion. The Pony Express was obsolete.

The $2 red Pony Express stamp was issued in April 1861 and today is collected Mint, used, and on cover. The cover is usually an embossed envelope issued by the U.S. Post Office Department. Letters carried by the Pony Express are rare, expensive, and eagerly sought by collectors whenever one comes on the market.

As governor, Milton Latham served the shortest term in California history. Covers that exhibit Latham's free franking privileges are scarce and very collectible.

		MARKET VALUES								
	1920	1930	1940	1950	1960	1970	1980	1990	2000	2007
MINT	N/A	N/A	$7.00	$7.00	$23.00	$45.00	$125.00	$100.00	$150.00	$175.00
USED	N/A	N/A	$50.00	$35.00	$50.00	$100.00	$250.00	$250.00	$500.00	$800.00

There were United States stamps with inverted centers long before an airplane flew upside down on a 24¢ airmail stamp. The four highest values of the 1869 series of regular-issue stamps were printed in two colors (bi-color stamps) and three of those values (the 15¢, 24¢, and 30¢) were printed with the frame and vignette (center design) inverted to one another. They were the first U.S. postage stamps to have this spectacular—and highly desired by collectors—kind of misprinting.

The stamps were printed by the National Bank Note Company. The 15¢ stamp illustrates "the landing of Columbus." What is commonly called an "inverted center" of this stamp is actually an inverted frame. The vignette of the stamp was printed first. Then the sheet bearing the images of the vignette was misfed upside down in the printing press. The frame was then printed inverted in relation to the vignette.

The Declaration of Independence 24¢ value and 30¢ Eagle and Shield stamps also are inverted frames rather than inverted vignettes. However, all of these stamps are usually illustrated or mounted in collections showing the frame in the upright position and the vignette inverted. The 15¢ and 24¢ inverts turned up within a year and a half of issue, and the 30¢ denomination was discovered after that.

The final bi-color of the series, the 90¢ Lincoln, was never found as an invert. Interestingly, 100 plate proofs on card stock were printed as inverts for the 90¢ Lincoln, as well as for the 15¢, 24¢, and 30¢ denominations. These plate proofs are imperforate and should not be confused with the actual stamps. Because they are scarce and

therefore valuable, these error stamps have been counterfeited. A certificate of authentication should be acquired before purchasing any inverts. The rarest of the rare 1869s are unused examples.

	MARKET VALUES										
	1920	1930	1940	1950	1960	1970	1980	1990	2000	2007
MINT	$50.00		$175.00		$225.00		$4,250.00		$7,500.00	$12,000.00
USED	$20.00		$50.00		$120.00		$750.00		$2,100.00	$2,250.00

1869 PICTORIAL ISSUE
3¢ LOCOMOTIVE

Scott #114 • Quantity Issued: 335,534,850

What appears today to be a quaint, old-fashioned steam engine that graces the 3¢ locomotive stamp in the 1869 series was high-tech state-of-the-art transportation for its day. The stamp arrived on the scene just as the first transcontinental railroad was approaching completion.

The Baltimore and Ohio Railroad was the first commercial line in the United States, beginning operation in 1830. Between 1830 and the 1860s, the network of rail lines expanded. Travel became more comfortable and expedient. Goods were brought to market faster. The U.S. Post Office Department used trains for transport of the mail.

The Pacific Railway Act of 1862 established a goal of completing a rail line to the Pacific coast. This would, it was believed, "bind the nation" that was engaged in civil war. Consider the achievement: the work of surveying, engineering, blasting, and tree felling was begun on a transcontinental railroad while the nation was at war with itself.

In an astoundingly short period of time, the Central Pacific Railroad (laying track eastward from Sacramento) and the Union Pacific (working west from Omaha) met on May 10, 1869, at Promontory Summit, Utah. A golden spike was driven into the last tie that linked the two lines. The feat had been accomplished in six years, despite inclement weather, disease, accidents, and raids from Indians who resented the incursion of the railroad on their land.

The completion of the transcontinental railroad reduced the time it took to travel from coast to coast from six months or more to one week.

The 3¢ ultramarine locomotive stamp, while not specifically issued for the opening of the transcontinental railroad, was certainly near-perfect timing. Amazingly, even though the stamp is more than 130 years old, it is still plentiful and affordable both on and off cover. The 3¢ locomotive stamp would have been used on ordinary day-to-day mail to pay for the first-class letter rate of the time. The Post Office Department released more than 330 million of the 3¢ stamps. In comparison, the next most plentiful denomination was the 2¢ Pony Express stamp with a known quantity of 72 million issued. The 3¢ locomotive stamp is a great entry point for collectors who want to tackle the 1869 series.

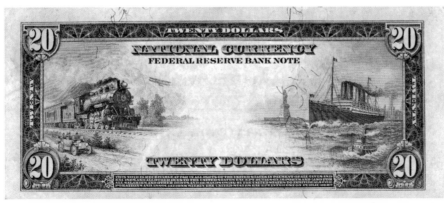

America's fascination with trains is evident in the number of times they appear on stamps and currency. Note the similarity of Scott #114 and this 1915 Federal Reserve Bank Note.

	MARKET VALUES									
	1920	**1930**	**1940**	**1950**	**1960**	**1970**	**1980**	**1990**	**2000**	**2007**
MINT	$1.00	$2.00	$2.00	$4.00	$5.00	$17.00	$85.00	$135.00	$300.00	$350.00
USED	N/A	$0.06	$0.15	$0.30	$1.00	$2.00	$4.00	$6.00	$20.00	$20.00

BLACK JACK
1863 2¢ ANDREW JACKSON
Scott #73 • Quantity Issued: 256,566,000

The first 2¢ United States stamp was introduced to pay the rate for the newly established free home-mail delivery service. Former president Andrew Jackson was selected as its subject. The design is based on the final portrait of Jackson completed before his death in 1845. Collectors nicknamed the stamp "Big Head" because Jackson's imposing portrait dominates the stamp. And that was no accident.

America had been embroiled in a tragic civil war for two years when Scott #73 was issued. Although he was the first Southern-born president, owned slaves, and was idolized by Southerners, Jackson strongly opposed secession. Placing his jumbo image on a United States stamp was meant to send a strong pro-Union message to the Confederate States of America. They responded by issuing their own 2¢ stamp featuring the same portrait of Jackson.

Andrew Jackson (1767–1845) was a veteran of the American Revolution, commander of American forces at the 1815 Battle of New Orleans, seventh president of the United States, and co-founder of the Democratic Party. He was the last American Revolutionary War veteran elected to the presidency and the only one who had been a prisoner of war.

Known for his toughness, Jackson earned the nickname "Old Hickory." Years before the Civil War broke out, he faced his own secession crisis over tariffs and federal versus states' rights. Although Jackson sympathized with the South in the debate, he favored a strong Union and a strong central government. After a heated debate with Vice President John C. Calhoun, Jackson sent warships to Charleston, South Carolina, to enforce the federal government's tariffs. The event, known to history as the Nullification Crisis, is considered an early prelude to the Civil War.

An important distinction is unique to Jackson: it was during his administration, for the first and only time, that the United States was debt-free.

The 2¢ Jackson stamp was issued in abundant quantities. However, it was produced during a time of war when resources were scarce and skilled craftsmen were called upon to serve in battle. Well-centered examples are difficult to find and command premium prices.

Issued by the Confederacy, CSA#8 also depicts Andrew Jackson.

Cover dated March 28, 1865, the final month before the Union was reunited.

	MARKET VALUES									
	1920	1930	1940	1950	1960	1970	1980	1990	2000	2007
MINT	$1.00	$3.00	$3.00	$5.00	$9.00	$27.00	$85.00	$110.00	$325.00	$400.00
USED	$0.20	$0.35	$1.00	$2.00	$3.00	$6.00	$14.00	$23.00	$50.00	$65.00

FATHER OF THE U.S. POSTAL SYSTEM
1857 1¢ BENJAMIN FRANKLIN
Scott #20 • Quantity Issued: Unknown

Few stamps have engendered as much scholarship as the 1¢ Franklin stamp, printed by Toppan, Carpenter, Casilear & Co. and in use from 1851 to 1861. The extensive studies made of this stamp rank among the very best in philatelic research. Entire books have been written about it, most notably a work by Mortimer L. Neinken entitled *The United States One Cent Stamp of 1851 to 1861.*

The 1¢ Franklin stamp was created to cover the postage fees for mailing unsealed printed circulars, as well as the fee for sealed "drop letters" (letters deposited at and picked up from the same post office) and, after 1856, the carrier fee. The 1¢ Franklin was issued either imperforate or, after 1857, with perforations that gauge 15. The stamp's design was engraved. Throughout the decade this 1¢ stamp design was in production, Toppan, Carpenter, Casilear & Co. used a total of 12 printing plates.

The *Scott Specialized Catalogue of U.S. Stamps* has 18 main listings for the 1¢ Franklin and many sub-varieties, but the one that made it to the 100 Greatest is known as Scott #20, 1¢ blue, Type II, printed from plate 2, with perforations that gauge 15.

The various types noted for this stamp are determined by comparing the scrollwork on the tops, bottoms, and sides of the stamp with illustrations and text in catalogs and other published works. Type I stamps have full scrollwork at the top and bottom. The scrollwork on the Type II stamp is described by both Neinken and Scott thus: "The little balls of the bottom scrolls and the bottoms of the lower plume ornaments are missing. The side ornaments are complete."

Neinken expands this description to state that the top and bottom outer curved frame lines are never broken, the side ornaments are generally complete with a few exceptions, and there may be complete or partially cut-away ornaments at the top.

Scott lists a host of sub-varieties for this stamp, including a double transfer, cracked plate, and "curl in hair."

Any collector may own an example of the 1857 1¢ Franklin, but it takes acquired skill, patience, and a generous hobby budget for those who wish to attain completion of all the collectible varieties.

Benjamin Franklin's career as a scientist was marked on a commemorative silver dollar in 2006.

		1920	1930	1940	1950	1960	1970	1980	1990	2000	2007
MARKET VALUES											
MINT		N/A	$14.00	N/A	$16.00	$35.00	$90.00	$300.00	$425.00	$850.00	$1,250.00
USED		N/A	$5.00	N/A	$13.00	$19.00	$35.00	$75.00	$150.00	$240.00	$275.00

Reflecting the speed theme that is common among the 1901 Pan-American stamps, the 10¢ Fast Ocean Navigation stamp pictures a passenger liner cutting through the sea. The design is based on the *St. Paul*, a 553-foot, 14,910-ton American Liner steamship launched in 1895.

The *St. Paul* was the first commercial ship to be commissioned during the Spanish-American War. The war was still fresh in the minds of many Americans in the early 1900s, and the *St. Paul's* fame almost certainly influenced the choice of ships to feature in the commemorative series.

In the late 1890s, the United States had threatened to intervene if Spain failed to resolve the mounting insurrection in Cuba. Tensions escalated. On February 15, 1898, the USS *Maine* (sent to Cuba to protect American interests there) exploded in Havana's harbor. Patriotic fervor spread, in spite of President William McKinley's desire to avoid all-out war. On March 19, 1898, Congress passed a joint resolution that authorized McKinley to use military force against Spain. Spain countered by declaring war on the United States.

Captain Charles D. Sigsbee boarded the passenger liner *St. Paul* on March 12, 1898, and pressed it into service as an auxiliary cruiser for the United States. The *St. Paul* cruised Jamaica and Haiti in search of Spanish admiral Pascual Cervera's squadron, which had been dispatched to run the U.S. blockade. The *St. Paul* captured the *Restormel* on May 25 before joining the force blockading San Juan, Puerto Rico. Off San Juan, ship and crew were fired upon by the Spanish cruiser *Isabel II* and the destroyer *Terror*. The *St. Paul* returned fire, heavily damaging the destroyer. After this action, the former passenger liner spent the rest of the Spanish-American War serving as a troop transport.

At the end of the 113-day naval war the *St. Paul* was decommissioned and returned to its owner. Almost 20 years later, during World War I, the steel ship was commissioned again and made 12 voyages between New York and Liverpool, England.

The outcome of the Spanish-American War led to the expansion of U.S. interests in Cuba, Puerto Rico, and the Philippines. The young nation that had fought for its independence little more than a century earlier was now a superpower in the eyes of the world. With the cry "Remember the Maine" fresh in their minds, a commemorative stamp bearing a symbol of the nation's military surely seemed appropriate to many Americans.

The steel passenger liner *St. Paul*, fitted out to serve in the Spanish-American War as an auxiliary cruiser.

	MARKET VALUES									
	1920	1930	1940	1950	1960	1970	1980	1990	2000	2007
MINT	$0.30	$1.00	$4.00	$8.00	$11.00	$30.00	$175.00	$150.00	$170.00	$175.00
USED	$0.12	$0.45	$2.00	$3.00	$4.00	$9.00	$20.00	$22.50	$25.00	$30.00

1871 "PERSIAN RUG"

$500 DOCUMENTARY REVENUE STAMP

Scott #R133 • Quantity Known: 77

The United States' Internal Revenue Act of 1861 was passed to help pay for the prolonged Civil War. Taxable goods and services included luxury items, liquor and tobacco, carriages, jewelry, processed meats, and the gross receipts of large businesses. Taxes raised by the act paid nearly 21% of the federal government's war expenses and helped prevent the kind of inflation that plagued the Confederate government.

After the war, the Bureau of Internal Revenue continued to tax many items to offset lingering bills and veterans' pensions—an expense that exceeded $3.3 billion by 1906.

The First Issue Documentary Revenue stamps were issued in 1862 and used as proof that taxes had been paid on transactions such as payment of promissory notes. After their release, officials received numerous reports of counterfeiting, fraudulent cleaning, and reuse.

The Second Issue was distributed in 1871. As an added precaution, the oversized $500-denomination stamps were printed on patented "chameleon" paper, featuring embedded colored silk threads. The elaborate stamps were printed with a three-piece plate. Each piece was individually inked, then assembled to print sheets of one stamp. The result was #R133, the beautifully complex revenue stamp known to collectors as the "Persian Rug" because of its similarity to the ornate carpets.

The $500 denomination was used for large transactions such as payment of promissory notes, whose tax rate in 1871 was 5¢ per $100. The $500 stamp indicated the revenue tax for a $10,000 transaction had been paid. In 1871, $10,000 was the monetary equivalent of more than $1.1 million today, so relatively few #R133 revenues were required. A mere 400 Persian Rug revenue stamps were printed, and only 210 are thought to have been issued. Of them, an estimated 77 stamps are known to survive today.

The intricate design and handsome orange-red, green, and black coloring make the $500 revenue stamp one of the more sought after of U.S. stamps. The large dimensions give the stamp presence and allow the viewer to fully appreciate its finest details. Some collectors suggest that the overall size and dimensions make the stamp resemble a banknote, a similarity that may also broaden the appeal of #R133.

MARKET VALUES										
	1920	1930	1940	1950	1960	1970	1980	1990	2000	2007
MINT	N/A	N/A	N/A	$1,250.00	N/A	$2,350.00	N/A	N/A	N/A	N/A
USED	$500.00	$700.00	$1,250.00	N/A	$1,500.00	N/A	$6,000.00	N/A	$5,000.00	$13,000.00

1901 PAN-AMERICAN COMMEMORATIVE
4¢ AUTOMOBILE
Scott #296 • Quantity Issued: 5,737,100

The 1901 Pan-American Exposition, held in Buffalo, New York, was the setting for a breathtaking display of American advances in transportation and technology. In honor of the occasion, the United States Postal Department issued the first bi-color U.S. commemorative stamp series.

The 4¢ denomination features a miniature engraving of an early electric automobile used for passenger service by the Baltimore and Ohio railroad. The vignette pictures a chauffeur driving the car along with a passenger reported to be Samuel Hedges (sometimes spelled "Hege"), a representative of the railroad. The United States Capitol can be seen directly behind the electric vehicle.

Inverted centers were discovered in the 1¢ and 2¢ denominations shortly after the 1901 Pan-American series was issued. Reports of the discovery of 4¢ inverts reached postal officials, who reacted by deliberately creating two sheets of 200 inverted stamps. Collectors were outraged by the intentional manipulation of the stamp market, and the government's plans to create inverted 5¢, 8¢, and 10¢ Pan-American commemoratives were dropped.

The electric vehicle depicted on the 4¢ Pan-American was a symbol of American innovation. At the end of the exposition, however, it was linked to a tragic event. President William McKinley was shot and wounded while attending the exposition. In a desperate bid to save the president's life, McKinley was rushed for help in a Riker Electric ambulance.

A lively debate continues among collectors regarding whether Hedges is the first distinguishable living person depicted on a U.S. stamp, or if the distinction belongs to Evan Nybakken of the 1898 2¢ Trans-Mississippi stamp. Nybakken reached for his hat, obscuring his face, as a gust of wind threatened to blow it away, just as the photographer snapped his picture.

1901 Columbia Electric Automobile advertisement.

	MARKET VALUES									
	1920	1930	1940	1950	1960	1970	1980	1990	2000	2007
MINT	$0.15	$0.35	$3.00	$4.00	$8.00	$17.00	$95.00	$70.00	$80.00	$100.00
USED	$0.10	$0.20	$1.00	$1.00	$3.00	$6.00	$12.00	$13.00	$15.00	$18.00

It is astonishing that Antonio Muñoz Degrain's painting *Isabella Pledging Her Jewels* was selected to grace the 1893 $1 Columbian stamp. This "historical painting" portrays an event that never happened.

Much of what we consider to be the history of Christopher Columbus and his voyages to the New World is more fiction than fact. The history is shrouded in mystery. The facts have been embellished beyond recognition.

Scholars now agree that, while it makes a great story, Queen Isabella I of Spain never pledged her jewels to help finance Columbus's expedition. In fact, Isabella's financial backing was quite limited. What is certain is that Columbus received the approval of Isabella and her husband Ferdinand for his quest to find a new route to the Indies by sailing west across the Atlantic. The bulk of the capital for the trip was fronted by a consortium of bankers who sought financial gain.

The stamp's central vignette was engraved by Robert Savage. The frame was engraved by D.S. Ronaldson. The stamp was printed by the American Bank Note Company.

The Columbians offer related collectibles of interest to stamp collectors. A host of essays (initial design work) exist. Some are preliminary drawings. Others are printed engravings of partially completed designs. Others show what the proposed design would look like if printed in a variety of colors. Collecting this "archival material" is expensive but illuminating: it beautifully illustrates the processes involved in creating stamp designs.

Once designs have been selected and approved, an engraved die is made by one or more engravers. Proof images are sometimes struck from the original engraved die, or, more commonly, from the master die made from the original. These are done on either large or small pieces of paper and are called accordingly "large die proofs" or "small die proofs." Once the printing plate has been made from the master die, proofs may be made from the entire plate. These, too, are known collectively as archival material, and

all are known to exist for the Columbians. The 1893 Columbian stamps were overprinted "Specimen," a practice that was done so examples of valid stamps could be distributed to other Universal Postal Union member nations. These, too, are collectible.

The glass front of the Aquaria at the 1893 World's Columbian Exposition measured 575 feet long and had a viewing surface of 3,000 square feet.

						MARKET VALUES					
	1920	1930	1940	1950	1960	1970	1980	1990	2000	2007
MINT	$3.00	$9.00	$22.00	$45.00	$58.00	$200.00	$1,000.00	$1,050.00	$1,500.00	$1,200.00
USED	$3.00	$9.00	$20.00	$38.00	$45.00	$130.00	$400.00	$475.00	$650.00	$650.00

1869 PICTORIAL ISSUE
2¢ POST HORSE AND RIDER

Scott #113 • Quantity Issued: 72,109,050

The 2¢ brown Post Horse and Rider was an interesting subject for the U.S. Post Office Department to select for the 1869 stamp series. The entire series had come under criticism for the shape, grills, subject matter, gum, and almost every other aspect about which complaints could be lodged.

The 2¢ Post Horse and Rider was certainly no exception. Some people immediately thought the image was that of the ill-fated Pony Express, which was not an official Post Office Department service. This is a mistake that is still made today. Others criticized the position of the horse, whose front and rear legs were splayed outward in an apparent gallop, an impossible position for a galloping horse to achieve.

The image of the Post Horse and Rider, however, predates its use on the 1869 series. According to the *History of the United States Postal Service 1775–1993*:

> The official seal used by the Post Office Department from 1837 to 1970 pictured, as directed by Postmaster General Amos Kendall, a post horse in speed, with mail bags and rider, encircled by the words "Post Office Department, United States of America."
>
> It is believed this seal was inspired by Benjamin Franklin. When Franklin was selected postmaster general by the Continental Congress, he issued a circular letter throughout the colonies, bearing a rude woodcut of a post rider on horseback, with saddle bags behind him for carrying the mail.

Thus the 2¢ Post Horse and Rider stamp illustrates the Post Office Department's official seal.

All of the stamps of the 1869 series were printed by the National Bank Note Company. The engravers for the 2¢ Post Horse and Rider stamp were Christian Rost and George W. Thurber. This denomination was the second most plentiful, behind the 3¢ locomotive, with an estimated 72 million issued. The 2¢ stamp paid several common rates for drop letters (which were handed in at a post office for delivery to an addressee at the same facility) and for unsealed circulars.

A rare use of the 2¢ stamps was as a bisect; that is, they were cut in half and used as a 1¢ stamp. These should always be collected on cover, with the cancel tying the stamp to the envelope.

The two-cent piece, minted from 1864 to 1873, would purchase a **Post Horse and Rider** stamp at its time of issue. (shown enlarged at 1.5x)

		1920	1930	1940	1950	1960	1970	1980	1990	2000	2007
MARKET VALUES											
MINT		$2.00	$3.00	$3.00	$6.00	$11.00	$33.00	$110.00	$160.00	$600.00	$800.00
USED		$0.35	$1.00	$1.00	$2.00	$3.00	$8.00	$20.00	$25.00	$50.00	$100.00

FIRST U.S. MOURNING STAMP
1866 15¢ ABRAHAM LINCOLN

Scott #77 • Quantity Known: 2,139,000

Issued one year after his death, the 1866 15¢ Abraham Lincoln stamp is America's first mourning stamp. Issued in relatively low quantities, Scott #77 is also the first United States stamp to bear a 15¢ denomination.

After four years of bitter division, America's Civil War drew to a close in the spring of 1865. General Robert E. Lee's surrender at Appomattox on April 9 signaled the end of the long national tragedy as war-weary Confederate soldiers laid down their arms and prepared for the journey home.

Together with a handful of co-conspirators, actor John Wilkes Booth had once planned to kidnap President Lincoln, transport him south, and exchange him for Confederate prisoners of war. Lee's surrender changed Booth's plans. As a military path to victory crumbled, Booth launched a conspiracy to topple the federal government.

The new plot called for the assassination of President Lincoln, Vice President Andrew Johnson, and Secretary of State William H. Seward—events designed to plunge the country into chaos.

Six days after the South fell, Booth shot the president as Lincoln watched the play *Our American Cousin* at Ford's Theater in Washington, DC. While Lincoln lay mortally wounded, another conspirator seriously injured Secretary of State Seward and members of his family and household. Only Vice President Johnson escaped injury.

With the first assassination of a U.S. president at hand, the provisions of the Constitution guided a stunned nation. Johnson, the only Southern senator who didn't quit his federal post when the South seceded, was sworn in as president on April 15, 1865. He was faced with reuniting and reconstructing the Southern states, as well as guiding the nation through its mourning.

One year later, the 15¢ Lincoln stamp was issued. Lincoln's likeness is based on an 1861 photograph of him as president-elect, taken by C.S. German.

At the time the stamp was issued, the most appropriate use was for letters sent to France, or, in combination with a 5¢ stamp, to pay the 20¢ postal registration fee.

Although a little ragged, this cover shows a typical international usage of #77, to Paris in 1867.

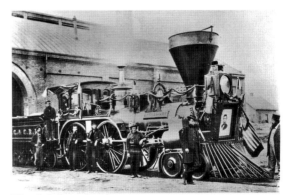

Lincoln's funeral train.

	MARKET VALUES									
	1920	1930	1940	1950	1960	1970	1980	1990	2000	2007
MINT	$13.00	$23.00	$30.00	$30.00	$38.00	$90.00	$325.00	$500.00	$1,200.00	$4,000.00
USED	$2.00	$4.00	$5.00	$9.00	$10.00	$16.00	$40.00	$68.00	$130.00	$200.00

AMERICA'S FIRST AIRMAIL STAMP
1918 24¢ CURTISS JENNY
Scott #C3 • Quantity Issued: 2,134,888

Shortly after the United States entered World War I, officials announced that airmail delivery service would begin on May 15, 1918. The news came as a surprise to many. Critics argued that every available resource was needed for the war effort. The government countered by using military pilots and planes to carry out the service, which provided sorely needed training for new recruits.

Officials decided that the airmail stamp should be printed in patriotic red, white, and blue. The 1918 24¢ stamp would be the first bi-color stamp since the 1901 Pan-Americans. The Bureau of Engraving and Printing was given less than two weeks to prepare the new airmail stamp.

Many skilled BEP employees were serving in the war effort overseas, and those who stayed on the home front were greatly overworked. They labored around the clock to produce the stamps in time for the May 15, 1918, inaugural flight. Using a War Department photo, BEP veteran Clair Aubrey Huston designed a blue vignette featuring the Curtiss JN-4 biplane, or "Jenny," surrounded by a red frame.

Manufactured to train Allied pilots, the Curtiss JN-4 was the first mass-produced plane. More than 6,000 Jenny planes were produced by the end of the war, which made it the most widely used and recognizable model. Six Jennys arrived at the airfield in crates on the night of May 13, and pilots worked around the clock to assemble the planes.

Several hundred people, including President Woodrow Wilson, turned out to watch the first airmail flight on May 15. One pilot left Belmont Park in New York for Philadelphia, where his bag of mail was transferred to a waiting plane bound for Washington, DC. A second plane left Washington for Philadelphia with mail destined for New York City. One pilot flew in the wrong direction and crash-

landed in a nearby field. But by the end of the day, America's first airmail service had been established.

The cost of sending an airmail letter quickly dropped to 16¢ in July and to 6¢ in December. New airmail stamps bearing the same design were issued in different colors for each price decrease.

The *Scott Catalogue* assigned numbers to the set of three 1918 airmail stamps based on denomination rather than chronology. This decision caused some confusion, as the first airmail stamp is identified as #C3, while the third is known as #C1.

Scott #C1 and #C2. In an unexplained twist of fate, the number inscribed on the plane on #C3 matched that of the actual plane flown in the inaugural flight.

	MARKET VALUES									
	1920	1930	1940	1950	1960	1970	1980	1990	2000	2007
MINT	N/A	$0.85	$3.00	$5.00	$9.00	$27.00	$200.00	$100.00	$105.00	$120.00
USED	N/A	$0.60	$2.00	$4.00	$7.00	$18.00	$40.00	$35.00	$35.00	$45.00

1901 PAN-AMERICAN COMMEMORATIVE
5¢ BRIDGE AT NIAGARA FALLS

Scott #297 • Quantity Issued: 7,201,300

The 1901 5¢ Pan-American Exposition stamp pictures Niagara Falls' legendary Honeymoon Bridge. The 19th-century engineering marvel was a suitable choice for the theme of the exposition, which was held in nearby Buffalo, New York, showcasing American advances in transportation and technology. Postal authorities at the time couldn't have foreseen the dramatic demise of the bridge featured on the handsome bi-color stamp.

The mighty Niagara River tumbles over a set of massive waterfalls at the rate of six million cubic feet of water per minute, making Niagara Falls the most powerful waterfall in North America. The Honeymoon Bridge was built 500 feet north of the American Falls. It was a two-hinged steel arch with a latticed rib and an 840-foot span that reached across the gorge to the top of the shorelines. The bridge was later dismantled and re-erected up the river in Queenston.

Frigid winters turn Niagara Falls' spray and mist to spectacular ice formations. A tremendous ice bridge, which rose up to 80 feet in the air, formed around the abutments of the Honeymoon Bridge in 1899. The pressure caused several steel pieces to bend. Laborers blasted the ice away, and protective walls were built around the abutments to shield them from the annual onslaught of ice.

On January 25, 1938, a warm wind pushed ice floes out of Lake Erie and down the Niagara River. Traffic across the bridge was stopped as authorities kept a wary eye on the ice jam that formed in the river. Large crowds gathered to keep a vigil. At 4:20 p.m. on January 27, the ice jam fell over Niagara Falls and hit the abutments of the Honeymoon Bridge. The bridge collapsed under the weight of the ice and fell into the frozen gorge below. Miraculously, there were no injuries.

The 5¢ Pan-American stamp chronicles the romance of the legendary Honeymoon Bridge. Two trolley cars can be seen crossing the bridge, with Niagara Falls in the background and both the Canadian and American shores visible. At the time of issue, Scott #297 paid the first-class letter rate to Europe, allowing Old World cousins to marvel at two of North America's natural and technological wonders.

Panoramic view of Niagara Falls, circa 1912.

						MARKET VALUES					
	1920	1930	1940	1950	1960	1970	1980	1990	2000	2007
MINT	$0.20	$0.50	$3.00	$4.00	$8.00	$17.00	$95.00	$82.50	$95.00	$95.00
USED	$0.15	$0.50	$2.00	$2.00	$3.00	$7.00	$13.00	$12.50	$14.00	$15.00

THE FIRST AMERICAN ORBITS EARTH
1962 4¢ PROJECT MERCURY

Scott #1193 • Quantity Issued: 289,240,000

It was 1962. The United States was in a competition with the Soviet Union that became known as the "Space Race," and the U.S. was losing. Five years earlier, the Soviet Union had successfully launched a satellite into Earth's orbit. Those of us who were alive then will remember venturing outdoors at night to marvel as *Sputnik* streaked across the evening sky.

Soviet cosmonaut Yuri Gagarin became the first human in space when he orbited Earth in 1961, 28 days before U.S. astronaut Alan Shepard made a successful suborbital space flight that lasted only 15 minutes.

On February 20, 1962, Marine Corps colonel John Glenn was launched aboard the Project Mercury capsule *Friendship 7*, becoming the first American to orbit Earth. The successful flight completed three orbits and lasted just less than five hours, splashing into the Atlantic at 2:42 p.m., Eastern Standard Time.

At 3:30 p.m., postmasters at 305 post offices across the United States received word to open parcels they had received as "top secret." The parcels contained panes of 4¢ Project Mercury "U.S. Man in Space" stamps that were to be released immediately in celebration of Glenn's successful orbital flight around Earth. Cancels applied to stamps at Cape Canaveral were the only ones to bear the words "First Day of Issue" within the cancellation.

The Bureau of Engraving and Printing had gone to great lengths to keep the stamp secret. Designer C.R. Chickering worked on the stamp art from home, claiming he was on vacation. The engraver, R.M. Bower, worked at night when no one else was present to see what he was doing. An estimated 400 people were "in" on the secret stamp. All things considered, it was amazing that the Post Office Department was able to pull off the big surprise. The clandestine Project Mercury stamps were an instant hit with stamp collectors and the general public.

John Glenn and President Kennedy with the Mercury capsule, February 23, 1962.

	MARKET VALUES								
	1920	1930	1940	1950	1960	1970	1980	1990	2000	2007
MINT						$0.08	$0.20	$0.08	$0.15	$0.20
USED						$0.04	$0.10	$0.05	$0.15	$0.20

1901 PAN-AMERICAN COMMEMORATIVE
4¢ AUTOMOBILE INVERT
Scott #296a • Quantity Known: 101

The 1901 Pan-American Exposition was a celebration of technological innovations suitable for the new century. The Bureau of Engraving and Printing produced its first bi-color stamps in honor of the event. The Pan-American stamps were the first commemoratives of the 20th century.

Although the nation had many reasons to be proud of its advances, the Pan-American issue demonstrated that no amount of engineering could overcome simple human error. Shortly after the bi-color series was issued, inverted frames were discovered in the 1¢ and 2¢ denominations.

Postal officials later received a report that inverted 4¢ stamps had also been discovered. Aware of the errors within the lower denominations, officials were convinced that the 4¢ inverts existed as well, even though they had no physical examples.

An order was issued to purposely print 400 inverted stamps to document the error. Some of them (an unknown quantity) were hand-stamped "Specimen." Officials later learned that the report of 4¢ inverted stamps was erroneous.

Third Assistant Postmaster General Edwin C. Madden took delivery of the intentionally created "error" stamps and distributed them among his acquaintances. Upon learning of Madden's generosity with the intentionally created rarities, authorities destroyed 194 stamps and placed a pane of 100 without overprints in the postal archives.

Stamp collectors were outraged. Based on their reaction, postal officials reportedly destroyed sheets of the 5¢, 8¢, and 10¢ denominations that had also been intentionally created with inverted frames.

While in storage, the pane of 100 4¢ invert stamps became stuck on a page. Eventually, 97 were traded with stamp dealers in exchange for stamp rarities missing from the archives. Today, virtually every 4¢ Pan-American invert stamp without an overprint can be traced to the archives and is found with disturbed gum as a result.

Although he was chided for his role in the Pan-American invert giveaway, Madden continued distributing philatelic rarities to political cronies. Between 1903 and 1905, he distributed up to 85 "Roosevelt Presentation Albums" to influential friends and political partisans with connections to President Theodore Roosevelt and his Cabinet. Although the practice was discontinued in 1905 in the wake of public protest, Madden kept his position in the Roosevelt administration until 1907.

The Electric Tower was the highlight of the Pan-American Exposition.

		1920	1930	1940	1950	1960	1970	1980	1990	2000	2007
	MARKET VALUES										
MINT		N/A	$850.00	$1,350.00	$1,000.00	$1,100.00	$4,750.00	$10,000.00	$13,000.00	$21,000.00	$35,000.00
USED		N/A	N/A	N/A	N/A	N/A	N/A	N/A	N/A	N/A	N/A

1901 PAN-AMERICAN COMMEMORATIVE
2¢ FAST EXPRESS
Scott #295 • Quantity Issued: 209,759,700

As the world's first high-speed passenger train, the *Empire State Express* was a logical choice for the Pan-American commemorative stamp series honoring American advances in technology.

At the time the 2¢ Pan-American stamp was issued, however, the choice of the passenger train to commemorate the Pan-American Exposition seemed unpleasantly political to some critics. They were concerned that the *Empire State Express* was still in use as the flagship of the New York Central and Hudson, a commercial railroad that served the Exposition's host city of Buffalo, New York.

Skeptics pointed to the commemorative's intended purpose and the longstanding prohibition against advertising on U.S. stamps. Perhaps to silence criticism, the stamps were merely inscribed "Commemorative Series, 1901."

G.H. Daniels, general passenger agent of the New York Central Railroad, lobbied strongly in favor of including the *Empire State Express* in the Pan-American series. Daniels argued that the *Empire State Express* was one of the most famous trains in history and that its widespread fame had focused worldwide attention on America's industrial superiority, which made it a natural choice in light of the Exposition's theme.

The *Empire State Express* had earned its fame in 1891, when it covered 436 miles between New York City and Buffalo in seven hours and six minutes, including stops. The train averaged 61.4 miles per hour, a new world record. It later made the longest scheduled nonstop run on record and was the first passenger train to maintain a regular-schedule speed greater than 52 miles per hour. In 1893, the *Empire State Express* was outfitted with a special 4-4-0 steam locomotive named *No. 999*, for the trip from Syracuse, New York, to the World's Columbian Exposition in Chicago. The train was recorded traveling an astonishing 121.5 miles per hour.

Ultimately, the *Empire State Express* transported as much as 60% of the Pan-American Exposition's visitors. And collectors have a striking black-and-red stamp that depicts one of history's more memorable locomotives.

These covers celebrated the Pan-American Exposition's host city (symbolized as a buffalo on top of the world).

	MARKET VALUES									
	1920	1930	1940	1950	1960	1970	1980	1990	2000	2007
MINT	$0.06	$0.10	$0.40	$0.50	$1.00	$4.00	$18.00	$14.00	$18.00	$20.00
USED	$0.01	$0.04	$0.05	$0.04	$0.15	$0.35	$1.00	$1.00	$1.00	$1.00

SERIES OF 1902–1903
1903 $5 JOHN MARSHALL

Scott #313 • Quantity Known: 49,211

The United States definitive stamp series of 1902 is often called the "Second Bureau Issue" because the Bureau of Engraving and Printing (BEP) produced the stamps. The ornate frames of the 1902 series stood in marked contrast to the plain (for its time) framing on the First Bureau Issue, whose dominant feature was nested triangles in the upper-left and upper-right corners.

The 1902 stamps produced a number of firsts. The 8¢ value bore the portrait of Martha Washington, whose appearance made her the first American woman to grace a United States postage stamp (see No. 86). This series was the first to contain the names of the individuals portrayed on the stamps.

The highest denomination in the series was a $5 value printed in dark green, featuring a portrait of early-1800s Supreme Court chief justice John Marshall. The BEP's chief designer, Raymond Ostrander Smith, designed all of the stamps in the series and they were printed by intaglio (engraved). Robert Ponickau and Marcus Baldwin engraved the die for the frame of the $5 Marshall stamp, and George F.C. Smillie engraved Marshall's portrait. A fourth engraver, Lyman F. Ellis, was responsible for the numerals and lettering. The stamps were printed on double-line watermarked paper with perforations that gauge 12.

The dollar denominations of the 1902 series were issued in 1903, but the $2 and $5 denominations were in use much longer than other stamps from the same series. In fact, the U.S. Post Office Department reissued both values in March 1917, long after the introduction of the Third Bureau Issue "Washington-Franklin" stamps. John Marshall's portrait also was used on the $5 First Bureau Issue issued in 1894.

The subject of this stamp, John Marshall, participated in the Revolutionary War, serving as a lieutenant with the Culpepper Minutemen. He studied law, and as an attorney entered politics as a representative to the Virginia House of Delegates. Later, Marshall was elected to the United States House of Representatives. In 1799, President John Adams appointed Marshall secretary of state, the fourth individual to hold that office. Marshall served in the position for only eight months. He was then appointed the fourth chief justice of the U.S. Supreme Court, a position he held for more than 34 years. The image of "blind justice" at the upper-right corner of the stamp pays tribute to Marshall's lengthy service to the nation as chief justice.

**In 2005 John Marshall's service on the Supreme Court
was commemorated by a silver dollar from the U.S. Mint.**

MARKET VALUES

	1920	1930	1940	1950	1960	1970	1980	1990	2000	2007
Mint	$10.00	$28.00	$50.00	$95.00	$135.00	$300.00	$1,750.00	$1,650.00	$2,900.00	$3,000.00
Used	$7.00	$17.00	$30.00	$60.00	$80.00	$160.00	$500.00	$450.00	$675.00	$750.00

On May 1, 1901, the Post Office Department issued the first United States commemorative stamp series of the 20th century. The series commemorates the Pan-American Exposition and World's Fair, a celebration of technology and its impact on America, held in Buffalo, New York, from May 1 through November 1, 1901.

Ironically, the Pan-American stamps could have been the last stamps of the 19th century. The Exposition was initially proposed in 1895, but was delayed because of the outbreak of the Spanish-American War. As plans to produce the 1898 Trans-Mississippi commemoratives in two colors were cancelled due to the war, collectors can only speculate on the fate of the bi-color Pan-Americans if the Exposition had been held as planned.

The vignette of each Pan-American stamp portrays an important innovation, resulting in a series that reflects American industry's growing dominance at the turn of the century. More than half of the stamp subjects focus on speed, reflecting its importance in the delivery of goods, and the resulting impact on the nation's growing economy.

The 1¢ Pan-American commemorative stamp depicts the Great Lakes steamer *City of Alpena*. Particularly well suited for inland waters, steamer boats replaced sailing ships along the water route during the mid-1800s. Steamers carried commercial freight and passengers throughout the 1,555-mile Great Lakes system, contributing to the rapid growth of Buffalo and several other major cities along the route.

The bi-color Pan-American stamps were printed in two steps. In the first step, the vignette depicting the steamship was printed

in black ink. The frame surrounding the steamship was then printed in green. This process made it very difficult for the printer to center the frame evenly around the central design. As a result, several stamps feature frames that are not aligned properly. Collectors have nicknamed these varieties based on the appearance of the ship in relation to the frame. These highly collectible stamps are known as the "fast," "slow," and "sinking" varieties. The rarest and most sought-after variety is the invert, which was produced when the frame was mistakenly printed upside down.

Based on the relationship of the frame to the vignette, varieties of Scott #294 include "fast," "slow," "sinking," and inverted.

Stock certificates were sold to offset the cost of the Pan-American Exposition. Shares cost $10 apiece, a sum equivalent to more than $1,000 in today's wages.

	MARKET VALUES									
	1920	1930	1940	1950	1960	1970	1980	1990	2000	2007
MINT	$0.05	$0.08	$0.40	$0.45	$1.00	$4.00	$18.00	$14.00	$18.00	$25.00
USED	$0.02	$0.06	$0.12	$0.20	$0.40	$1.00	$4.00	$3.00	$3.00	$3.00

MESSENGER RUNNING
1885 10¢ SPECIAL DELIVERY

Scott #E1 • Quantity Known: 6,634,450

In 1885, the U.S. Postal Department brought a revolutionary new service to America. For the first time in United States history, speedy delivery of very important messages could be guaranteed from 555 special post offices located in America's largest cities.

The experimental Special Delivery service was well received by the public. Letters were delivered within minutes of their arrival at the recipient's local post office, and the hours of service were extended late into the evening. Special Delivery service was the most reliable way to send an urgent message in the era before telephones, email, and text messaging.

The fee for Special Delivery service was 10¢ in addition to the first-class rate, regardless of weight or distance. A handsomely engraved stamp was printed by the American Bank Note Company to indicate payment of the fee. The 1885 Special Delivery stamp depicts a messenger running, lending #E1 and its successors the nickname "Speedy."

Only cities of more than 4,000 residents were eligible for the service. Young men aged 13 to 16 were paid 8¢ per letter, with a limit of $30.00 per month, to provide special delivery. Some major cities averaged delivery times of just six minutes from the time the letter was received.

Throughout the years, a certain romance has been associated with Special Delivery. Americans received marriage proposals, important business papers, news of the death of a loved one, birth announcements, and many other life-altering personal messages in letters brought by Special Delivery messenger.

This new form of communication captured the imagination of the American public, somewhat like the Pony Express system had 25 years earlier. References to Special Delivery became common in American pop culture. Perhaps the most famous example can be found in Elvis Presley's "Return to Sender," in which he sends his girlfriend a letter by "Special D."

Special Delivery service was expanded to include all post offices on October 1, 1886, prompting the need for a new stamp. Successive stamps featured messengers promptly delivering letters on bicycles and motorcycles, and in post-office trucks.

On June 8, 1997, Special Delivery service was discontinued in favor of Express Mail.

	1920	1930	1940	1950	1960	1970	1980	1990	2000	2007
MARKET VALUES										
MINT	N/A	$2.00	$4.00	$5.00	$11.00	$35.00	$200.00	$175.00	$300.00	$500.00
USED	N/A	$0.60	$2.00	$3.00	$5.00	$10.00	$25.00	$20.00	$45.00	$70.00

HIGH-VALUE THIRD BUREAU ISSUE
1918 $5 BENJAMIN FRANKLIN

Scott #524 • Quantity Issued: 296,653

When the Washington-Franklin Third Bureau Issue series of 1908 appeared, the highest denomination printed was a $1 stamp with a portrait of George Washington. When higher-denomination stamps were needed, the earlier Second Bureau Issue $2 Madison and $5 Marshall stamps were pulled into service. The U.S. Post Office Department had believed it to be a sufficient quantity.

Things changed nine years after the Washington-Franklin series began. The United States was being drawn into the Great War. Suddenly, there was more demand for stamps with face values of $2 and $5 to send heavy parcels to Europe and Russia. In March 1917, the Post Office Department had the 1902-series $2 Madison and $5 Marshall stamps reprinted to accommodate the demand. Seventeen months later, in August 1918, the Post Office Department released newly designed $2 and $5 Franklin stamps.

Both the $2 and $5 Franklin stamps of 1918 are considered to be a part of the Third Bureau Issue Washington-Franklin series, but they also serve as design precursors to the 1922 Fourth Bureau Issue series. The frames surrounding the head of Franklin on the $2 and $5 stamps bear a number of similarities to the Fourth Bureau series that would come three years later. The $2 and $5 Franklin stamps both used the same printing plate for the vignette. The Bureau of Engraving and Printing's Claire A. Huston designed the $5 Franklin. He also designed the 1922 Fourth Bureau Issue series.

The $5 Franklin was printed in two colors, the frame in green and the vignette in black. This required two passes through the printing press. Unlike with the 24¢ Jenny bi-color airmail stamp that had been printed a few months earlier, care was taken so that there were no inverts made of either the $2 or $5 Franklin bi-color stamps.

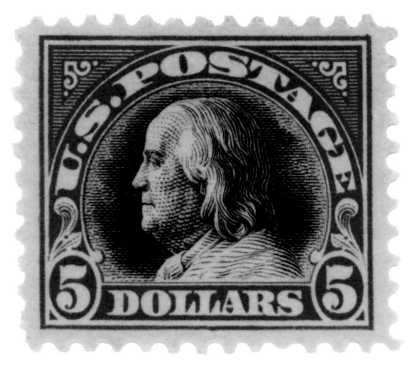

The $5 Franklin had a long period of use, from 1918 until 1933, well into the Fourth Bureau issue period. It was in use concurrently with the $5 Statue of Freedom stamp from the 1922 series.

Five dollars was a lot of money in the period of use for these stamps—the equivalent of more than $220 in today's wages. They were used primarily on large, heavy parcels and for registration fees for valuable items.

A perennial favorite on American stamps and coins, Benjamin Franklin would be honored on silver commemorative dollars in 2006.

MARKET VALUES										
	1920	1930	1940	1950	1960	1970	1980	1990	2000	2007
MINT	$8.00	$10.00	$10.00	$15.00	$23.00	$45.00	$400.00	$275.00	$220.00	$250.00
USED	$1.00	$4.00	$2.00	$3.00	$4.00	$8.00	$20.00	$20.00	$35.00	$40.00

COLUMBUS DESCRIBING HIS THIRD VOYAGE
1893 $3 COLUMBIAN COMMEMORATIVE
Scott #243 • Quantity Issued: 27,350

The $3 Columbian design is based on a painting by Francisco Jover y Casanova, who died at age 54, just three years prior to the stamp's release. It depicts the painting *Columbus Describing His Third Voyage*. Unfortunately, Columbus's third voyage was not one of his crowning glories. He ended up in chains, as illustrated on the $2 Columbian, and then imprisoned.

The reason this happened begins with Columbus's second voyage in 1493. He was commissioned as admiral and appointed viceroy of "the Indies." Columbus carried to his death his belief that these voyages had taken him to India. His orders were to convert the populations he found to Christianity and establish a colony at the stockade he began on Hispaniola, the land he had claimed for Spain during his first voyage.

Columbus set sail with 17 ships and 1,500 men under his command. When the flotilla arrived in Hispaniola, they discovered the 39 men left behind at the stockade on the first voyage had been killed and the settlement destroyed by indigenous people. Columbus established a new colony despite the hostile local population, many of whom were captured and enslaved with promises that their freedom could be obtained once Columbus had been paid in gold.

The troubles with the second voyage made gathering the financial backing necessary for a third voyage more difficult, but by 1498 Columbus was back at sea. This time he sailed farther south and explored an island he called Trinidad, after the Holy Trinity, and then went on to what would become Venezuela, believing that King Solomon's mine was nearby.

Columbus then returned to Hispaniola. The colony was in shambles. Insufficient gold had been collected to bring wealth to everyone in the colony. The food available was unfamiliar and unpalatable to the colonists, and they returned to Spain in disgust, demanding reparation. The colonists also charged Columbus with mismanagement. Upon hearing their reports, King Ferdinand and Queen Isabella sent another vessel to return with Columbus. He and his two brothers, Diego and Bartholomew, who governed Hispaniola when Columbus was away, were brought back to Spain in chains and imprisoned for a short time in 1500.

Columbus was able to convince Ferdinand and Isabella of his innocence and his superior navigation skills. In September 1501, he began his fourth and final voyage.

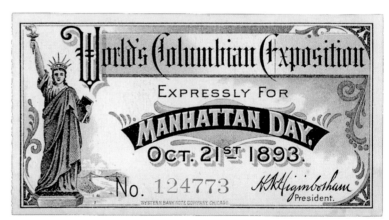

Held October 21, 1893, Manhattan Day was one of the highlights of the Columbian exposition.

	1920	1930	1940	1950	1960	1970	1980	1990	2000	2007
MARKET VALUES										
Mint	$6.00	$15.00	$45.00	$70.00	$95.00	$325.00	$1,850.00	$1,950.00	$2,400.00	$1,900.00
Used	$6.00	$15.00	$33.00	$63.00	$85.00	$225.00	$650.00	$700.00	$1,000.00	$1,000.00

1938 PRESIDENTIAL SERIES
$5 CALVIN COOLIDGE
Scott #834 • Quantity Issued: 9,318,026

The United States Post Office Department launched a new series of regular-issue (or "definitive") stamps in 1938 that replaced the 1922 series known as the "Fourth Bureau" issues. The 1938 series is called the Presidential Series, or more commonly the "Prexies," even though not all of the stamps in the series illustrate U.S. presidents.

It was an interesting and novel approach to stamp issuing. Each president was shown in chronological order from the 1¢ value showing first president George Washington to the top value depicting the 30th president, Calvin Coolidge. Only two chief executives were not shown: the sitting president, Franklin Roosevelt, and his immediate predecessor, Herbert Hoover, who was still alive. Children and adults who took an interest in stamps could recite the sequence of successive presidents by remembering how the stamps were mounted in their albums.

The Prexies evolved from a design competition suggested by President Roosevelt, who was a keen stamp collector. The winner of the competition was Elaine Rawlinson, a 25-year-old artist. In addition to winning the $500 prize, she also made history by being the first woman to design a series of United States stamps. Her design was vastly different from the heavily ornamented stamps that preceded the Prexies, relying on the Art Deco style that was the beginning of mid-century minimalism.

The cent-value Prexies were rotary printed in one color. This type of printing uses curved plates mounted on a cylinder. The bi-color dollar values were flat-plate printed. President Coolidge graced the highest denomination of the series with a face value of $5. Coolidge had been president from 1923 to 1929, completing Warren Harding's term after Harding's death and serving one elected term of his own. A conservative Republican, he earned the nickname "Silent Cal" for his taciturn demeanor. (A story is told of a young woman sitting next to Coolidge at a dinner party, who confided that she had bet she could get at least three words of conversation from him. Silent Cal's retort: "You lose.") This was in sharp contrast to his vivacious wife, Grace, and his well-connected vice president, Charles Dawes, who was awarded the Nobel Peace Prize in 1925.

The $5 Coolidge stamps, printed in carmine and black, were released on November 17, 1938. A scarce color variety in red-brown and black may also be found, but because colors can be chemically altered, collectors are well advised to acquire a certificate of genuineness before buying.

The designs of the high-value Prexies are reversed compared to the lower denominations, which feature a variety of colored backgrounds and white lettering.

	MARKET VALUES								
	1920	1930	1940	1950	1960	1970	1980	1990	2000	2007
MINT			$8.00	$8.00	$10.00	$18.00	$225.00	$105.00	$95.00	$90.00
USED			$1.00	$0.60	$1.00	$1.00	$5.00	$4.00	$3.00	$3.00

SERIES OF 1922-1925
14¢ AMERICAN INDIAN
Scott #565 • Quantity Issued: 151,114,177

The Series of 1922–1925 can be thought of as progressive in some respects. It was the first U.S. stamp series in 20 years to honor a wide variety of distinguished Americans. It was the first to include a 14¢ stamp, and the first to portray an American Indian in traditional dress as its subject. More importantly, the Series of 1922–1925 was the first to benefit from the oversight of a postmaster general familiar with the preferences of stamp collectors.

Warren Harding's 1921 presidential inauguration ushered in sweeping changes at many levels of the U.S. Post Office Department. Harding selected W. Irving Glover to serve as third assistant postmaster general, the person traditionally in charge of stamps and their production. Although Glover never spoke openly about his hobbies, his wife is known to have owned an extensive worldwide stamp collection.

Glover made many immediate changes. A window at the Washington Post Office was opened specifically to service the needs of stamp collectors. Older stamps were made available to collectors. Extensive information was given regarding new issues, and efforts were made to make them more appealing to collectors.

Glover immediately requested a new stamp series to replace the Washington-Franklins. Operating under his direction, BEP veteran Claire Huston engraved a 23-stamp series featuring the ornate details that are his signature.

A photograph of Brule Sioux chief Hollow Horn Bear was used as the model for the 14¢ stamp in the Series of 1922–1925. Hollow Horn Bear had once fought to drive white men from the Great Plains. By the 1870s, however, he advocated peace, helped negotiate terms for the Rosebud Indian reservation in South Dakota, and became a minor celebrity in Washington, DC. He traveled to the

capital to take part in Theodore Roosevelt's 1905 inaugural parade. While in Washington, Hollow Horn Bear was photographed by a Smithsonian Institute photographer. Close examination of the photograph reveals a Roosevelt campaign button.

Hollow Horn Bear also took part in Woodrow Wilson's 1913 inaugural parade, where he caught cold and died of pneumonia a few days later.

To ensure that registered mail was being checked for tampering, the Post Office briefly forbade postmasters from showing the name and date on the front of a cover—but the stamps still needed cancelling. Enterprising postmasters created fancy cancels such as the Ear of Corn cancel from Fairfield, Iowa, as shown above.

This World's Columbian Exposition ticket pictures an Indian chief in full regalia.

		MARKET VALUES								
	1920	1930	1940	1950	1960	1970	1980	1990	2000	2007
MINT		$0.24	$0.40	$0.45	$1.00	$1.00	$5.00	$3.00	$4.00	$4.00
USED		$0.05	$0.10	$0.08	$0.20	$0.30	$0.45	$1.00	$1.00	$1.00

ONE GIANT LEAP FOR MANKIND
1969 10¢ MOON LANDING

Scott #C76 • Quantity Issued: 152,364,800

The world held its breath on July 20, 1969. Hundreds of millions watched scratchy television images beamed from a spacecraft nearly 240,000 miles away.

"Houston, Tranquility Base here. The *Eagle* has landed."

Astronauts Neil Armstrong and Edwin "Buzz" Aldrin had just set the lunar landing module of the *Apollo 11* mission on the Moon, fulfilling John F. Kennedy's promise in 1961 to land a man on the Moon and return him safely to Earth before the end of the decade. Seven hours after the landing, *Eagle's* hatch opened. Armstrong, encapsulated in a cumbersome space suit, backed down the ladder and placed his foot on the Moon.

"That's one small step for [a] man; one giant leap for Mankind," became the first words a human being uttered on the Moon. In his excitement, Neil Armstrong, commander of the expedition, omitted the article "a."

Buzz Aldrin, the lunar module pilot, joined Armstrong on the lunar surface. Together they spent two hours on the surface, erecting an American flag, deploying instruments, taking photographs, and collecting more than 40 pounds of lunar rocks and dust. In less than 24 hours, the *Eagle's* rockets fired and the module returned to the orbiting command module piloted by Michael Collins. The three-man crew concluded the eight-day *Apollo 11* mission by splashing into the Pacific Ocean on July 24, 1969. The men and their capsule were recovered by the aircraft carrier USS *Hornet*.

Anticipating the success of this mission, the U.S. Postal Service commissioned a stamp design for the lunar landing. The artwork was done by Paul Calle, who has designed many other stamps for the Postal Service. A metal die of the stamp art was prepared and placed in the lunar landing module, and this went to the Moon with Armstrong and Aldrin.

Rock specimens, equipment, and the metal stamp die all were transferred from the lunar module to the command module before it was jettisoned prior to re-entry into Earth's atmosphere. The die was used to produce the plates from which the stamps were printed, giving everyone who owns one of these extraordinary stamps a piece of lunar history.

More than 500 million people watched Neil Armstrong's historic moon walk on television.

MARKET VALUES										
	1920	1930	1940	1950	1960	1970	1980	1990	2000	2007
MINT						$0.20	$0.35	$0.20	$0.25	$0.25
USED						$0.10	$0.10	$0.15	$0.15	$0.20

ISABELLA AND COLUMBUS
1893 $4 COLUMBIAN COMMEMORATIVE
Scott #244 • Quantity Issued: 26,350

The term "first ladies" in the United States usually refers to presidents' wives, but the first ladies to appear on United States stamps were featured on the 1893 Columbians. The 1¢ denomination has an Indian woman and a child who could be either male or female. The 5¢ value shows Columbus speaking at Court in front of Isabella, queen of Spain, and several ladies in waiting. An unnamed woman is shown on the 6¢ stamp; many women are shown on the 8¢. The 10¢, 15¢, $1, and $3 values all show Queen Isabella as part of the design, but only the $4 value shows her in a prominent portrait, thus making it the first U.S. stamp to show a portrait of a woman. Nine years later, Martha Washington would become the first American woman to have her portrait featured on a stamp.

Queen Isabella of Castille was Christopher Columbus's champion and patron. It was Isabella to whom Columbus made his pitch for the voyage to find a new route to the Indies by sailing west instead of east. Although unconvinced at first, she eventually capitulated, and together with her husband, King Ferdinand of Aragon, saw to it that Columbus received the financial backing necessary to outfit the expedition.

The two portraits were engraved by Alfred Jones of the American Bank Note Co., who also worked on several other stamps in the series. The stamp is listed in the *Scott Catalogue* as being "crimson lake," with a sub-variety "carmine" also listed. The $4 Isabella and Columbus stamp had the lowest distribution number of the 16-stamp series, variously recorded as ranging from 24,700 to 26,350.

The origin of the queen's portrait is not known, but the image of Columbus was taken from a painting done in 1512 by Lorenzo Lotto. This portrait was used often for stamps, including those from Chile and other nations.

In 1992 the United States, Italy, Portugal, and Spain jointly released souvenir sheets that reproduced the original U.S. 1893 Columbian series stamps. This provided an easy way for collectors to own the designs of the high values that were never inexpensive or plentiful.

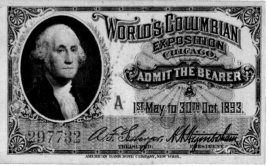

World's Columbian Exposition ticket.

						MARKET VALUES					
	1920	1930	1940	1950	1960	1970	1980	1990	2000	2007
MINT	$8.00	$18.00	$50.00	$80.00	$110.00	$400.00	$2,850.00	$2,750.00	$3,250.00	$2,600.00
USED	$8.00	$18.00	$40.00	$73.00	$90.00	$265.00	$900.00	$1,000.00	$1,350.00	$1,300.00

Shortly after the Pan-American commemorative series was issued, two fortunate men each purchased a sheet of 100 inverted 2¢ Fast Express stamps.

Mr. Davis of Mergenthaler Linotype Co. discovered his inverted stamps after a visit to a Brooklyn post office and quickly sold them to stamp dealers along New York's famed Nassau Street for $5 each. The second sheet of 100 stamps was purchased by a Sunday School teacher, who gave a few to his friends and sold the remainder for $1,000.

More than a century later, only 158 examples of the dramatic inverted stamp are known. As one of the inverted sheets featured a distinct shade of carmine and the other an equally distinct shade of scarlet, individual stamps can often be traced to their specific sheet of origin.

Centering also varies widely among the Fast Express inverted stamps. Some examples are very well centered, while others are rather poor. Most are missing their original gum.

Although Scott #295a is frequently described as having an inverted center, the black vignette was printed before the red frame. Therefore, it is the frame that is inverted.

Inverts were also created while printing the 1¢ and 4¢ denominations. However, the 4¢ Pan-American invert was purposely created and distributed among dignitaries. While still desirable, 1,000 1¢ inverted Pan-American stamps reached the public. They are much more common than their 2¢ cousins.

Non-error Scott #295.

Railroad poster, early 1900s.

MARKET VALUES										
	1920	1930	1940	1950	1960	1970	1980	1990	2000	2007
MINT	$750.00	$1,750.00	$3,500.00	$2,500.00	$3,250.00	$15,000.00	$35,000.00	$45,000.00	$37,500.00	$45,000.00
USED	N/A	N/A	$2,500.00	$2,500.00	$2,600.00	$5,500.00	$8,000.00	$13,500.00	$15,000.00	$55,000.00

1 8 6 9 PICTORIAL ISSUE
1¢ BENJAMIN FRANKLIN
Scott #112 • Quantity Issued: 12,020,550

The design of the 1¢ stamp from the 1869 series is based on a sculpture of Benjamin Franklin. The stamp is listed in the *Scott Catalogue* as being in buff, with additional color varieties listed of brown-orange and dark brown-orange. The various shades differ dramatically from one another. As with all stamps of the 1869 series, it was printed by the National Bank Note Company and issued with grills and without grills.

Within a series of stamps that were vastly different from all that had come before, the 1¢ denomination is even more dissimilar. Compared with the heavily ornamented frames of the 1851 series, the 1869 1¢ Franklin is almost a stark precursor to simpler modern design that would dominate the stamp scene a century later. It is curious that the first value of the first nearly-square U.S. stamps would have an image that was completely contained within a circle. It was as if the Post Office Department were attempting to put a round peg in a square hole.

The entire 1869 series was reissued as special printings done again by the National Bank Note Company in 1875 for the Centennial Exhibition of 1876. This event was held in Philadelphia for the 100th anniversary of the signing of the Declaration of Independence. However, Lester Brookman wrote in *The United States Postage Stamps of the 19th Century, volume III*, "so far as can be determined, none of the Special Printings that were issued for the Centennial Exposition of 1876 were on sale at the Exhibition post office." This made hollow the professed desire of the Post Office Department that all past issues of U.S. stamps be available for purchase by stamp collectors.

The 1875 reissue of the 1¢ Franklin was printed using a new plate. Like the other 1869 reissues, the 1¢ was not grilled. The stamps were valid postage and were used on ordinary mail. According to Brookman, 8,252 of the 1¢ 1875 reissues were sold.

In 1880, the American Bank Note Company reissued the 1869 1¢ Franklin. This time the stamp was printed on soft, porous paper and without a grill. There are two varieties of the 1880 special printing. One was printed in buff and issued with gum. The other was printed in brown-orange and issued without gum. Again, these stamps were valid for postage and may be found postally used.

Considering the original 1869 printing, the special printings, grills, and stamps without grills, color shades and varieties, essays, proofs, color trials, and a vast assortment of other varieties, there is much for philatelists to collect. No wonder the 1869s are so popular.

Benjamin Franklin's visage is familiar to generations of Americans from a wide variety of stamp, coin, and paper currency designs.

	1920	1930	1940	1950	1960	1970	1980	1990	2000	2007
MINT	$2.00	$6.00	$7.00	$10.00	$18.00	$58.00	$165.00	$225.00	$650.00	$850.00
USED	$1.00	$3.00	$4.00	$7.00	$10.00	$20.00	$45.00	$60.00	$140.00	$175.00

MARKET VALUES

CONTINENTAL BANK NOTE CO.
1873 90¢ PERRY WITH SECRET MARKS

Scott #166 • Quantity Known: 197,000

Several competing bank-note printing companies vied for lucrative contracts with the United States Post Office Department in the 1870s. In the end, three won the right to produce U.S. postage stamps at different times.

The first to get the Post Office Department nod was the National Bank Note Co., which held the contract from 1870 to 1873. They produced 11 face-different denominations, ranging from 1¢ to 90¢, with grills and without them.

In 1873 National lost out to the Continental Bank Note Co., whose pricing was more competitive. The Post Office Department required that Continental use the same designs, done by B. Packard of the National Bank Note Co. The department made it compulsory that National hand over the stamp dies and plates to Continental. "Secret marks" were engraved into the dies that Continental used to create new printing plates. These secret marks are found on 1873 Continental 1¢, 2¢, 3¢, 6¢, 7¢, 10¢, 12¢, and 15¢ stamps.

It is presumed that Continental used the original National plates to print the 90¢ Perry stamps rather than making new plates from a die with secret marks, as no such marks have been found on the 90¢ denomination produced by Continental. This makes identifying a Continental printing of the 90¢ Perry more difficult. It was printed in rose-carmine, whereas the National Bank Note Co.'s version was in carmine . . . but colors change and fade over time.

Oliver Hazard Perry was an interesting subject choice for a stamp. He entered the United States Navy as a midshipman at the age of 13, following his father's example. In 1812, Perry rose to the rank of master-commandant. Shortly thereafter, the United States and Great Britain were at war. Perry requested sea duty but was sent to Erie, Pennsylvania, to oversee building of a fleet of naval vessels, which he later commanded against a British squadron in Lake Erie. Perry defeated the entire British squadron and captured every ship as a prize of war. In his report summarizing the Battle of Erie, the 28-year-old Perry wrote, "We have met the enemy and they are ours."

This engraving shows Oliver Hazard Perry's gold medal, awarded with the thanks of the Legislature of Pennsylvania. (from *Lossing's Pictorial Field Book of the War of 1812*)

MARKET VALUES										
	1920	1930	1940	1950	1960	1970	1980	1990	2000	2007
MINT	$6.00	$12.00	$20.00	$50.00	$70.00	$185.00	$775.00	$1,350.00	$2,750.00	$2,750.00
USED	$3.00	$7.00	$9.00	$15.00	$19.00	$40.00	$100.00	$185.00	$250.00	$275.00

Historic Sault Ste. Marie is situated along the banks of St. Mary's River between Lake Superior and Lake Huron. Its strategic location makes Sault Ste. Marie an important navigational link between America's Midwest, the Great Lakes, and the Atlantic Ocean. Until 1895, the swirling rapids of St. Mary's River interfered with this critical shipping route.

The Sault Ste. Marie canal and locks were completed in 1895. The locks allowed vessels to bypass the perilous rapids, ensuring that commerce from "America's Breadbasket" reached Eastern markets. At the time it opened, the Sault Ste. Marie locks were the largest in the world, and the first to be operated electrically.

As organizers planned the 1901 Pan-American Exposition, postal officials prepared a commemorative stamp series to coincide with the celebration. Each stamp design fit the theme of the Expo, which chronicled the dawn of the industrial age and America's fascination with machinery. As the United States and Canada had cooperated on the lock project, the subject choice was also a gesture of goodwill to the nation's closest neighbor and ally.

Collectors were still attempting to complete their Columbian series when the bi-color Pan-American stamps were issued. Mindful of the criticism caused by the large 16-stamp series and its high denominations, officials were more modest with the Pan-Americans. Six designs were selected, and the total face value was a moderate 30¢.

Shortly after the first Pan-American stamps reached the public, inverts were discovered in the 1¢ and 2¢ denominations. Officials were erroneously told that inverts had occurred in the 4¢ denominations as well.

Specially printed 4¢ inverts were purposely created as specimens. Postal authorities had reportedly planned to intentionally create similar inverts of the 5¢, 8¢, and 10¢ Pan-American stamps as well, but cancelled the project due to biting criticism from the philatelic community.

Lock at Sault Ste. Marie, circa 1855.

MARKET VALUES										
	1920	1930	1940	1950	1960	1970	1980	1990	2000	2007
Mint	$0.30	$1.00	$4.00	$5.00	$8.00	$20.00	$125.00	$100.00	$120.00	$130.00
Used	$0.18	$1.00	$3.00	$4.00	$6.00	$13.00	$40.00	$50.00	$50.00	$50.00

1869 PICTORIAL ISSUE
12¢ SS ADRIATIC
Scott #117 • Quantity Issued: 3,012,700

In the mid-19th century, the United States and Great Britain were engaged in a race to dominate Atlantic shipping, the likes of which would not be repeated until the "space race" between the Soviet Union and the United States a century later. More than just bragging rights were at stake. The winner would attain power, money, control of commerce, the latest technology, and prestige.

Edward Knight Collins founded the New York & Liverpool United States' Mail Steamship Company, commonly known as the Collins Line. This company sprung from a much smaller and older company of packet ships that was formed by his father, Captain Israel Collins.

Speed was everything if the Collins Line was going to vie for a lucrative contract with the U.S. government to carry mail. Edward Collins began having massive wooden ocean-going side-wheelers built for the Atlantic trade. They would be powered by steam, and the first of them were named *Atlantic, Baltic, Pacific,* and *Arctic.* The initial launch was *Atlantic,* whose maiden trans-Atlantic voyage from New York was fraught with mechanical difficulties. In spite of the troubles, Atlantic broke a westbound speed record on her return trip to New York. On her second voyage, she broke all records in both directions. The Collins Line became renowned for speed and luxury, and was awarded the coveted Blue Riband for speed, a distinction Collins held between 1851 and 1856.

The U.S. government contract became an increasingly important source of revenue that subsidized the high costs of coal and repairs for the expensive fleet. In January 1852, Collins successfully petitioned Congress for an increase from $385,000 to $858,000 annually.

Four years later, the Collins Line suffered the loss of the steamer *Arctic* off the coast of Newfoundland. Collins's wife, daughter, and youngest son perished along with 319 other passengers and crew. The following year, the Collins steamer *Pacific* disappeared on a westbound sailing from Liverpool.

Edward Collins persevered. He contracted with naval architect George Steers to build a new ship, *Adriatic,* the vessel seen speeding through the waves on the 12¢ denomination of the 1869

series. Steers was killed in an accident before completion of the vessel, leaving behind a work in progress with mechanical problems that delayed its completion. In the meantime, Congress had reduced the Collins Line subsidy to $346,000.

Finally, on November 23, 1857, the 355-foot-long *Adriatic* departed New York on her maiden voyage. She had two 40-foot-diameter side paddle wheels, two smokestacks, and two masts. *Adriatic* was the largest and most luxurious liner afloat at the time, but was carrying only a tenth of the number of passengers she could accommodate. Her maiden voyage was also her last as a Collins liner. The company was bankrupt. The remaining ships were sold to the principal creditors at a sheriff's sale.

MARKET VALUES										
	1920	1930	1940	1950	1960	1970	1980	1990	2000	2007
MINT	$5.00	$8.00	$12.00	$23.00	$30.00	$90.00	$475.00	$750.00	$1,750.00	$2,600.00
USED	$3.00	$5.00	$5.00	$9.00	$9.00	$19.00	$65.00	$90.00	$150.00	$160.00

Land! There it was on the horizon, five weeks after the little flotilla of ships under command of Christopher Columbus had left the Canary Islands.

The first stamp in the series of 16 denominations shows Columbus "in sight of land." It was actually a sailor aboard the *Pinta* who made that first sighting of land at 2:00 a.m. on October 12, 1492, while Columbus presumably slumbered peacefully aboard the *Niña*. Columbus, never a man of great humility, claimed the first sighting for himself.

That is the scene illustrated on the 1¢ Columbian series of stamps issued in 1893. The central portion of the design shows part of a painting by William H. Powell. Alfred Jones of the American Bank Note Co., printer of the stamps, engraved the die used to produce the plates from which the stamps were printed. Jones added three "Indians" to either side of the encircled Columbus to complete the stamp design. A woman and child are at the left of the Columbus scene, and on the right is a male Indian chief with headdress.

Columbus saw potential for the natives. He wrote, "The people are ingenious and would make good servants." In later voyages, Columbus would indenture indigenous people who could buy their freedom for gold.

The 1¢ Columbian stamps are readily available today at nominal cost for collectors who wish to own one. Nearly a half billion of the 1¢ denomination were sold. They were used primarily to pay the correct rate for first-class postcards that were becoming increasingly popular, and for third-class mail such as circulars. Collecting them "on cover" (still affixed to an envelope or postcard that was sent through the mail) is also an affordable, achievable goal for collectors. Though not voted in as one of the 100 Greatest, the 2¢ Columbian is even more plentiful and affordable for budget-minded collectors.

For those collectors who like to look for varieties, there are examples that show a double transfer and cracked plate. A "cracked plate" variety occurs when the printing plate develops a crack. Ink collects in the crack and is transferred to the printed stamp, leaving a line of color where it is not supposed to be.

Double transfer varieties on the 1¢ Columbian are more common and easier to find, but not always as easy to spot. A double transfer occurs in the process of making a printing plate. A transfer die rocks the stamp design into a master plate. If, during the rocking of the transfer die, the die should slip even minutely, a doubling will occur. This is usually most visible at the tops, bottoms, or sides of the stamps. A good magnifier is helpful in looking for all stamp varieties.

	MARKET VALUES									
	1920	1930	1940	1950	1960	1970	1980	1990	2000	2007
MINT	$0.05	$0.06	$0.30	$0.60	$1.00	$4.00	$24.00	$17.50	$25.00	$23.00
USED	$0.01	$0.02	$0.03	$0.03	$0.10	$0.18	$0.25	$0.25	$0.40	$0.40

1869 PICTORIAL ISSUE
15¢ LANDING OF COLUMBUS (TYPE II)
Scott #119 • Quantity Issued: 1,576,700

The 15¢ denomination of the 1869 series illustrates *The Landing of Columbus*, a painting by John Vanderlyn that is in the rotunda of the Capitol in Washington, DC. This image became a stamp subject for the 2¢ value in the 1893 Columbian series and again in the 1992 29¢ World Columbian Stamp Expo stamp.

Three distinct variations (known as "types" by stamp collectors) may be found on the 15¢ denomination in this series. These types are sought by stamp collectors and listed in catalogs. The differences are easy to spot by looking at the bottom of the brown frame just below the letter T in POSTAGE and around the edges of the central vignette area.

If there is no diamond-shaped ornament within the indented area and there is brown shading within the vignette area along the sides, the stamp is a Type I. If a diamond shape appears in that indented area below the T in POSTAGE, it is a Type II. Type III stamps are those reissued in 1875. The reissues have no diamond below the T, just as the stamps of Type I, but unlike the latter, there is no brown shading within the vignette area.

Why were there different types? In his book *The United States Postage Stamps of the 19th Century*, Lester Brookman states "the reason for the slight change in design, which gives us Type II, was that the extra bands of lines around the inside of the frame were placed there to make less noticeable any slight misplacing of the frame in relation to its proper place around the vignette."

This worked less well than hoped as the Type II stamps may be found with the frame and vignette inverted to one another, making this a highly desirable and costly stamp for collectors to acquire.

The 15¢ denomination was primarily used to pay the fee for registration service, although this stamp is not common on cover.

A postal customer could pay for this stamp with three "half dimes"—tiny silver coins minted from 1794 to 1873. (shown enlarged at 2x)

		MARKET VALUES								
	1920	1930	1940	1950	1960	1970	1980	1990	2000	2007
MINT	$8.00	$15.00	$20.00	$28.00	$33.00	$110.00	$550.00	$850.00	$2,500.00	$4,000.00
USED	$2.00	$4.00	$6.00	$9.00	$10.00	$24.00	$80.00	$150.00	$250.00	$275.00

COLUMBUS IN CHAINS
1893 $2 COLUMBIAN COMMEMORATIVE

Scott #242 • Quantity Issued: 45,550

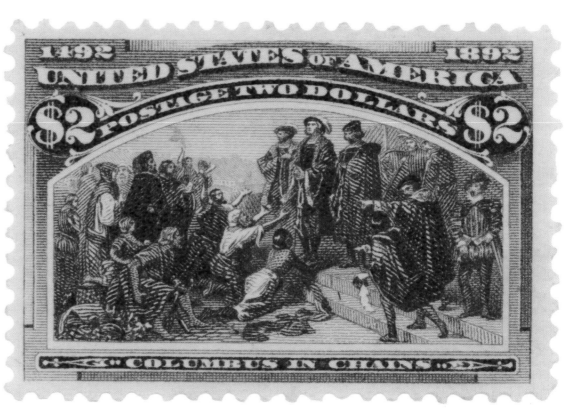

The $2 denomination of the 1893 Columbian series of commemorative stamps reproduces a painting entitled *The Return of Columbus in Chains to Cadiz*. It was painted by Emmanuel Gottlieb Leutze, a German-born artist who worked in Germany, Italy, and the United States.

Leutze's name may not be as famous as other artists who painted historical scenes or portraits, such as Gilbert Stuart, John Trumbull, or Charles Wilson Peale. However, one of Leutze's paintings has become so iconic that nearly every school in the nation displays a print. That painting is *Washington Crossing the Delaware*, created in 1851 and most notably reproduced in a souvenir sheet issued in 1976 by the United States for its bicentennial.

Leutze was a master of historical painting, and he was especially good at capturing dramatic events, such as Christopher Columbus being placed in chains and imprisoned at the settlement Santo Domingo, which he had founded in Hispaniola.

This event happened on Columbus's third voyage in 1498. Discovering the community in a shambles after his absence, the explorer sent to Spain for a judge to help officiate. Ferdinand and Isabella sent Francisco de Bobbadilla. The monarchs gave him considerably more power and control than Columbus expected. After a brief investigation, Bobbadilla seized Columbus's house and records, placed him and his two brothers, Diego and Bartholomew, in chains, and locked them up in prison. There the Columbus brothers remained until they could be returned to Spain.

It must have come as a shock to Columbus, but serious charges had been levied against him, including tyranny. Columbus wrote a letter to Ferdinand and Isabella on the return journey to Spain in defense of his actions. Although the royal couple returned Columbus's possessions, he was stripped of his titles as governor and viceroy of the Spanish possessions in the New World.

Two years later, Columbus began his fourth and last voyage.

Official postcard bearing the signature of World's Columbian Exposition president Harlow N. Higginbotham.

	1920	1930	1940	1950	1960	1970	1980	1990	2000	2007
MARKET VALUES										
MINT	$4.00	$8.00	$25.00	$48.00	$65.00	$230.00	$1,100.00	$1,150.00	$1,550.00	$1,250.00
USED	$4.00	$6.00	$14.00	$32.00	$45.00	$120.00	$350.00	$400.00	$600.00	$600.00

COLOR ERROR STAMP
1918 $2 BENJAMIN FRANKLIN
Scott #523 • Quantity Known: 60,000

In 1918, a $2 Benjamin Franklin stamp was issued with the Founding Father's likeness in black, surrounded by a striking orange-red frame. The stamp had been requested much earlier, but was delayed while the Bureau of Engraving and Printing struggled to meet the demands caused by World War I.

The handsome rectangular stamp was issued on August 19, 1918, along with a deep-green and black $5 Franklin (Scott #524). Both were printed using a single plate. The 1918 $2 and $5 Franklins were the first bi-colored definitive stamps in United States history.

The 1918 issue replaced the stamps of 1902, which were still available in a fairly large quantity. Records indicate that a mere 40,561 Scott #523 stamps were distributed in 1919, and only 28,670 in 1920. The high denomination was frequently used for heavy letters to foreign destinations and relief packages to war-ravaged Europe.

With a cost equivalent of nearly $90 today, relatively few collectors were able to afford the luxury of adding the high-value stamp to their collections.

In November of 1920, the $2 Franklin stamp suddenly appeared with a carmine frame. The stamp-collecting world buzzed with talk of the newly discovered color error.

Postal officials steadfastly denied that an error had occurred. After investigating, it was learned that the original specifications had called for a carmine frame, and that the earlier Franklin stamp was in fact the color error.

More than two years after it had been issued, collectors who had overlooked Scott #523 scrambled to acquire it. Without doubt, many of the stamps had been discarded after serving their function, and were lost to philately forever.

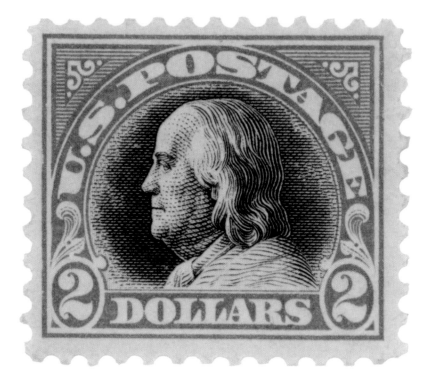

Although postal authorities never distinguished between the stamps, the orange-red and black 1918 stamp is designated Scott #523, and the carmine and black stamp is designated Scott #547.

Modern collectors can expect to pay several hundred dollars for a Mint 1918 $2 Franklin stamp, and more than twice that amount for a never-hinged example.

Benjamin Franklin occupied the central vignette of a 19th-century $2 note of the Farmers & Merchants Bank of St. Joseph, Michigan. (from *Obsolete Paper Money Issued by Banks in the United States 1782–1866*)

	1920	1930	1940	1950	1960	1970	1980	1990	2000	2007
					MARKET VALUES					
MINT	$4.00	$9.00	$25.00	$48.00	$75.00	$110.00	$1,150.00	$675.00	$625.00	$625.00
USED	$1.00	$4.00	$12.00	$24.00	$40.00	$55.00	$140.00	$250.00	$230.00	$240.00

1895 BUREAU ISSUE
$1 OLIVER HAZARD PERRY (TYPE I)
Scott #276 • Quantity Issued: 192,449

When the Bureau of Engraving and Printing took on the job of producing stamps for the U.S. Post Office Department in 1894, there were no dollar-value regular-issue stamps (although a year earlier the first United States commemorative stamps, the Columbian series, had denominations ranging from $1 to $5). Nevertheless, the Post Office Department instructed the BEP to create $1, $2, and $5 stamps for the new 1894 series.

The Bureau produced the $1 Commodore Oliver Hazard Perry stamp of the 1895 regular-issue series using the same vignette as had been used on the 1890 90¢ stamp done by the American Bank Note Co. The die for the vignette had been engraved by E.C. Steimle. The frame needed to be reworked, inserting the words ONE DOLLAR in written text in the semi-circle beneath the portrait, and "$1" in the two ornamented circles at the bottom-left and right corners of the stamp.

Two varieties occurred when the work was undertaken, resulting in two collectible types. It is easy to spot the two types without the aid of a magnifying glass. On Type I stamps, the circular ornaments (in the bottom corners that contain the $1 denomination) are broken by the outer frame line of the semi-circle below the portrait, making the round value ornament appear to go behind the portrait's framing. On Type II stamps, those two round ornaments completely form a circle that meshes with the outer frame for a short time. Both varieties occurred on the same printing plate. The left 15 vertical rows of stamps on plate 76 were Type I and the remainder of stamps were Type II. It is possible to collect Type I and Type II as a se-tenant (joined together) pair.

The 1894 $1 Perry stamp was printed on un-watermarked paper with perforations that gauge 12. In 1895, the stamps were printed on double-line watermarked paper with perforations that gauge 12. The two types occur on both printings. The stamps were printed in black ink of which shades are known, most noticeably a greenish-black variety.

A silver Morgan dollar (minted from 1878 to 1904, and again in 1921) would have paid for the handsome Scott #276 stamp.

		1920	1930	1940	1950	1960	1970	1980	1990	2000	2007
MARKET VALUES											
MINT		$3.00	$8.00	$18.00	$70.00	$38.00	$90.00	$450.00	$375.00	$600.00	$700.00
USED		$1.00	$1.00	$4.00	$14.00	$9.00	$15.00	$40.00	$45.00	$65.00	$95.00

Unrestrained plundering of America's natural resources during the 1800s underscored the need to protect these vital assets for future generations. In response, President Ulysses Grant established Yellowstone, the world's first national park, in 1872. Yet three decades passed before rising public sentiment and a president with a passion for the environment expanded the national park system.

Theodore Roosevelt was the first president to take a proactive role in the conservationist effort. An outdoorsman by nature, Roosevelt declared in his first State of the Union address that natural resource issues were "the most vital internal problems of the United States."

During Roosevelt's administration, lands designated as national forests increased three-fold to 148 million acres. Four wildlife refuges were created along with 51 protected bird sanctuaries.

A generation later the president's second cousin, Franklin D. Roosevelt, was elected to the White House. FDR's New Deal, with programs focused on resource conservation, was the second significant chapter in the conservationist movement. More land renewal occurred during his first term in office than in any other time in United States history.

Roosevelt proclaimed 1934 National Parks Year to call attention to the fact that the U.S. had set aside millions of acres for the public's enjoyment. A series of stamps depicting the outstanding features of 10 prominent national parks was issued to promote interest and increase attendance at the parks.

The National Parks issue reveals the diversity of America's natural resources, including the giant sequoia trees of Yosemite, the grandeur of the Grand Canyon, majestic Mt. Rainier, the cliff dwellings of Mesa Verde, Yellowstone's "Old Faithful," Crater Lake, the spectacular cliffs of Acadia, the Great White Throne of Zion, northern Montana's Glacier National Park, and the breathtaking beauty of the Great Smoky Mountains.

Today, the National Park System boasts 84.3 million acres and is visited by 266,000,000 people each year. As James Bryce, the former British ambassador to the United States, once said, national parks may be the "best idea America ever had."

As was his custom, President Franklin D. Roosevelt personally approved each of the National Parks stamps.

	1920	1930	1940	1950	1960	1970	1980	1990	2000	2007
MINT			$1.00	$2.00	$3.00	$6.00	$12.00	$9.00	$9.00	$10.00
USED			$0.48	$1.00	$2.00	$3.00	$6.00	$6.00	$7.00	$7.00

MARKET VALUES

Missionary stamps are historic links to the sun-drenched Kingdom of Hawaii. Printed on fragile pelure paper and now more than 150 years old, the "Missionaries" are among the most elusive of all stamp issues. Only 51 of the 13¢ "H.I. & U.S." stamps are known.

The Missionary stamps are named for the Americans who traveled to the islands to spread Christianity during the 19th century. Collectors learned of the seldom-seen stamps after letters began arriving in the United States from the exotic island paradise.

As the volume of mail from missionaries, teachers, and traders increased, Hawaii's King Kamehameha III was asked to establish a more systematic arrangement for the mail. On June 18, 1851, the legislature of the Kingdom of Hawaii authorized the printing of stamps of useful denominations.

Postage stamps were printed by Henry Whitney, an employee of Hawaii's Government Printing Office, appointed postmaster in 1850. The industrious young man was also responsible for printing the island's weekly government paper and ran a general stationery store plus a printing office. Whitney printed postage stamps in 2¢ and 5¢ denominations, as well as a 13¢ stamp for foreign mail.

The fees for letters sent from Hawaii to the United States were 5¢ for Hawaiian postage, 2¢ for the ship captain's fee, and 6¢ for U.S. postage on letters sent to destinations over 3,000 miles.

A complicated accounting system was used to distribute the U.S. postage correctly. The 13¢ stamp was inscribed "Hawaiian Postage." The designation confused many American postmasters stateside, who were uncertain if the U.S. postage had been prepaid. Some recipients reported that properly franked mail arrived with an additional 6¢ postage due.

To eliminate the confusion, a new 13¢ Hawaii stamp was issued in the spring of 1852. The stamp's inscription clearly indicates pre-payment of both "H.I. & U.S. Postage."

Missionary stamps are among the most famous of all stamp issues, and interest in them has been strong for more than a century. In 1918, a Los Angeles high-school teacher named George Grinnell reported his discovery of a small hoard of Hawaii Missionary stamps. The authenticity of the "Grinnells" has been debated for decades and remains one of philately's most intriguing controversies.

Many American postmasters misunderstood that the 13¢ Hawaii stamp included the 6¢ U.S. fee.

13¢ Grinnell Missionary stamp.

MARKET VALUES										
	1920	1930	1940	1950	1960	1970	1980	1990	2000	2007
MINT				$9,000.00	$9,000.00	$16,000.00	$30,000.00	$45,000.00	$40,000.00	$55,000.00
USED				$4,000.00	$4,000.00	$7,500.00	$17,500.00	$21,000.00	$27,500.00	$32,500.00

1869 PICTORIAL ISSUE
6¢ GEORGE WASHINGTON
Scott #115 • Quantity Issued: 4,293,100

Various branches and departments of the United States federal government have utilized Gilbert Stuart's paintings of George Washington to maximum advantage. Postage stamps, revenue stamps, and the familiar Federal Reserve one-dollar note all bear images of George Washington painted by Stuart. There was much from which to choose. Washington posed for the artist three times, and from those sittings, Stuart made more than 100 paintings of the "Father of Our Country."

The 1869 6¢ denomination is the same Gilbert Stuart image that was on the 1847 10¢ stamp and which currently appears on the dollar bill. Interestingly, the first time George Washington's face was featured on a U.S. one-dollar bill was this same year, 1869, but it was a different Stuart portrait than is used today.

Three portraits grace different values within the 1869 pictorial series. The first is the 1¢ Benjamin Franklin, the second the 6¢ George Washington, and the third the 90¢ Abraham Lincoln. In each case, the stamps look very different. The 6¢ value uses the nearly square format to good advantage, with the portrait within a circle that is set like a jewel in a square filled with latticework.

E. Pitcher designed the stamp. The vignette was engraved by W.E. Marshall, and the frame was engraved by W.D. Nichols. All of the stamps of the 1869 series were printed by the National Bank Note Co. of New York.

The stamp was useful for paying the postage on domestic first-class double-weight letters and for letters to Canada. Six cents also became the rate for letters sent to Great Britain, in January 1870.

Both Lester Brookman (in his book *The United States Postage Stamps of the 19th Century*, Volume II) and the *Scott Specialized Catalogue of U.S. Stamps* agree that this value is the most difficult to find well centered, creating a challenge for collectors.

A spectacular Mint block of 16 1869 6¢ Washington pictorials with Very Fine centering, fresh color, and original gum was part of the fabulous Ryohei Ishikawa named sale conducted by Christie's auction house in 1993. It sold for 50% more than the top estimate.

In the 1850s and early 1860s, tokens and medals depicting George Washington were popular collectibles. (Painting by Henry Alexander Ogden, published by the U.S. Army Quartermaster General in 1890)

MARKET VALUES										
	1920	1930	1940	1950	1960	1970	1980	1990	2000	2007
MINT	$6.00	$10.00	$12.00	$22.00	$29.00	$90.00	$525.00	$775.00	$2,000.00	$3,250.00
USED	$2.00	$4.00	$5.00	$9.00	$9.00	$19.00	$65.00	$100.00	$180.00	$250.00

CONFEDERATE STATES OF AMERICA
1861 5¢ JEFFERSON DAVIS

Scott CSA#1 • Quantity Known: 9,250,000

The early Confederate States of America stamps were the only such stamps produced by stone lithography. For Southerners enduring the uncertainty of the Civil War, they represented a glimmer of hope that their new government could provide essential services.

The 1861 CSA 5¢ stamp is also the only stamp issued on American soil to picture a living president. A promising politician with an outstanding record of military service to the United States, Jefferson Davis had earlier denounced secession. Nevertheless, he was named the provisional president of the Confederate States of America on February 9, 1861, and later elected to a six-year term.

Although 11 states joined the Confederacy during the tense spring months, federal mail service continued throughout the nation until June 1, 1861. On that date, service to Southern states was suspended, while existing U.S. stamps were demonetized and replaced with a new series. Southern postmasters were asked to return their supplies of U.S. stamps for credit.

The change created a hardship for the Confederacy. The majority of industry and commerce was in the Northern states, which left the South at a disadvantage as it tried to provide day-to-day services at the same time it prepared for war.

Although the Confederate States of America Postal Service was established in February, arrangements to print CSA stamps proved difficult. Postmaster provisionals, handstamps, and manuscript markings were used to indicate prepayment of postal fees until the Richmond firm of Hoyer and Ludwig produced the first Confederate stamps.

Ill equipped for the task, Hoyer and Ludwig relied on stone lithography to print the 1861 5¢ Jefferson Davis stamp. Stone lithography is a process that relies on the natural repulsion between oil and water. A design is drawn directly onto a stone surface with a grease-based medium. The stone is then soaked in water. When ink is applied, it is soaked into the greased portion of the design. The stone is then pressed against paper to leave an inked impression.

Issued on October 16, 1861, the imperforate 5¢ Jefferson Davis stamp satisfied the rate for letters that weighed up to one-half ounce sent distances of less than 500 miles. A 10¢ stamp bearing the likeness of Thomas Jefferson was also issued to pay the rate for letters sent further distances.

Former Texas congressman John Henninger Reagan served as the Confederate postmaster throughout the Civil War. With every resource and revenue funneled into the war, Reagan was required

to make the Postal Service self-sustaining. His was the only Confederate government agency to make a profit.

Reagan was captured along with Jefferson Davis on May 10, 1865, just days after the Confederate States of America formally dissolved. Reagan was the last Confederate Cabinet member to stand by Davis's side. He was offered a similar position in the United States Post Office Department during Reconstruction, but declined the offer. Reagan died in 1905, the last surviving Cabinet member of the Confederate States of America.

Cover mailed from Gettysburg on October 5, 1863, bearing Union and Confederate postage. Jefferson Davis appeared on 10 of the 14 stamps issued by the Confederacy.

MARKET VALUES										
	1920	1930	1940	1950	1960	1970	1980	1990	2000	2007
MINT	$3.00	$12.00	$6.00	$6.00	$13.00	$14.00	$65.00	$140.00	$225.00	$275.00
USED	$2.00	$6.00	$8.00	$8.00	$8.00	$14.00	$30.00	$100.00	$150.00	$175.00

1869 PICTORIAL ISSUE
10¢ SHIELD AND EAGLE

Scott #116 • Quantity Issued: 3,299,550

The 10¢ Shield and Eagle 1869 pictorial stamp is similar to the 30¢ value in the same series. The flags that flank the shield on the latter are missing on the 10¢ value, and the 10¢ value is one color instead of bi-color carmine and blue. The 10¢ Shield and Eagle was printed in yellow or yellowish orange, although many shades within those ranges may be found.

Both values were designed by J. Macdonough of the National Bank Note Co. The design was engraved by Douglas S. Ronaldson, who also worked on the 30¢ stamp.

The National Bank Note Co. placed their bid to produce the 1869 series. They submitted an "essay" (a proposed design) for the 10¢ stamp that bore a portrait of Abraham Lincoln. The head on the essay is similar to the one that eventually appeared on the 1869 90¢ pictorial stamp, but it was cropped more closely to the head. The frame surrounding the vignette includes a pair of fasces, or bundles of rods bound around an axe. This ancient Roman symbol forms the base of the ceremonial mace of the United States House of Representatives. It represents official authority as well as strength through unity. The essay exists in many color variations, paper types and formats, but it was not adopted for either the 10¢ denomination or the 90¢ Lincoln value.

The National Bank Note Co. created essays more closely resembling the adopted Shield and Eagle design. One version has incomplete shading and was printed in black. Another version was a more complete design. This exists in black, orange, or blue.

The 10¢ denomination of the 1869 pictorial series paid the postage fees for single-rate letters to Brazil, Austria, Germany, Mexico, Cuba, and some other nations—depending on the routes used.

Postally used examples of the 10¢ Shield and Eagle are difficult to find in pleasing condition. The light color makes the design of stamp fade in contrast to a heavy cancel, and any smearing of the cancel becomes very noticeable.

The 30¢ Pictorial stamp features additional design elements such as the United States flag.

A postal customer who wanted a 10¢ Shield and Eagle stamp in 1869 might have tendered two Shield nickels. (shown here enlarged at 1.5x)

	MARKET VALUES									
	1920	1930	1940	1950	1960	1970	1980	1990	2000	2007
MINT	$8.00	$10.00	$14.00	$25.00	$33.00	$98.00	$550.00	$850.00	$1,600.00	$2,500.00
USED	$2.00	$4.00	$5.00	$9.00	$9.00	$19.00	$70.00	$95.00	$140.00	$150.00

1926 2¢ WHITE PLAINS

Scott #630 • Quantity Issued: 107,398

The Revolutionary War battle of White Plains took place on October 29, 1776. General William Howe, commander of the British occupation force sent to New York to quell dissension, had been aggressively pursuing General George Washington's colonial troops from New York City up the East River. Washington's army took a favorable position on high ground in White Plains. Howe's Redcoats, supported by Hessian soldiers, outflanked the colonials, but Washington was able to retreat to safety into the surrounding wooded hills. He was aided in part by a young captain and the artillery battery under his command, who were guarding Chatterton's Hill. That captain was Alexander Hamilton.

The U.S. Army's present-day Alexander Hamilton Battery (formally, the 1st Battalion, 5th Field Artillery) is the direct descendant of the battery commanded by Hamilton. It is the oldest unit in the Regular Army.

In 1926, the second International Philatelic Exhibition held in the United States took place in New York City. The show ran from October 16 to 23, and the United States Post Office Department released two versions of the Battle of White Plains stamps on the third day of the show, October 18, to commemorate the 150th anniversary of the battle. The stamps were released simultaneously at the show venue in New York City and in White Plains, New York.

The stamp was printed in sheets of 400 examples. The sheets were cut down (before being distributed to post offices) to panes of 100. These were easier for postal clerks and customers to handle.

The Post Office Department additionally created a first-ever collectible designed just for stamp collectors: a souvenir sheet of 25 stamps. Plate numbers appeared in the selvage (margins) on all four sides of the souvenir sheet. Additionally, the top margin contained the words INTERNATIONAL PHILATELIC EXHIBITION, OCT. 16TH TO 23RD 1926 and in the bottom selvedge the words NEW YORK N.Y. U.S.A.

The Bureau of Engraving and Printing set up a flat plate press at the show and demonstrated stamp production by printing ungummed and imperforate White Plains souvenir sheets using plate number 18772. None of these demonstration sheets was sold and all were destroyed.

	MARKET VALUES								
	1920	1930	1940	1950	1960	1970	1980	1990	2000	2007
MINT		N/A	$7.00	$24.00	$60.00	$115.00	$650.00	$350.00	$400.00	$375.00
USED		N/A	$7.00	$23.00	$58.00	$90.00	$400.00	$300.00	$450.00	$450.00

NEVER INTENDED FOR THE PUBLIC
1873 $20 STATE DEPARTMENT OFFICIAL

Scott #O71 • Quantity Issued: Unknown

In 1873, United States federal government departments lost their "franking privileges"—they were no longer permitted to send mail for free by using a signature or official imprint in place of a postage stamp. The Post Office Department gladly issued stamps for each government department on July 1, 1873, because it meant the end of the financial drain caused by the franking privilege.

The Continental Bank Note Co. printed the stamps using vignettes of the then-current 1870 American Bank Note regular-issue stamps, except for those of the Post Office Department itself. That department's stamps were simple numerals within the vignette area. The frames were adjusted to contain the name of the government department or branch.

Most of the government departments had stamps that went to a 90¢ denomination. The Department of State was the exception, with denominations of $2, $5, $10, and $20. These denominations were necessary because the Department of State sent parcels all over the world, although only one cover is known that bears any of the dollar denominations (a $2 stamp). The $20 denomination and all other Department of State dollar values were printed in green and black.

William Henry Seward had never been on a stamp before and it was not until the 1909 Alaska-Yukon Pacific Exposition commemorative stamps that Seward would be so honored again.

Seward was a lawyer and abolitionist who was elected to the United States Senate in 1848 as a member of the Whig party. Abraham Lincoln appointed him secretary of state in 1861. It was in this office that Seward received his greatest claim to fame. A strong supporter of United States westward expansion, Seward negotiated an agreement with Russia for the U.S. to purchase Alaska at a cost of $7.2 million. This proved to be controversial. At the time of the purchase, few understood the vast natural resources that would be found in Alaska. The purchase became known as "Seward's Folly."

Seward was vindicated when gold, oil, and other natural resources were discovered in Alaska, and because of that it is fitting that he should grace the high-value Department of State official stamps. Government department official stamps were abolished six years after their issue, replaced by envelopes imprinted with several lines of text saying that they were invalid for private use.

Proof sheet.

	1920	1930	1940	1950	1960	1970	1980	1990	2000	2007
MARKET VALUES										
MINT	$65.00	$150.00	$150.00	$150.00	$150.00	$225.00	$1,350.00	$2,250.00	$3,250.00	$4,500.00
USED	$65.00	$150.00	$150.00	$150.00	$150.00	$225.00	$850.00	$1,100.00	$1,700.00	$3,250.00

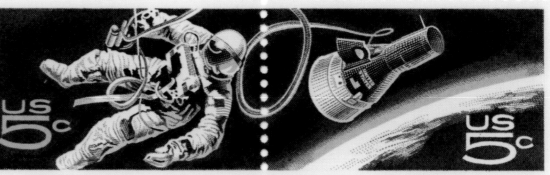

On June 3, 1965, a Titan II rocket lifted from Launch Complex 19 at the John F. Kennedy Space Center in Florida. The rocket bore a two-man capsule, *Gemini 4*, into Earth orbit. The two astronauts on board were James McDivitt (command pilot) and Edward White (pilot).

The crew of *Gemini 4* had the task of doing something no American had ever done: walking in space. The National Air and Space Administration (NASA) called this "extravehicular activity" or "EVA." White exited the capsule on the third orbit. He was attached to a tether and controlled the space walk with a hand-held maneuvering unit that used nitrogen as a propellant. White spent a total of 20 minutes outside the *Gemini 4* capsule.

On September 29, 1967, the U.S. Post Office issued a pair of stamps to commemorate the first American space walk. The design created by Paul Calle spread across two conjoined stamps so that it took both stamps to complete the picture. One stamp showed an astronaut floating in space attached to a tether. The other stamp showed the *Gemini 4* space capsule orbiting Earth with a part of a tether drifting off the left side of the stamp. The se-tenant (joined together) pair has become known as the "Space Twins."

The U.S. Postal Service had a longstanding rule that a person had to be dead at least 10 years to be honored with a stamp. The sole exception to the rule was those individuals who had been president of the United States (the time period was reduced to five years in 2006). The space-walking astronaut in the *Gemini 4* stamp was Edward White, who died tragically during an Apollo mission test at Cape Canaveral just eight months earlier, on January 27, 1967. Although White's face is not shown on the stamp, he was the only *Gemini 4* astronaut who performed the historic walk, and thus he became an exception to the Post Office's 10-year rule.

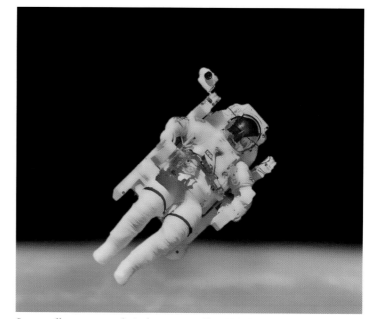

Spacewalks are now relatively common. In 1984, astronaut Bruce McCandless made the first untethered spacewalk.

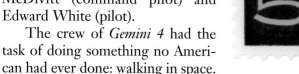

This cover, with a specially prepared cachet (illustration), was cancelled at the Kennedy Space Center in Florida on the first day of issue of these stamps.

	MARKET VALUES									
	1920	1930	1940	1950	1960	1970	1980	1990	2000	2007
MINT						$0.20	$6.00	$2.00	$1.00	$1.00
USED						$0.08	$2.00	$1.00	$1.00	$1.00

1895 BUREAU ISSUE
$5 JOHN MARSHALL
Scott #278 • Quantity Issued: 26,965

The Bureau of Printing and Engraving produced its first regular-issue postage stamps for the U.S. Post Office Department in 1894, using designs that were largely the work of the American Bank Note Co.'s regular-issue series of 1890. According to a report by the third assistant postmaster general dated October 31, 1894, "All the dies, rolls, and working plates of postage stamps, of present and past series, were transferred . . . and are now in the custody of the Bureau of Engraving and Printing."

This made producing some of the 1895 denominations quite easy. The BEP added an arrangement of triangles and dots to the top-left and -right corners on the old American Bank Note Co. dies. According to Lester Brookman's *United States Postage Stamps of the 19th Century, Volume III*, "The method by which triangles were added to the corners was simple enough. The Bureau, when they took over the printing job, obtained all of the old dies, plates, transfer rolls, and other effects from the American Bank Note Company. Triangles were cut into the dies or duplicate dies of the 1890 series and new plates were laid down from transfer rolls made from these altered dies."

This worked perfectly for the 1¢, 2¢, 3¢, 4¢, 5¢, 6¢, 8¢, 10¢, and 15¢ values, but there had been no American Bank Note Co. $5 value in the 1890 series. The stamp was designed by T.F. Morris. The central portrait (vignette) was engraved by W.G. Phillips and the frame, border, and lettering were engraved by J. Kennedy and E.M. Hall. The stamps were intaglio printed.

The first $5 Marshall "First Bureau Issue" stamps were printed on un-watermarked paper with perforations that gauge 12, and issued in December 1894. This stamp is the most difficult to acquire of all of the First Bureaus, with only 6,251 having been

issued. In August 1895, the $5 Marshall was released on double-line-watermarked paper.

A small quantity of the 1895 $5 Marshall stamps was over-printed PHILIPPINES in red in 1901 for use there during the United States administration.

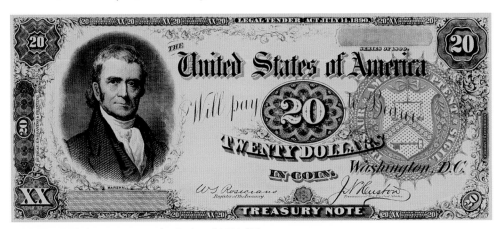

John Marshall also appears on the Series of 1891 $20 currency note.

MARKET VALUES										
	1920	1930	1940	1950	1960	1970	1980	1990	2000	2007
MINT	$14.00	$28.00	$50.00	$88.00	$110.00	$260.00	$1,350.00	$2,000.00	$2,250.00	$2,400.00
USED	$7.00	$14.00	$15.00	$33.00	$45.00	$75.00	$225.00	$425.00	$425.00	$650.00

A STAMP THAT LAUNCHED A REVOLUTION
1766 BRITISH REVENUE STAMP

Scott #RM19 • Quantity Issued: Unknown

Ranking in 60th place of the 100 Greatest American Stamps is what, arguably, should be the world's most famous stamp. You learned about it in grade school and studied it in college. It is the stamp that changed the world.

On March 22, 1765, Great Britain passed the Duties in American Colonies Act, more commonly known as the "Stamp Act." This levied additional taxes on the already heavily taxed American colonies. All legal documents, contracts, pamphlets, newspapers, wills, and playing cards would be required to bear a tax stamp. The fees thus collected would be used to maintain British troops in the American colonies.

None of this sat very well with disgruntled colonists. On May 30, 29-year-old Patrick Henry, a lawyer who was serving his first term in the Virginia House of Burgesses, condemned the British Parliament for taxing the American colonists at rates much higher than those in Britain. Henry, accused by the House Speaker of treason, responded, "If this be treason, make the most of it!"

Riots ensued throughout the colonies. The home of the lieutenant governor of Massachusetts was burned by a mob calling themselves the "Sons of Liberty."

The first "Stamp Act Congress" convened in October and adopted a Declaration of Rights and Grievances, as well as petitioning King George III. The Stamp Act nevertheless took effect on November 1, 1765.

The British government appointed trusted colonists as tax agents, with salaries of £300 per year, and began imposing the fees that were represented by a tax "stamp" that was embossed into the document. Demonstrators burned effigies of tax collectors in public places. Britain's American colonies were on the brink of revolution.

On March 4, 1766, the British House of Commons overturned the Stamp Act. This was based on the testimony of British merchants who claimed the American colonies were importing fewer goods from Britain because of the taxes, and that was bad for business. As a result of the relatively short period that the embossed stamps were used—and the fear of the tax agents to impose the taxes—the 1766 British revenues are not often found.

Although the 1765 Stamp Act was set aside, the British government set new taxes again in 1767 on such common items as paper, paint, and tea. The seeds of a revolution in the American colonies had been sown, and colonists whose names have become etched forever in the minds of all Americans took a stand against taxation without representation.

Proof of Scott #RM19.

						MARKET VALUES				
	1920	1930	1940	1950	1960	1970	1980	1990	2000	2007
MINT			N/A	N/A	N/A	N/A	N/A	N/A	N/A	N/A
USED			N/A	N/A	N/A	$400.00	$1,750.00	N/A	$2,000.00	$2,000.00

As the only known example in existence, the 1847 Alexandria Postmaster Provisional stamp is unique. Dubbed "Blue Boy," the stamp and its cover survived in spite of specific instructions written on the enclosed letter that advised the recipient to "burn as usual." It is considered one of the rarest philatelic items in the world, one that also offers a glimpse into forbidden love during the Victorian era.

Effective July 1, 1847, a Congressional act allowed for uniform rates and the prepayment of postage rates; however, it didn't specifically provide for stamps. Postmasters were allowed to issue provisional stamps valid at their local post office as they awaited government-issued stamps.

Collectors were aware that Alexandria postmaster Daniel Bryan had produced a provisional stamp consisting of 40 rosettes arranged around the words ALEXANDRIA POST OFFICE. However, examples were unknown until 1907, when Mary Fawcett found an envelope in her sewing box and sold it for $3,000.

The enclosed letter remained in a family scrapbook for nearly 100 years. The cover, however, began a journey among the elite of the philatelic community, commanding record prices. In 1981, the Blue Boy sold for $1 million. Its estimated value has multiplied several times since then.

In 2006, the cover bearing the Alexandria Postmaster Provisional was reunited with the letter it once carried, and the ending to a love story was revealed.

In 1847, James Hooff was a 24-year-old Presbyterian, and Jannett H. Brown was a 23-year-old Episcopalian. Both were neighbors of Postmaster Bryan. James and Jannett were also second cousins, living under the watchful eyes of relatives who disapproved of their romance.

While visiting an aunt in Richmond, Jannett received a letter from her cousin James. Dated November 24, 1847, the letter by modern standards is restrained. One line offers a clue to the subdued tone. "And Mother laughingly remarked that if there was any love going on Aunt Julia was sure to find it out, and while making that remark, I think, looked at me." The letter was signed "Yours with the greatest affection," and "Burn as Usual" was scrawled across the bottom. James and Jannett were married in 1853. Mary Fawcett, their eldest daughter, was born a few years later.

The famous Alexandria Blue Boy letter.

MARKET VALUES										
	1920	1930	1940	1950	1960	1970	1980	1990	2000	2007
MINT	N/A	N/A	N/A	N/A	N/A	N/A	N/A	N/A	N/A	N/A
USED	N/A	N/A	$15,000.00	$15,000.00	$15,000.00	$32,000.00	$85,000.00	N/A	N/A	$3,000,000.00

USPO DESPATCH
1851 1¢ CARRIER STAMP
Scott #L02 • Quantity Issued: Unknown

America's early postal system delivered mail from one post office to another. Home delivery was a development introduced on July 1, 1863. Prior to that date, "carriers" would take letters to or from the post office, or between people living in the same city, for a fee. Carriers worked with the knowledge and cooperation of the local postmasters.

The carrier fee was set by each jurisdiction's postmaster, who balanced the cost against the need to compete with local posts. The fee was typically 1¢ or 2¢ per letter.

Carrier stamps provided a convenient method to prepay the service. The first carrier stamps were issued in 1842 after the U.S. Post Office Department purchased Alexander Greig's privately owned City Despatch Post, a delivery firm in New York City. After the government took over operations, Greig's carrier stamps were canceled by a "U.S. City Despatch Post"—or simply "U.S."—handstamp.

In 1849, the Post Office Department issued carrier stamps to satisfy a mandatory 1¢ carrier fee in major U.S. cities. Known as "Semi-Official Issues," or "tickets," the stamps were only valid for use in the city in which they were issued.

The first Official U.S. carrier stamp was printed by Toppan, Carpenter, Casilear & Co. and issued in 1851. It also indicated the prepayment of the carrier fee, but was valid in all major U.S. cities.

The original 1851 1¢ carrier stamp pictured Benjamin Franklin, America's first postmaster general and the father of the United States postal system. It closely resembled the 1851 1¢ postage stamp, which caused confusion among postal employees and the public as well.

Two months later, a 1¢ Official carrier stamp picturing an American eagle in rich shades of blue replaced the 1¢ Franklin carrier stamp.

The Official carrier stamps helped meet the demands of a rapidly expanding industrial nation. The Franklin and Eagle carrier stamps are known to have been used in New York City, Philadelphia, New Orleans, Wilmington, Washington, DC, and Cincinnati.

Use of the carrier stamps was discontinued on July 1, 1863. On that date, free mail-delivery service became available in large cities and all mail carriers became U.S. Post Office Department employees.

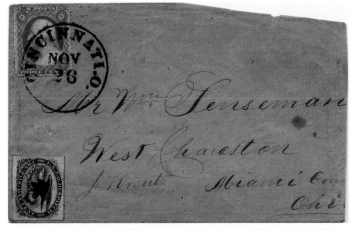

Mailed from Cincinnati, Ohio, to West Charleston, Ohio, #LO2 paid the fee for delivery to the post office; Scott #26 paid for the rest of the trip.

A copper large cent paid the rate for this carrier stamp. These coins were made in various designs from 1793 to 1857. (shown enlarged at 1.25x)

	1920	1930	1940	1950	1960	1970	1980	1990	2000	2007
MARKET VALUES										
MINT	$1.00	$2.00	$2.00	$2.00	$4.00	$7.00	$15.00	$20.00	$25.00	$25.00
USED	$3.00	$5.00	$5.00	$5.00	$7.00	$10.00	$20.00	$20.00	$50.00	$60.00

FIRST ADHESIVE U.S. POSTAGE STAMP
1842 3¢ CITY DESPATCH POST

Scott #40L1 • Quantity Issued: Unknown

Alexander M. Greig founded the City Despatch Post on February 1, 1842. The privately owned firm offered prompt mail delivery within New York City for a fraction of the cost charged by the U.S. Post Office Department. Greig produced the 3¢ City Despatch Post stamp to indicate the pre-payment of the delivery fee. The handsome stamp, which bears the likeness of President George Washington, is America's first adhesive postage stamp.

"Despatch, Punctuality, and Security" was the motto of the City Despatch Post. Letters franked with City Despatch Post stamps could be placed in letter boxes located throughout the city at any time of the day. Mail was picked up three times daily and promptly delivered to homes and businesses within the city. The rate was 3¢ for letters up to two ounces in weight—half the 6¢ average amount charged by the government agency.

Shortly after it was established, the City Despatch Post was handling an average of 450 letters per day as opposed to the 250 per day carried by the U.S. Post Office Department. The service offered a convenient and affordable delivery alternative for New York City's businesses and its population of 312,710 residents.

Four months after it was established, the federal government purchased the City Despatch Post and re-established it as the carrier branch of the New York Post Office.

The 3¢ City Despatch Post stamp continued to be used, which made it the first stamp produced for use by the Post Office Department. When used after the August 16, 1842, federal-government acquisition date, the 3¢ City Despatch Post stamp is referred to as carrier stamp #6LB1.

The 3¢ City Despatch Post was printed in sheets of 42 stamps. The plate used to produce the historic stamp was also used by four other mail-delivery proprietors in several different colors, and by the U.S. government. At least eight major Scott-listed stamps can be traced directly to the original plate.

The only known first day cover bearing carrier stamp #6LB1, the first government-issued adhesive. In preparation, the postmark device was altered to include "U.S." at the foot and the stamps were canceled with a boxed "US" handstamp.

		MARKET VALUES								
	1920	1930	1940	1950	1960	1970	1980	1990	2000	2007
MINT	N/A	N/A	$25.00	$38.00	$63.00	$110.00	$175.00	$350.00	$400.00	$375.00
USED	N/A	N/A	$75.00	$75.00	$75.00	$110.00	$125.00	$250.00	$250.00	$275.00

The Registered Mail system was introduced in the United States on July 1, 1855, promising special care and handling in exchange for an extra fee. However, a special 10¢ Registry stamp indicating prepayment for the mail service wasn't issued until December 1, 1911.

Placed beside a regular-issue U.S. stamp, #F1 was intended to guarantee that Registered Mail was carefully tracked and recorded along its route. The special service was a convenient and inexpensive way to guarantee safe delivery of valuable letters, documents, and materials.

In spite of the dramatic American Eagle design printed in bold blue ink, confusion and misuse of the Registration stamp was widespread. Ten months after it was issued, the postmaster general announced that the use of Registration stamps would be limited to the existing supply.

The need for the service, however, continued to play out in the daily headlines. Pockets of untamed frontier still existed in the West, and electronic fund transfers were decades away. Cash was frequently mailed to cover payrolls, transfers from the Federal Reserve to local banks, and other financial transactions.

Shipments were especially vulnerable while in transport. In 1916, the last known stage robber in the United States shot and killed the driver for the mail he was transporting. Ben E. Kuhl, a drifter who had a long criminal history, netted $4,000 in the crime. Ironically, a bloody palm print on a piece of mail incriminated him. It was the first time palm prints were allowed as evidence in a U.S. criminal trial.

Trains also offered a fast, economical method of transporting mail and other valuable commodities. They were considered safe. In 1937, $200 million in gold bullion was transported securely by rail from New York City to the new depository at Fort Knox, Kentucky. But optimistic thieves weren't always deterred. During their prime, train robbers carried out 28 mail-car robberies in just a two-year period.

In 1923, brothers Ray, Roy, and Hugh DeAutremont ambushed South Pacific train No.13 in hopes of stealing $40,000 rumored to be aboard. The robbery was botched when too much dynamite set the mail car on fire. Four men, including the postal clerk, died in the robbery.

As the brothers fled, Roy DeAutremont dropped his revolver and his overalls. Investigators discovered a crumpled Registered Mail receipt signed by him in the overalls pocket. The receipt led to the conviction of all three brothers.

Cover that survived the explosion aboard train No. 13. A Registered Mail receipt found in an overalls pocket led to the arrest of the DeAutremont brothers.

	MARKET VALUES									
	1920	1930	1940	1950	1960	1970	1980	1990	2000	2007
MINT	N/A	$0.25	$2.00	$4.00	$5.00	$11.00	$100.00	$55.00	$75.00	$70.00
USED	N/A	$0.06	$0.25	$0.40	$1.00	$1.00	$4.00	$2.00	$8.00	$9.00

The 1925 5¢ Viking Ship stamp was issued to commemorate the centennial of the first organized Norwegian emigration to America. A mistake made by a rookie Bureau of Engraving and Printing employee made it one of the most eye-pleasing of all United States stamps.

Original plans called for a monochromatic 2¢ stamp depicting the immigrants' vessel, the *Restaurationen*, to commemorate the 1825 voyage. A 5¢ denomination featuring the Viking ship was later added to pay postage overseas.

Unaware of the usual procedures, a new Bureau of Engraving and Printing employee prepared bi-color models for each of the Norse-American stamps. The striking designs created a sensation among postal officials and were quickly approved, becoming the first bi-color U.S. commemorative stamps since the 1901 Pan-Americans.

With limited demand anticipated, the 5¢ Viking Ship stamp was printed in sheets of 100 subjects rather than the typical 400, which meant that no straight edges were produced. Fewer than two million stamps were distributed, and no more than 300 post offices received a supply.

Demand was overwhelming, especially within the large population of Norse-Americans living in communities in the Midwest, and supplies quickly sold out.

Upon close examination of the stamp, collectors detected a mistake. The handsome stamp pictures a circa 1000 A.D. Viking ship with a United States flag, which wouldn't come into existence for hundreds of years.

The image bears a striking resemblance to a photo of a Viking ship replica, also flying an American flag, taken at the 1893 World's Columbian Exposition. The replica had sailed from Norway across the ocean and through the Great Lakes to Chicago, retracing the route taken by the Norwegian immigrants.

Nearly one third of Norway's population emigrated to the U.S. between 1825 and 1925 in search of religious freedom. While many of the early settlers came for faith-based reasons, later immigrants were motivated by crop failures and other economic concerns. More than 800,000 Norwegians immigrated to America in a single century. James Cagney, Hubert Humphrey, Renee Zellweger, Earl Warren, Knute Rockne, Eliot Ness, Walter Mondale, and Marilyn Monroe are among their notable descendants.

The 2¢ Norse-American Centennial.

Norse-American medal authorized by a Congressional act.

	1920	1930	1940	1950	1960	1970	1980	1990	2000	2007
MINT	N/A	$0.40	$2.00	$4.00	$7.00	$10.00	$33.00	$14.00	$15.00	$12.00
USED	N/A	$0.30	$2.00	$3.00	$5.00	$9.00	$20.00	$11.00	$11.00	$11.00

MARKET VALUES

CIA INVERT
1986 $1 RUSH LAMP ERROR
Scott #1610c • Quantity Known: 95

The discovery of inverted Rush Lamp stamps was the biggest invert-error story in generations, and it was cloaked in secrecy. It took a determined stamp dealer armed with a Freedom of Information Act request to peel back the layers of the mystery. What he found took him to the upper echelons of the Central Intelligence Agency and made headlines around the country.

The first public offering of a Rush Lamp invert occurred at the Schiff auction at AMERIPEX '86. The stamp sold for $5,500 and was quickly resold for a handsome profit. A few months later Mystic Stamp Company, along with two partners, purchased 50 of the inverts for more than $400,000. Mystic president Don Sundman donated one Rush Lamp invert to the Smithsonian Institution's National Philatelic Collection.

Sundman was puzzled by the lack of information surrounding the inverts and filed a Freedom of Information Act request with the Bureau of Engraving and Printing. He was shocked when he received a 35-page report with names blocked out and a cover letter from the Central Intelligence Agency.

As the story unfolded, it was learned that CIA employee Stephen Lambert had purchased a partial sheet of 95 $1 Rush Lamp stamps on March 27, 1986, while on duty near his office in McLean, Virginia. A few days passed before Lambert and his coworkers realized they possessed 95 inverted error stamps. The group substituted 95 non-error stamps for the inverts, which they claimed was consistent with their common practice of purchasing stamps for personal use from the office inventory.

One of the CIA employees contacted dealer Jacques Schiff, who offered $25,000 for the sheet of 85 stamps (plus one damaged stamp thrown in for free). Schiff was unaware that each of the nine co-workers had kept a stamp for themselves. Each CIA employee received a check in the amount of $2,777.78.

The existence of nine additional inverts became known when one of the co-workers arranged to sell a stamp through a dealer. The CIA discovered the identities of the employees, and threatened each with fines and years in prison. Five returned their stamps to the agency, one claimed to have lost his, and three employees resigned.

Although the courts later ruled in favor of the co-workers, those who lost their jobs were unable to regain their positions. Lambert was one of them. In a twist of fate, Lambert sold his CIA Invert (pictured top right) to Mystic Stamp Company in 2006, nearly 20 years after it was first discovered!

Non-error Scott #1610.

MARKET VALUES										
	1920	1930	1940	1950	1960	1970	1980	1990	2000	2007
Mint	N/A	N/A	N/A	N/A	N/A	N/A	N/A	$15,000.00	$15,000.00	$22,500.00
Used	N/A	N/A	N/A	N/A	N/A	N/A	N/A	N/A	N/A	N/A

1895 INDIAN MAIDEN STAMP
$100 NEWSPAPER AND PERIODICAL

Scott #PR113 • Quantity Issued: Unknown

Obsolete for more than a century and never valid as postage, high-value Newspaper and Periodical stamps are as scarce as they are desirable.

Based on the belief that information is essential to democracy, American newspapers and periodicals have always enjoyed a favorable postal rate. However, the lower rates didn't speed delivery time. Many publishers found that it was less expensive and faster to use private carriers. An 1851 rate decrease slashed the cost of delivery in half, yet failed to sway business back to the U.S. Postal Department.

To thwart competition, the government established lower uniform rates in 1863. Congress also allowed route agents to accept payments for bulk shipments on trains and vessels, eliminating the need to physically route the packages through a post office.

By 1865, officials realized that a significant amount of revenue was being withheld by postal employees. The first Newspaper and Periodical stamps were introduced that year as an accounting method for cash payments. The stamps were made large and colorful for easy identification on bulk shipments in transit. They were rendered obsolete four years later when the cash system was resumed.

In 1874, Congress learned that up to two-thirds of the fees had been embezzled. A new accounting system was established whereby the publisher was given a receipt for payment, and a canceled Newspaper and Periodical stamp was attached to the stub of the receipt book. Under this system, stamps would not enter the mails. A rate of 2¢ per pound for daily or weekly publications was set, with a 3¢ rate for those issued less frequently.

Prompted by a rate change, a new Newspaper and Periodical stamp series was produced by the Bureau of Engraving and Printing in 1895. A $100 denomination was added for large bulk shipments. Under the new 1¢-per-pound rate, #PR113 prepaid postage for shipments weighing 10,000 pounds. Printed in purple ink, the "Indian Maiden" design was fairly provocative for the Victorian era.

Newspaper and Periodical stamps were discontinued on July 1, 1898. In 1899, a public sale of the demonetized stamps was held. Only 26,989 complete sets were sold.

For collectors, #PR113 is the key to a complete Newspaper and Periodical stamp collection. Mint examples are scarce, and used stamps are nearly impossible to acquire.

MARKET VALUES										
	1920	1930	1940	1950	1960	1970	1980	1990	2000	2007
MINT	$40.00	$40.00	$45.00	$27.00	$33.00	$55.00	$300.00	$775.00	$1,600.00	$3,500.00
USED	$10.00	$10.00	$10.00	$13.00	$19.00	$43.00	$150.00	$350.00	$525.00	$2,500.00

Commerce in the United States depended heavily on waterways in the years before railroads, tractor trailers, and commercial aircraft. None were more important to national interests than the mighty Mississippi River and the port city of New Orleans.

In the early 1800s, fearful that the United States might lose navigational rights along the Mississippi, President Thomas Jefferson sent James Monroe and Robert R. Livingston to Paris to negotiate the purchase of New Orleans and its immediate surrounding area.

The U.S. was prepared to pay $10 million for the Louisiana parcel. Jefferson anticipated resistance to his proposal. However, war between France and England seemed inevitable in 1803, and the Louisiana Territory was a distraction for France. So Napoleon Bonaparte abandoned his plan to rebuild a French New World empire and offered the entire territory of 530 million acres to the United States for $15 million.

The purchase was the American government's largest financial transaction to date, and it doubled the size of the United States at a cost of less than 3¢ per acre. Control of the Mississippi River and the port of New Orleans provided a convenient venue for transportation necessary for the development of the new region. Acquiring the land also distanced France, a potential enemy, from the young nation.

Jefferson quickly dispatched the Lewis and Clark expedition to explore the unknown region and locate a waterway to the Pacific Ocean. Westward expansion, the discovery of gold, and the completion of the transcontinental railroad helped to make the territory a vital part of the American fabric by the end of the 19th century.

St. Louis, Missouri, hosted the Louisiana Purchase Exposition in 1904. This World's Fair, the largest up to that date, celebrated the centennial of the purchase with seven months of festivities.

The United States Postal Department issued a set of five commemorative stamps to honor the centennial. Livingston, Monroe, and Jefferson were honored along with President William McKinley, who had been assassinated in 1901. The 10¢ Louisiana Purchase commemorative stamp depicts a map of the continental United States with the territory highlighted and inscribed with the year the property (today accounting for 23% of the U.S.) was acquired.

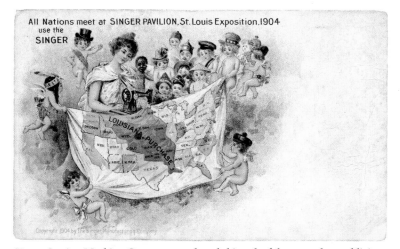

Singer Sewing Machine Company produced this colorful postcard to publicize its booth at the Louisiana Purchase Exhibition.

MARKET VALUES										
	1920	1930	1940	1950	1960	1970	1980	1990	2000	2007
MINT	$0.15	$2.00	$10.00	$14.00	$25.00	$58.00	$225.00	$115.00	$180.00	$175.00
USED	$0.01	$0.65	$3.00	$5.00	$8.00	$12.00	$25.00	$20.00	$28.00	$30.00

1879 1¢ POSTAGE DUE

Scott #J1 • Quantity Issued: 1,530,000

The understated elegance of the 1879 Postage Due stamps reflects their utilitarian purpose. Introduced as an internal accounting tool to prevent the embezzlement of fees collected by postal clerks, Postage Due stamps were first issued in 1879, with a series of seven engraved stamps in denominations of 1¢ to 50¢. The 1879 Series is important postal history that can be both challenging and rewarding to acquire.

Prior to 1879, there was no system to record the amount postal workers collected from addressees. Postmasters were frequently appointed not for their experience as civil servants, but for political patronage by incoming presidential administrations. Some dishonest postmasters collected money for insufficient postage and kept it without fear of recourse.

Twenty years before the United States took steps to correct the oversight, France introduced the world's first Postage Due stamp. Its plain, functional design apparently served as the model for future issues by countries around the world.

Intended for internal accounting use, Postage Due stamps often don't carry an inscription denoting the country that issued them. Unlike other stamps issued for this purpose, #J1, the United States' first Postage Due stamp, specifies its origins with the letters "U" and "S" on either side of the frame.

The introduction of Postage Due stamps required postmasters to keep careful accounting that balanced the value of postage stamps received against the funds collected. Postal revenues increased as a result, providing accurate receipts for services rendered by the agency.

Postage Due stamps were typically affixed to the cover on which insufficient postage had been paid. A cancel was applied when the money was collected.

Parcel Post Postage Due stamps were issued in 1913 to indicate the payment of insufficient postage on packages mailed through the postal service. In less than one year, this new category of stamps was allowed to be used interchangeably with Postage Due stamps.

Replaced by specially marked meter stamps, Postage Due stamps were discontinued in 1985. Over their 100-year history, more than 100 Postage Due stamps were issued using only four basic designs in a variety of red and brown shades.

Australian postage due stamp.

	MARKET VALUES									
	1920	1930	1940	1950	1960	1970	1980	1990	2000	2007
MINT	N/A	$0.20	$0.40	$0.40	$1.00	$2.00	$12.00	$30.00	$50.00	$90.00
USED	N/A	$0.12	$0.30	$0.35	$1.00	$1.00	$3.00	$5.00	$9.00	$14.00

WASHINGTON-FRANKLIN SERIES OF 1908
1920 $2 BENJAMIN FRANKLIN
Scott #547 • Quantity Known: 750,000

The $2 and $5 denominations arrived late in the life of the Washington-Franklin Third Bureau Issues: in August 1918 those two values were added to the series that had begun in 1908. They were the only two denominations in the series issued in horizontal format, and the only two bi-color denominations.

The U.S. Post Office Department instructed the Bureau of Engraving and Printing to print the $2 stamp with a red frame and a black vignette, but when the stamp was released in August 1918, the frame was decidedly orange. The Scott Catalogue calls this color "orange red" or "red orange," but the stamp is definitely more orange than red.

The Bureau of Engraving and Printing corrected their error of color with new $2 stamps printed in the correct red (carmine) and black, released in November 1920. The 1918 orange-red and black stamp (Scott No. 523) is scarcer than the later issue in the proper colors.

This was not the first time a stamp printer made an error of color. In 1893, the American Bank Note Co. produced a series of 16 stamps for the 400th anniversary of the first voyage of Christopher Columbus. The Post Office Department ordered the 4¢ value printed in ultramarine. The American Bank Note Co. complied, but at some time they printed an estimated two sheets in a very different, darker shade of blue that has been described as similar to, but not exactly matching, the 1¢ denomination.

Color errors and varieties are problematic for stamp collectors. Every person sees colors a little differently, and color appears different depending upon the kind of light used for viewing. There

are some excellent philatelic color guides that are helpful. A color guide is similar to a paint chart, with blocks of color identified by name. By comparing the darkest area of a stamp against the range of similar colors, it is possible to find a close match. However, the names on any given color guide may not match the names used by catalog makers.

A recognized philatelic expertizing service should authenticate any stamp that is suspected to be a color error.

A plate number single of Scott #547, used on an air post stamped envelope (#UC1) along with high-value stamps from the series that replaced the Washington-Franklin stamps, carried this cover on the 1929 *Graf Zeppelin* Around-the-World flight.

A quarter eagle ($2.50 gold coin, minted in various designs from 1796 to 1929) would have purchased this stamp and brought 50¢ in change. (shown enlarged at 1.5x)

	MARKET VALUES									
	1920	1930	1940	1950	1960	1970	1980	1990	2000	2007
MINT	N/A	$4.00	$7.00	$14.00	$5.00	$38.00	$400.00	$225.00	$190.00	$160.00
USED	N/A	$0.60	$2.00	$2.00	$5.00	$9.00	$20.00	$25.00	$40.00	$40.00

MOST EXPENSIVE STAMP OF 1983
$9.35 EXPRESS MAIL
Scott #1909 • Quantity Issued: 18,000,000

In 1977, the United States Postal Service introduced a new class of mail called Express Mail. Its purpose was to address the needs of "I want it now" postal customers who were increasingly taking their business to competitors who offered expedited delivery. (Ironically, in 2000, the U.S. Postal Service contracted with FedEx, its chief competitor in expedited delivery, to carry USPS overnight mail through its system.)

Express Mail rates were initially structured much the same way as parcel post rates, that is, by distance (calculated in "zones") and by weight. In 1981, zone rates were eliminated for Express Mail weighing less than two pounds. Express Mail guarantees next-day delivery for most addresses, or second-day delivery where next-day is not available.

At first, Express Mail letters and parcels used ordinary postage stamps or postage meters, and no special stamps were available. A large-format stamp, issued in booklets containing three stamps that sold for $28.05, was released by the Postal Service on August 12, 1983. The stamp featured a prominent bald eagle in the foreground with a full moon in the background, and it was intended for use on Express Mail. Since the stamp was not inscribed specifically for that service, it could be used on all classes of mail, a fact that was not uniformly recognized by postal employees.

More than 260,000 covers franked with the new $9.35 Express Mail Stamps were loaded aboard the space shuttle *Challenger* in advance of the shuttle's August 30, 1983, launch from Kennedy Space Center. The covers were carried into space and, upon the safe landing of *Challenger* on September 5 at Edwards Air Force Base in California, were placed on sale by the USPS at a price of $15.35. The covers sold out within two months.

The USPS used the proceeds from sale of the *Challenger*-flown covers to promote philately.

Flown cover that traveled aboard the Space Shuttle *Challenger*.

	1920	1930	1940	1950	1960	1970	1980	1990	2000	2007
MARKET VALUES										
MINT								$26.00	$21.00	$23.00
USED								$8.00	$14.00	$15.00

5¢ POCAHONTAS

Scott #330 • Quantity Issued: 7,980,594

An aura of mystery and romance surrounds Pocahontas, the Indian princess who befriended the residents of the first permanent English community in America. Although modern historians question her legendary romance with Captain John Smith, Pocahontas is known to have brought food to the starving settlers and kept peace with the neighboring Powhatan Confederacy. For her contributions to their success, Pocahontas was honored on a 1907 stamp commemorating the founding of Jamestown.

Pocahontas never learned to write, and what is known about her comes from accounts left by Smith and other contemporaries. Over time, fact and fiction melded into an inspiring tale that is uniquely American.

The daughter of Chief Powhatan by one of his many wives, Pocahontas was 10 to 12 years old when the colonists arrived. According to legend, Captain Smith, the colonists' leader, was captured by Powhatan and saved from execution by the girl's pleading. In 1608, she is said to have warned the Jamestown residents of an ambush that would have taken the lives of the community's leaders.

Injured in a gunpowder explosion in 1609, Smith returned to England to recover. On April 5, 1614, Pocahontas married John Rolfe, a widowed tobacco farmer, and was christened Lady Rebecca. The union brought a climate of peace to the colonists and the Powhatans. A son, Thomas Rolfe, was born in January of 1615.

To convince other Englishmen to join the Jamestown community, the Virginia Colony investors persuaded the Rolfes and a group of Powhatan natives to visit England. Pocahontas was

entertained among the highest circles of society and met the king at Whitehall Palace. During her journey home to America, Pocahontas fell ill and died.

Many prominent Virginians were (and are) direct descendants of John Rolfe and Pocahontas, including George Wythe Randolph, the Confederate States of America's secretary of war, and former first lady Edith Wilson.

This registered, forwarded cover from 1907 features all three stamps from the Jamestown Commemorative series.

The Baptism of Pocahontas is depicted on this 1875 $20 note.

	1920	1930	1940	1950	1960	1970	1980	1990	2000	2007
MARKET VALUES										
MINT	$0.30	$0.50	$5.00	$7.00	$12.00	$30.00	$110.00	$67.50	$135.00	$150.00
USED	$0.01	$0.25	$2.00	$4.00	$5.00	$9.00	$24.00	$15.00	$28.00	$30.00

In 1942, with the memory of Pearl Harbor fresh in their minds, the American public demanded stamps showing the nation's resolve to win World War II. The result was the simple yet powerful "Win the War" stamp. With more than 20 billion issued, Win the War stamps franked letters from home to servicemen stationed overseas and brought hope to an embattled nation.

The 3¢ stamp featuring an American eagle was issued on Independence Day, 1942. American society had changed drastically in the seven months since the attack on Pearl Harbor. American servicemen had been deployed across Europe and to tiny islands in the South Pacific. Women took their husbands' places in factories. Singapore and the Philippines had fallen to the Japanese Empire, but the United States had just delivered a stunning defeat at the Battle of Midway. In spite of the victory, it was clear that the world was embroiled in a protracted war on many fronts.

As a lifelong stamp collector, President Franklin D. Roosevelt had been actively involved in stamp design throughout his administration. Roosevelt resisted calls for images that showcased American weaponry or military power. The Win the War stamp was based on a poster used by the Maritime Commission. The 3¢ stamp features an American eagle, subtly engraved to stand out against the deep purple background. Thirteen stars representing the original colonies surround the eagle.

Critics immediately denounced the heraldry and symbolism of the stamp design. In their opinion, it was pacifist and served directly the opposite of its intended purpose.

The debate stemmed from the eagle's head, which critics believed had been changed to point to the viewer's left. In the Great Seal of the United States, this would be in the direction of the olive branch rather than toward the arrows clutched in his talons.

This belief surrounding the change stemmed from the myth that the eagle's head faces different directions during war and peace. In fact, on the Great Seal, the eagle's head has always faced to its right rather than toward the talon holding the arrows of war. The change was actually a correction of a mistake made more than six decades prior.

For unknown reasons, President Rutherford Hayes designed a presidential seal in 1880 that portrayed the eagle facing to the viewer's right, in contrast to the normal position for heraldic eagles. By coincidence, the correction of the design approved by Hayes occurred during a time of war, which led to the critics' misconception over the meaning of the eagle's direction.

World War II–era National Recovery Administration label. Notice the direction the eagle's head is facing.

		1920	1930	1940	1950	1960	1970	1980	1990	2000	2007
MARKET VALUES											
MINT					$0.08	$0.08	$0.08	$0.10	$0.08	$0.15	$0.30
USED					$0.02	$0.02	$0.02	$0.03	$0.05	$0.15	$0.20

SERIES OF 1916–1917
1917 $5 JOHN MARSHALL
Scott #480 • Quantity Issued: Unknown

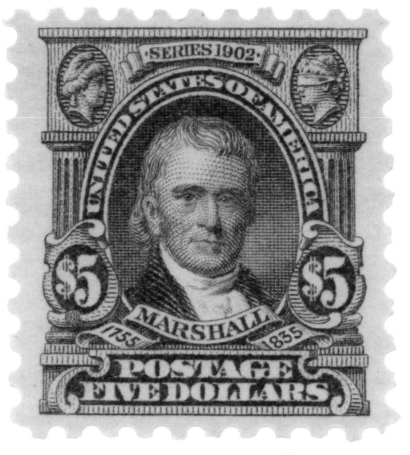

Like its twin issued in 1903 (see No. 32), the 1917 $5 Marshall stamp was designed by Raymond Ostrander Smith. Four engravers worked on producing the die from which the stamps would be printed. Robert Ponickau and Marcus Baldwin engraved the ornate frame, George F.C. Smillie engraved the portrait, and Lyman F. Ellis engraved the numerals and lettering.

Unlike its 1903 twin, the 1917 $5 Marshall stamp was printed on un-watermarked paper and had perforations that gauge 10. The color of the 1917 stamp is also a little different: light green instead of the dark green of the 1903 version. One would think these differences should be easy for collectors to spot; nevertheless the 1903 $5 Marshall and the 1917 $5 Marshall stamps are frequently confused.

The 1917 version of the $5 Marshall stamp was released well into the time period of the series' successor, the Washington-Franklin Third Bureau Issue. The reason for this late printing is that the U.S. Post Office Department did not order $2 and $5 stamps for this Washington-Franklin series, believing they had enough stock of those values of the 1902 series to suffice.

The winds of war changed everything. Suddenly, there was a greater demand for high-value stamps. The $5 Marshall stamp was useful for sending parcels to Russia and Europe, and for paying registration fees on domestic mail containing valuable documents and Liberty Bonds. To meet the demand, it was easier and quicker for the Bureau of Engraving and Printing to make more of the old designs than it would have been to create new designs that matched the other Washington-Franklin stamps.

Collectors should be cautious when purchasing either the 1903 or the 1917 versions of the $5 Marshall stamps. The 1903 $5 Marshall stamp is worth approximately 10 times more than the 1917 version, either Mint or postally used. Occasionally, sellers do not properly identify the stamps. If in doubt, buyers should be diligent in examining the stamps prior to purchase, and should obtain a certificate of genuineness made by a reputable expertizing service.

In 1916 the new Standing Liberty quarter design showed Miss Liberty bare-breasted. By 1917—the year this stamp was issued—she would be covered by chain-mail armor, perhaps girded for the European war that had not yet reached America. (shown enlarged at 1.5x)

	MARKET VALUES									
	1920	1930	1940	1950	1960	1970	1980	1990	2000	2007
MINT	$8.00	$10.00	$11.00	$16.00	$25.00	$50.00	$375.00	$250.00	$240.00	$220.00
USED	$2.00	$2.00	$2.00	$4.00	$7.00	$13.00	$25.00	$32.50	$43.00	$40.00

Joe Rosenthal's Pulitzer Prize–winning photograph of six Marines raising a United States flag during the Battle of Iwo Jima defines the essence of courage and valor. Public demand prompted Congress to push for a U.S. stamp to commemorate the event. On the day it was issued, lines formed around city blocks and village streets as people waited to purchase the 1945 Iwo Jima stamp.

Caught off guard, Rosenthal had snapped the photograph of the battle-weary Marines without looking through his camera's viewfinder, and sent it off to the Associated Press sight unseen. Seventeen hours after the flag was raised, newspapers around the world ran the photograph on their front page.

Strategically located 500 miles from Tokyo, the volcanic island was used by the Japanese as an early-warning station to warn of incoming American long-range bombers. Control of the island would allow the U.S. to disrupt the warning system, provide an emergency landing strip for American bomber planes, and maintain escort fighters for the B-29 Superfortresses.

As more than 110,000 Marines prepared for an amphibious landing on Iwo Jima, the Japanese used the time to become firmly entrenched on the island. Using volcanic ash mixed with cement, the Japanese built pillboxes fortified with four-foot thick walls into the side of Mount Suribachi, and more than 11 miles of underground tunnels with rooms capable of holding hundreds of artillerymen. Certain they would be outnumbered, the Japanese strategy was to hide and wait for the Marines to come ashore. As they moved closer to the mountain, the Marines would become easy targets.

Iwo Jima was one of the hardest-fought battles in history and the casualties were horrendous. The Marines landed on the island unaware that the previous day's bombings had left the Japanese unscathed. Exposed on the beaches and unable to see their enemy, the Marines suffered crippling losses. After four days of intense fighting, they reached the top of Mount Suribachi and raised a United States flag.

Secretary of the Navy James Forrestal had witnessed the battle from a nearby ship and prepared to come ashore. Advised that Forrestal wanted the flag as a souvenir, the feisty commander of "Easy Company" decided the flag belonged to the men who had fought for it. Another flag was located and Michael Strank, Harlon Block, Franklin Sousley, Ira Hayes, John Bradley, and Rene Gagnon were sent to make the switch. Joe Rosenthal's photograph captures the second flag-raising on Iwo Jima on February 23, 1945. Six days later, Strank and Block were killed in action. Sousley was killed on March 21, just days before the U.S. Marines secured Iwo Jima.

John Bradley beside a War Bond poster depicting the famous photograph. The three surviving flag raisers traveled with the seventh bond tour, raising more than $26 million for the war effort.

MARKET VALUES										
	1920	1930	1940	1950	1960	1970	1980	1990	2000	2007
MINT				$0.06	$0.09	$0.10	$0.10	$0.08	$0.15	$0.30
USED				$0.02	$0.05	$0.05	$0.05	$0.05	$0.15	$0.20

1913 $1 PARCEL POST

Scott #Q12 • Quantity Issued: 1,053,273

Sending packages through the mail is known as "parcel post." Introduced in the United States in 1913, parcel post greatly improved life for rural Americans and nurtured America's mail-order industry. The 1913 $1 Parcel Post stamp (#Q12) is the highest denomination issued and the key to owning a complete set.

Parcel post was actually an extension of existing fourth-class mail service. The service expanded the size and weight limits for packages, and the stamps were an accounting tool used to determine the cost of the program.

Together with the free rural-delivery service introduced in 1896, parcel post provided an inexpensive method to send packages weighing up to 70 pounds to the most isolated areas of the country. The service was an instant success, with more than four million parcel-post packages handled in the first five days of service. More than 300 million were sent in the first six months.

The impact was enormous. Farmers were able to save time and money by sending produce through the mail. Rural Americans, who comprised 54% of the nation, were able to receive a wide array of commodities including seeds, books, baby chicks, and clothing. Companies such as Montgomery Ward and Sears, Roebuck and Company grew into retail giants. Mail-order catalogs, affectionately known as "the Bible," were the primary sources of goods for many Americans. Box manufacturers thrived as they developed new packaging to ship the variety of materials.

A new regulation was introduced in 1914 to forbid the mailing of humans. At least three people had been sent through the service, including a four-year-old girl whose parents attached 53¢ in parcel-post stamps to her coat and mailed her to her grandmother. The postal fee was a fraction of the train fare.

Although the service was very popular, the stamps were not. While each of the 12 denominations featured a different vignette, all were printed in the same shade of red ink. Clerks had difficulty telling the stamps apart, and the panes, printed in sheets of 45, were difficult to store. Occasionally, the stamps were larger than the packages they franked. After six months, parcel-post stamps became interchangeable with standard postage stamps.

Although each parcel-post denomination featured a different design, postal clerks had difficulty telling the stamps apart.

	1920	1930	1940	1950	1960	1970	1980	1990	2000	2007
MARKET VALUES										
MINT	$2.00	$5.00	$15.00	$25.00	$33.00	$68.00	$275.00	$300.00	$350.00	$375.00
USED	$0.25	$1.00	$1.00	$2.00	$3.00	$7.00	$15.00	$20.00	$30.00	$45.00

THE BRITISH BULLDOG
1965 5¢ WINSTON CHURCHILL

Scott #1264 • Quantity Issued: 125,180,000

Winston Churchill became the prime minister of Great Britain just hours before Nazi Germany invaded France in 1940. Nicknamed the "British Bulldog," he remained steadfast in his determination to defeat Adolph Hitler during World War II. Churchill forged a strong alliance with President Franklin D. Roosevelt during the conflict and later, in 1963, was named the first Honorary United States Citizen. The 5¢ Winston Churchill commemorative stamp was issued May 13, 1965, less than four months after his death at age 90.

Churchill was born in 1874, the third son of Lord Randolph Churchill, seventh duke of Marlborough, and his American-born wife, Jennie. After a lackluster academic career, Churchill was accepted at the Royal Military Academy Sandhurst. He saw combat in India and Cuba, served as a war correspondent during the Second Boer War, and became a national hero after his daring escape from a POW camp. Churchill began his political career with a seat in Parliament in 1900. In 1911, he was appointed first lord of the Admiralty, a post he held throughout World War I.

Adolph Hitler rose to power in post-World War I Germany, gradually rearming the nation and threatening to dominate Europe. As World War II loomed, Churchill was again appointed first lord of the Admiralty and a member of the War Cabinet. He became a vocal critic of British prime minister Neville Chamberlain's policy of appeasement toward the newly expansionist Germany. Churchill was appointed to replace Chamberlain on May 10, 1940.

Historians credit Britain's survival during World War II to Churchill's refusal to capitulate to Hitler even as the nation's defeat seemed likely. "We shall fight on the beaches, we shall fight on the landing grounds, we shall fight in the fields and in the streets, we shall fight in the hills; we shall never surrender." His resolve buoyed his countrymen, and his refusal to surrender preserved England as a base for the Allied counterattacks that eventually liberated Western Europe.

By Queen Elizabeth's decree, Churchill was honored with a state funeral service, the first for a non-royal family member in more than 50 years. The funeral was held on January 30, 1965, the birthday of his friend Franklin D. Roosevelt.

Great Britain's philatelic tribute to Churchill.

		1920	1930	1940	1950	1960	1970	1980	1990	2000	2007
MARKET VALUES											
MINT							$0.10	$0.12	$0.10	$0.15	$0.20
USED							$0.04	$0.05	$0.05	$0.15	$0.20

Personally designed by President Franklin D. Roosevelt, the 1933 Byrd Expedition stamp was issued to help fund Admiral Richard E. Byrd's second trip to the South Pole. For an extra charge of 50¢, covers could be transported to "Little America" in the Antarctic and canceled at a special post office, giving collectors a tangible connection to the daring journey.

Undertaken during the Great Depression, the expedition relied on private and corporate donations, government loans of equipment, and funds received for newspaper rights, photographs, and the sale of advertising aired during weekly radio broadcasts from Little America.

Collectors hoping to have their covers transported aboard Byrd's ship were instructed to have them delivered to Norfolk, Virginia, no later than October 8, 1933. Covers sent to Washington, DC, by November 10, 1933, would be forwarded to Dunedin, New Zealand, where they would be placed aboard the ship bound for the South Pole. All collectors were informed that it would be some time in 1934 before they would receive their canceled covers.

Chosen to be the postmaster general's special representative at the Antarctic base, Charles F. Anderson sailed from San Francisco on November 10, 1934, with five full pouches of mail and other equipment. Transported 10 miles across the continent by dogsled, Anderson discovered that the canceling machine was assembled incorrectly, the ink was frozen, and most of the mail sent with the 1933 crew members was frozen under several layers of ice and snow. Anderson had 16 days to unpack, organize his postal facility, cancel the mail, and pack it up for his return trip.

For 16 days, he averaged less than two hours of sleep per day. He canceled more than 150,000 pieces of mail, wrapped the letters in waterproof paper, packed it in cartons, enclosed the cartons in heavy mail sacks, and locked the sacks.

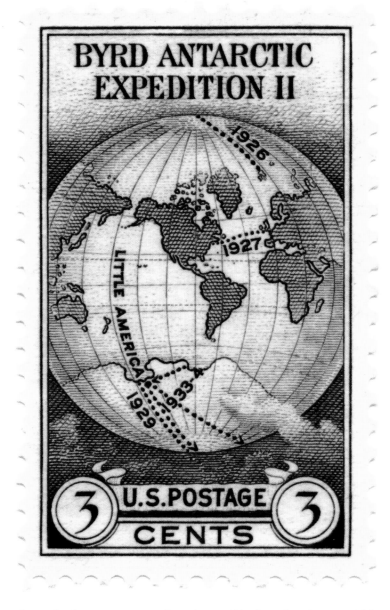

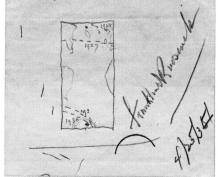

Anderson departed Little America on February 4, 1935, with a dogsled team pulling his load of mail. Upon his arrival at Eleanor Bolling Bay, he discovered the waiting ship stranded offshore by ice. Anderson spent 26 hours, without food or water, guarding the mail before the ship was able to break through the ice. Upon his arrival in San Francisco, the dedicated postal employee joined 16 other clerks and worked five and a half days processing the mail from Little America.

FDR's hand-drawn concept for the Byrd Expedition stamp.

		MARKET VALUES								
	1920	1930	1940	1950	1960	1970	1980	1990	2000	2007
MINT			$0.08	$0.30	$1.00	$0.65	$1.00	$0.40	$1.00	$1.00
USED			$0.06	$0.20	$1.00	$0.60	$1.00	$0.40	$1.00	$1.00

In 1874, a congress of 22 nations gathered in Switzerland to form the General Postal Union. That embryonic organization became known as the Universal Postal Union (UPU) in 1878. The UPU, now a part of the United Nations, establishes how international mails are exchanged between member nations.

The founding congress of 1874 implemented the first of many reforms. These reforms included the instruction that postal fees for international mail between member nations must be prepaid by using stamps, and that the basic letter rate for international mails would be 25 French gold centimes. That was the equivalent of 5¢ in the United States.

In June 1875, the United States Post Office Department released a new 5¢ stamp for the purpose of carrying half-ounce letters to international destinations, a rate that became effective July 1, 1875.

The stamp featured a portrait of Zachary Taylor, 12th president of the United States, whose short term of office lasted only 16 months (from March 1849 to July 1850). Prior to his election as president, Taylor had a distinguished 40-year career as a military officer, serving with distinction in the War of 1812 and the Mexican-American War.

The 1875 5¢ Taylor stamp was produced by the Continental Bank Note Company of New York. The design of the stamp was done by B. Packard, and the engraving of the die has been attributed to Skinner and Ronaldson. The portrait of Taylor was copied from a daguerreotype. The stamp was issued with and without grills.

Stamp collectors like to find this stamp used by itself on cover to a foreign destination that was a member nation of the General Postal Union. This is called a "solo usage" by stamp collectors, and illustrates the stamp being used for precisely the purpose it was created.

Essays exist of this stamp, as do trial color proofs in the unissued colors of black, deep green, dull gray-blue, deep brown, dull red, and scarlet. The Continental Bank Note Co. also produced a special printing of the 5¢ Taylor in 1875. The special printing was on hard white wove paper and issued without gum.

Zachary Taylor was a descendant of Britain's King George III, and a distant cousin of Robert E. Lee. His daughter Sarah married Jefferson Davis in spite of her father's strenuous objections. (Sarah died shortly after the marriage.) This campaign poster shows Taylor and his vice president Millard Fillmore, who became president upon Taylor's death.

MARKET VALUES										
	1920	1930	1940	1950	1960	1970	1980	1990	2000	2007
MINT	$4.00	$7.00	$8.00	$9.00	$10.00	$28.00	$110.00	$175.00	$475.00	$850.00
USED	$0.15	$0.45	$1.00	$1.00	$1.00	$3.00	$5.00	$9.00	$18.00	$25.00

SERIES OF 1902-1903
$2 JAMES MADISON
Scott #312 • Quantity Known: 37,862

The United States Post Office Department issued the $1 Farragut, $2 Madison, and $5 Marshall stamps that concluded the "1902 Series" Second Bureau Issue on June 5, 1903. Even today, more than 100 years later, the elaborately designed stamps set themselves apart and command attention.

The $2 Madison and all the other stamps in the 1902 series were designed by Raymond R. Ostrander Smith, who took his inspiration for the portrait from a painting. The engraving of the portrait was done by George F.C. Smillie, the frame by Robert F. Ponickau, and the numerals and lettering by George U. Rose Jr. The $2 Madison stamps issued in 1903 were printed on double-line-watermarked paper, with perforations that gauge 12.

James Madison was the fourth president of the United States, serving from 1809 to 1817. He was one of the young nation's Founding Fathers, and a delegate to both the Continental Congress and the Constitutional Convention. Madison, John Jay, and Alexander Hamilton together wrote the *Federalist* essays and helped frame the Bill of Rights.

American relations with Great Britain deteriorated halfway through Madison's presidency, and he petitioned Congress to declare war on June 1, 1812. Britain had failed to give up western forts as promised in the Treaty of Paris (which concluded the Revolutionary War) and had stopped and searched American vessels on the high seas, impressing American seamen into British service. The war dragged on for more than two years and ended in a deadlock with the signing of the Treaty of Ghent.

Like the $5 denomination in the same series (No. 32 among the 100 Greatest), the $2 Madison was reissued on March 22, 1917, in the midst of the Third Bureau Issue Washington-Franklin period. The Washington-Franklin series did not have $2 and $5 denominations. The 1917 $2 Madison was printed on un-watermarked paper and has perforations that gauge 10. Collectors should take heed to examine any $2 Madison stamp carefully before making a purchase. Check the paper to see if it has a double line watermark, and check the perforations to see if they gauge 12. The 1903 $2 Madison should sell for considerably less than its 1917 look-alike un-watermarked stamp with gauge 10 perforations.

$5,000 Madison note.

MARKET VALUES										
	1920	1930	1940	1950	1960	1970	1980	1990	2000	2007
MINT	$5.00	$13.00	$25.00	$50.00	$70.00	$150.00	$900.00	$600.00	$1,100.00	$1,200.00
USED	$2.00	$7.00	$10.00	$23.00	$25.00	$50.00	$135.00	$125.00	$170.00	$200.00

BEST-SELLING STAMP IN U.S. HISTORY
1993 29¢ ELVIS PRESLEY

Scott #2721 • Quantity Issued: 517,000,000

S trains of the hit rock 'n' roll song "Return to Sender" reverberated from post offices throughout the United States on January 8, 1993, while millions of postal customers waited in line to buy stamps. Some disappointed customers were turned away that day when demand exceeded supply, but eventually everyone who wanted their stamps got them. The heavily hyped stamps honored the "King of Rock and Roll," Elvis Presley, who would have turned 58 years old on the day the stamps were released.

The buildup for these stamps began a year earlier. The United States Postal Service distributed pre-addressed ballots illustrating a youthful, crooning Elvis with a "come hither" look (the creation of graphic designer Mark Stutzman), and a more mature, rhinestone-costumed "Vegas" Elvis (created by John Berkey). Postal customers were asked to vote for the image they preferred for a stamp that would be issued the following year.

A riot of newspaper editorials was published decrying the proposed stamp and its subject. Op-ed pages of daily papers all over the country reminded readers that, as a young performer, television cameras were allowed to film Elvis only from the waist up because his hip-swiveling gyrations were considered indecent. Others postulated that the King of Rock 'n' Roll should not be on a stamp because he reportedly died from a drug overdose and served as a poor role model for young people.

But Elvis fans rallied. More than one million postcards were returned to the Postal Service. The people had spoken. America—and the world—would be admiring a young Elvis on the 29¢ stamp.

In 2006, the United States released a list of its 25 most popular stamps based upon the number of stamps that were saved by collectors. Thirteen years after the stamp was first issued, Elvis still finished in first place, a whopping 44% higher than the next most popular, a sheet of 40 different designs issued in 2006 depicting the "Wonders of America."

Elvis Presley

Ceremonies for the first day of issue of the Elvis stamp took place at his famous residence, Graceland, in Memphis, Tennessee.

This ballot, available at post offices throughout the U.S., shows both the "young" Elvis and the "old" Elvis. Americans overwhelmingly favored the young Elvis.

	1920	1930	1940	1950	1960	1970	1980	1990	2000	2007
MARKET VALUES										
MINT									$0.50	$1.00
USED									$0.12	$0.20

Issued to commemorate the end of World War I, the richly symbolic 1919 3¢ Victory stamp is worthy of study by historians and collectors alike.

World War I began in 1914 after the assassination of Archduke Franz Ferdinand of Austria-Hungary. A complex web of treaties drew several nations into the resulting turmoil, which quickly escalated into full-scale war.

In spite of intense pressure at home and abroad, President Woodrow Wilson rejected United States involvement for more than three years. Increased German U-boat (submarine) attacks against American merchant ships led to a U.S. declaration of war on April 6, 1917. The United States joined the Allied Powers of France, Italy, Russia, and the British Empire against the Central Powers of Austria-Hungary, the German and Ottoman empires, and Bulgaria.

Arriving at the rate of 10,000 per day, American troops poured into Europe. Although the war raged on for another year and a half, the Allies were ultimately victorious and the conflict officially ended on November 11, 1918.

Issued on April 3, 1919, the 3¢ Victory stamp depicts Liberty Victorious against a background comprised of the flags of the Allied Powers. Close examination reveals that the Russian flag is absent, due perhaps to its withdrawal from the war in the wake of the Russian Revolution.

Prior to the outbreak of war, the first-class domestic postage rate was 2¢. That amount was raised one cent on November 3, 1917, to offset the cost of the war, and decreased on June 30, 1919. The Victory stamp was the only 3¢ U.S. commemorative issued to pay the first-class letter rate during that period.

The violet ink used to produce Scott #537 greatly influences the catalog value of several color varieties. The ink is very light, sensitive to solvents, and prone to fading. The most common shades are violet (#537) and light reddish-violet (#537b). Red-violet (#537c) has a catalog value at least 10 times that of the most common variety. Deep red-violet (#537a), however, is extremely scarce and is valued at least 125 times more than #537. Opinions on color may differ drastically, so guarantee certificates are recommended for #537a.

Posters urging the public to buy War Bonds and Savings stamps helped raise millions of dollars for the prolonged war effort.

The Fourth Liberty Loan War Bond was initiated on September 28, 1918. The cover above carried such a bond, on a special flight from the Atlantic to the Pacific across the Canal Zone.

		MARKET VALUES								
	1920	1930	1940	1950	1960	1970	1980	1990	2000	2007
MINT	$0.06	$0.12	$1.00	$1.00	$2.00	$4.00	$11.00	$6.00	$10.00	$10.00
USED	$0.02	$0.08	$0.25	$0.60	$1.00	$2.00	$4.00	$3.00	$3.00	$3.00

SERIES OF 1908-1909
$1 GEORGE WASHINGTON
Scott #342 • Quantity Issued: 313,590

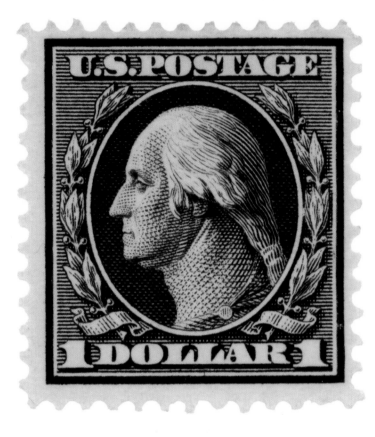

The highest denomination of the Third Bureau Issue, also known as the "Washington-Franklins," had a face value of $1.

The complexities of the Washington-Franklin series have perplexed stamp collectors for nearly a century. There is much to collect. Many of the varieties collectors seek were created by advances in production and printing. The $1 Washington is one of the least complicated stamps in the series—although not the most economical, because it was replaced just three years after its introduction.

The United States Post Office Department released a $1 denomination on January 29, 1909. It was a flat-plate printing, made on double line watermarked paper with perforations that gauge 12. The production work was done by the Bureau of Engraving and Printing.

The Post Office Department originally requested the BEP print the $1 denomination in pink, and pink trial color proofs of the stamp exist. It turned out that the pink was too close to the carmine color used for the 2¢ Washington stamps, so the $1 stamps were printed in violet-brown.

The $1 Washington stamp had the same portrait and frame as the 3¢, 4¢, 5¢, 6¢, 8¢, 10¢, 13¢, 15¢, and 50¢ stamps, all of which were printed in various shades of six different colors. The stamps looked alike. Similar colors could be confused unless postal clerks, mail handlers, and postal customers took the time to read the denominations.

In July 1911, the Post Office Department issued a statement saying: "The postage stamps of the 1908 issue, while possessing high artistic merit, had given considerable trouble to the public and to the Postal service on account of the similarity of designs of the different denominations. . . . To give more marked contrast, a change was made in the border design. With these changes the stamps . . . will have the head of the first President on the first six denominations and that of the first Postmaster General, with a different border design" for the denominations from 8¢ upward.

On February 12, 1912, a $1 stamp featuring a portrait of "the first Postmaster General," Benjamin Franklin, replaced the $1 Washington stamp.

Ninety years after the debut of Scott #342, the U.S. Mint would issue a commemorative coin with a similar design: the $5 gold piece marking the bicentennial of George Washington's death. (shown enlarged at 1.5x)

		1920	1930	1940	1950	1960	1970	1980	1990	2000	2007
	MARKET VALUES										
MINT		$0.12	$7.00	$15.00	$23.00	$35.00	$75.00	$325.00	$300.00	$500.00	$550.00
USED		$0.01	$1.00	$5.00	$8.00	$13.00	$20.00	$45.00	$50.00	$75.00	$100.00

RARE IMPERFORATE GRANT STAMP
1902 4¢ WITH SCHERMACK COIL

Scott #314A • Quantity Known: 59

The Second Bureau Issue 4¢ brown stamp showing a portrait of President Ulysses S. Grant looks innocuous enough. As originally issued with perforations that gauge 12, it is a handsome stamp, but not a great rarity. If you check a recent catalog you will find that the 4¢ Grant stamp issued in 1903 has a nominal value in postally used condition. It is more valuable in Mint condition, but not so much that an "ordinary" collector would be unable to own one.

Beginning in 1906, something extraordinary happened to some United States stamps, thanks to the invention of new equipment. Some of the machinery would automatically affix stamps to envelopes. However, the stamps needed to be in a different format.

The U.S. Post Office Department aided the manufacturers of this new equipment by providing them sheets of uncut, imperforate postage stamps that could be configured to the specifications of the machinery. One of those companies was the Schermack Mailing Machine Co. of Detroit.

The Post Office Department sent to Schermack 25 uncut, imperforate sheets containing 400 stamps each (10,000 stamps total) of the 1902 series 4¢ Ulysses S. Grant stamp. The company prepared these stamps in coil rolls, into which they punched their distinctive twin rectangular holes between each stamp. This type of perforation is known as Schermack Type III.

All 10,000 of the Schermack Type III 4¢ U.S. Grant stamps were sent to the Winfield Printing Co., which was preparing several mass mailings. An estimated 6,000 of the stamps were used to send advertising for Hamilton Carhartt Manufacturer, a producer

of work clothing that was popular at the time with railroad workers. (That company is still in business today.) The remaining 4,000 were used on a mailing for Burroughs Adding Machine Co.

A Detroit stamp collector reportedly acquired 50 Mint stamps while they were still in production by Schermack, but the stamps are very rare both in Mint condition and used on cover.

President Grant was later honored on a commemorative half dollar that showed his Point Pleasant, Ohio, birthplace. (shown enlarged at 1.5x)

MARKET VALUES										
	1920	1930	1940	1950	1960	1970	1980	1990	2000	2007
MINT	N/A	N/A	$1,500.00	$1,250.00	$1,500.00	$4,350.00	$12,000.00	$17,500.00	$27,500.00	$75,000.00
USED	N/A	N/A	$1,500.00	$750.00	$850.00	$2,350.00	$6,000.00	$9,000.00	$22,500.00	$45,000.00

WORLD'S FIRST AIRMAIL STAMP
1877 5¢ BUFFALO BALLOON
Scott #CL1 • Quantity Issued: 300

The 1877 5¢ Buffalo Balloon stamp was privately produced for use along with a standard 3¢ United States stamp to pay for airmail service. Many collectors consider the Buffalo Balloon to be the world's first adhesive "airmail" stamp.

Professional balloonist Samuel Archer King (1828–1914) made his first ascent in 1851 in a flight that reportedly ended with his ride over a dam in Pennsylvania's Schuylkill River. Undaunted, King returned to the skies and eventually developed the technique of using a drag rope to slow his balloon's motion.

The U.S. Army Signal Service established its national weather service in 1870. King, who theorized that meteorology was best pursued with a balloon, began collaborating with Signal Service officials in 1872, and made several flights with them aboard his enormous 92,000-cubic-foot *Buffalo Balloon*.

The romance of people floating through the sky in immense balloons guaranteed crowds of onlookers whenever such an event was publicized. To capitalize on the interest, an article in Nashville's *Daily American* announced that stamps would be available for anyone who wished to send letters aboard the *Buffalo* on its June 18, 1877, flight from Nashville to Gallatin, Tennessee.

Three hundred stamps bearing the likeness of the *Buffalo* were printed by Wheeler Brothers Printers and Publishers of Nashville. BALLOON POSTAGE appears across the top of the stamp and FIVE CENTS is inscribed along the bottom to indicate the denomination. The stamps were designed by a reporter for the *Daily American*, and engraved by a scientist who also provided materials for experiments performed during the flight.

After one side of the stamp sheet was printed, the sheet was rotated and fed back into the press to print the second side upside-down in relation to the first (tête-bêche format). The stamps were issued adhesive and imperforate.

The Buffalo Balloon stamps indicated payment for the private airmail delivery service rendered by King. Upon landing, a 3¢ regular U.S. stamp was added to satisfy the rate for conventional postal delivery.

Approximately 200 stamps are believed to have been carried aboard the flight. Of them, only 23 are thought to have been used on June 18, 1877.

MARKET VALUES										
	1920	1930	1940	1950	1960	1970	1980	1990	2000	2007
MINT	N/A	N/A	N/A	N/A	N/A	N/A	$4,000.00	N/A	$6,500.00	$7,500.00
USED	N/A	N/A	N/A	N/A	N/A	N/A	N/A	N/A	N/A	N/A

SERIES OF 1902–1903
8¢ MARTHA WASHINGTON
Scott #306 • Quantity Issued: 176,841,474

The ornate stamps of the Series of 1902 are favorites among collectors. Cherished for its elaborate engraving and warm, rich ink tones, the series was the first to honor a number of distinguished Americans.

The 8¢ stamp of the series is the first United States issue to depict an American woman as its subject. Martha Washington, the nation's original first lady, was chosen for the honor. Frequently overshadowed by the accomplishments of her husband, Martha can accurately be called one of America's greatest and most selfless patriots.

Born in 1731, Martha Dandridge was the eldest daughter of a wealthy Virginia planter. By the age of 26, she had lost two of her four children as well as her husband, Daniel Parke Custis, a wealthy planter several years her senior. Martha raised her surviving children and managed her 15,000-acre plantation until her 1759 wedding to Colonel George Washington.

George adopted Martha's children, and the couple lived happily at their Mount Vernon estate, disturbed only by the 1773 death of their daughter Patsy. Their genteel lifestyle was interrupted when George was appointed commander-in-chief of the Continental Army, an assignment that kept him from home for several years.

Martha joined George near the battlefields often and spent the dreadful winter of 1777 with his army in Valley Forge. Her son, John Parke Custis, served as Washington's aide until John's death of typhus during the 1781 Siege of Yorktown. Now childless themselves, the Washingtons adopted John's children and raised them.

After a brief retirement, George was again called upon to serve his country, becoming the nation's first president in a unanimous election. Martha, who strongly preferred a return to private life after years of public service, refused to attend the inauguration. Yet her conduct during George's terms in office set a standard of elegance and refinement for America's first ladies.

If one considers that Scott #306 was issued 18 years before women gained the right to vote, it appears the

Martha Washington, America's original first lady.

Martha Washington stamp may have reflected an emerging appreciation of females and their role in history. Noting its handsome shade of violet-black, many collectors also consider it the most beautiful stamp of the Series of 1902.

An interesting registered usage of #306 in combination with #327 (100 Greatest No. 68) to Saxony, Germany, in 1904 (the registry label has fallen off).

	MARKET VALUES									
	1920	1930	1940	1950	1960	1970	1980	1990	2000	2007
MINT	$0.20	$0.45	$1.00	$1.00	$2.00	$4.00	$25.00	$25.00	$40.00	$45.00
USED	$0.02	$0.05	$0.10	$0.12	$0.25	$0.50	$2.00	$1.00	$2.00	$3.00

ALMOST LOST TO COLLECTORS FOREVER
1908 5¢ ABRAHAM LINCOLN IMPERFORATE
Scott #315 • Quantity Known: 13,500

Acentury ago, fast-acting stamp collectors saved some of America's great stamp rarities for posterity. Thanks to their efforts, 1,575 stamps that were never intended for sale to collectors or the general public are now preserved in Mint condition.

The find occurred a few years after the issuance of Scott #304, the 5¢ Lincoln stamp of the Series of 1902–1903. Imperforate stamps were in demand by private companies, who perforated them specially for use in coil vending machines.

To satisfy the private companies' needs, 29 sheets of 400 imperforate 5¢ Lincoln stamps each were printed using the same plates as Scott #304. Only 13,500 examples of #315 were created, and 10,000 of those were sent to the Indianapolis Post Office.

A sharp-eyed member of the Detroit Philatelic Society discovered that the stamps were being sold at the Indianapolis Post Office. He notified the club's president of the mistake, and his fellow stamp-club members helped purchase 825 imperforate Scott #315 stamps in Mint condition. The stamps were divided among the members on a pro-rata basis, with most preserved in blocks of 25 and 50 stamps each.

Collectors also purchased approximately 350 copies at the Washington Post Office, and a full sheet of 400 stamps in New York. Some used copies are known on cover.

The 1908 5¢ Lincoln stamp features the ornate frame the Series of 1902–1903 is noted for. Several stamp collectors observed that President Lincoln appears haggard and worn in the portrait, burdened by the tragedy of the Civil War. In the frame above Lincoln are two female figures with outstretched hands and an olive branch of peace, representing a reunited country.

The imperforate 1908 5¢ Lincoln stamp is valued at more than 10 times the amount of the perforated 1902 stamp. In the past, individuals have trimmed the perforated edges of the 1902 stamp in an attempt to duplicate the genuine rarity. Collectors who seek to acquire a genuine imperforate 1908 5¢ Lincoln stamp should purchase it in pairs or blocks, or be especially careful to look for wide margins—a feature that trimmed copies can't have.

Abraham Lincoln in 1863, during America's devastating Civil War.

Private companies added perforations to the imperforate 5¢ Lincoln stamps.

MARKET VALUES										
	1920	1930	1940	1950	1960	1970	1980	1990	2000	2007
MINT	$0.05	$10.00	$28.00	$73.00	$100.00	$140.00	$525.00	$375.00	$290.00	$240.00
USED	$0.02	N/A	N/A	$48.00	$65.00	$120.00	$250.00	$150.00	$475.00	$1,000.00

MIGRATORY BIRD HUNTING STAMP
1959 $3 DOG AND MALLARD DUCK
Scott #RW26 • Quantity Issued: 1,626,115

Federal Migratory Bird Hunting and Conservation stamps were introduced in 1934. Outdoorsmen are required to purchase the stamps and carry them when they hunt fowl. Of each dollar generated by their sale, 98¢ is used to acquire wetland for the National Wildlife Refuge System. Since 1934, the program has raised more than $670 million, allowing 5.2 million acres of land to be set aside for waterfowl habitat. It is one of the most successful conservation programs in United States history.

The pictorial stamps feature original art selected from annual contests that attract some of the nation's most promising wildlife artists. The 1959 issue is the only Duck Stamp to feature a dog, and it will remain unique because new rules prohibit the depiction of anything other than a living bird.

Maynard Reece, the son of a Quaker minister, won his first Federal Duck Stamp Contest in 1948 and was honored again in 1951. In the late 1950s, he began searching for a subject for his next attempt. Reece found King Buck at Nilo Kennels, owned by Winchester Ammunition heir and fellow conservationist John Olin.

King Buck had overcome canine distemper to become a National Championship Stake winner in 1952, earning recognition as the finest field-trial retriever in the nation. He defended his crown again in 1953. King Buck eventually finished nearly every event in seven consecutive Nationals, establishing a record that remains unbroken today.

The pairing of Maynard Reece and King Buck would also prove to be a winner. Reece's artwork was selected for the 1959 Duck Stamp, which made him the only person to win the contest three times. Reece also won in 1969 and 1971, establishing an unbroken record of his own.

Maynard Reece remained an active outdoorsman, donating original works of art to raise funds for wildlife conservation. King Buck retired to Nilo Kennels, where he lived to the age of 14. A black statue of him stands guard over his grave.

Other hunting stamps by Maynard Reece.

MARKET VALUES										
	1920	1930	1940	1950	1960	1970	1980	1990	2000	2007
MINT					$6.00	$6.00	$55.00	$65.00	$93.00	$120.00
USED					$1.00	$1.00	$4.00	$5.00	$10.00	$11.00

1894 FIRST BUREAU ISSUE
50¢ THOMAS JEFFERSON
Scott #275 • Quantity Issued: 1,065,390

Looking at the 1894 50¢ stamp you have to ask yourself, "Who is that man?" Believe it or not, the portrait is of Thomas Jefferson.

Most of the stamps in the 1894 First Bureau Issue series are similar in design to the American Bank Note Co. 1890 series of regular-issue stamps. The similarity ceases with the 1894 First Bureau Issue 50¢ denomination. A comparable profile of Jefferson appeared in the 1890 series, but that earlier stamp was a 30¢ denomination printed in black.

The First Bureau Issue series of 1894 converted the 30¢ denomination to 50¢ and changed the color from black to orange. Several shades within the orange "family" are known and collected.

The profile portrait of Thomas Jefferson, third president of the United States, was an interesting, if uninspired, design choice. A similar Jefferson profile was first used on the 10¢ denomination in the 1870 series produced by the National Bank Note Company. Butler Packard designed that stamp and the vignette was engraved by L. Delnoce after a Hiram Powers sculpture of Jefferson. That statue is on display in the national Capitol. One would be hard pressed to identify this stamp's subject as being Jefferson, since it lacks identification and it looks nothing like the same man whose pleasantly familiar profile graces the United States five-cent coin known as the "nickel." A bust by sculptor Jean-Antoine Houdon served as the inspiration for that image.

Now fast-forward 20 years to 1890, and the American Bank Note Co.'s 30¢ Jefferson (Scott #228). T.F. Morris designed the stamp. Alfred Jones engraved the vignette, also modeled on the same Hiram Powers sculpture of Jefferson. The 1870 vignette and the 1890 vignette do not look much alike, but then neither does the 1894 vignette, which is even less like the well-known Jefferson on the nickel. That is because a third engraver was involved—W.G. Phillips. The president's mouth has a slight upturn, his chin is very flat and weak, and his hair almost resembles a close-fitting woman's hat in the art deco style. Is that really Thomas Jefferson?

Fortunately, the Second Bureau Issue series of 1902 solved Jefferson's identity crisis. Not only did all of the stamps have labels stating who they were supposed to be, but the stamp designer selected a very familiar Gilbert Stuart portrait of Thomas Jefferson as the vignette.

Thomas Jefferson's portrait has also taken various forms on the nickel.

MARKET VALUES										
	1920	1930	1940	1950	1960	1970	1980	1990	2000	2007
MINT	$2.00	$4.00	$9.00	$15.00	$18.00	$34.00	$175.00	$160.00	$275.00	$325.00
USED	$0.30	$0.65	$1.00	$2.00	$3.00	$5.00	$12.00	$14.00	$20.00	$35.00

1962 ERROR STAMP
4¢ DAG HAMMARSKJÖLD INVERT

Scott #1204 • Quantity Issued: 40,270,000

Leonard Sherman, a resident of Irvington, New Jersey, and a stamp collector, went to the post office on October 24, 1962. This was the first day of sale for new stamps commemorating Dag Hammarskjöld, who had been secretary-general of the United Nations from 1953 until his death in an airplane crash in 1961.

Hammarskjöld was awarded the Nobel Peace Prize posthumously in 1961 for work he had done to quell strife over the Suez Canal and in the Congo. In issuing the 4¢ Hammarskjöld stamp, the United States Post Office Department broke its own rule of not honoring an individual (other than a U.S. president) by issuing a stamp until the person had been deceased for at least 10 years. That made the Hammarskjöld stamp more interesting than most for collectors.

Sherman put his purchase of a pane of 50 Hammarskjöld stamps in his desk drawer until the following day, when he took it out to look at it. Something was not right. The yellow background was oddly placed—perhaps it was a color shift. He looked at it more carefully. The yellow background appeared inverted to the rest of the stamp.

Imagine what it must be like to go to your local post office, purchase a pane of stamps, and suddenly realize that one of the colors has been printed upside down just like the famous "Inverted Jenny." Your palms go sweaty, your heart beats a little faster, and dollar signs—lots of them—do a jig in your head.

Sherman did the sensible thing and kept quiet.

Meanwhile in Ohio another stamp collector, Gerald Clark, had purchased a pane of Hammarskjöld stamps and used most of them to mail letters before noticing that the yellow background was inverted. Clark reported his find and estimated the 19 Mint inverts he had left were worth a couple of hundred thousand dollars. Sherman saw that report, and calculated his complete Mint pane must be worth a half million dollars. He quickly called his local newspaper to report his good fortune.

Edward Day, postmaster general of the United States, was embarrassed. He ordered millions more Hammarskjöld stamps be deliberately printed with inverted yellow backgrounds and released to the public so that all stamp collectors could experience the joy of having a Hammarskjöld invert, thus depriving Leonard Sherman and Gerald Clark of their windfalls. Their inverted Hammarskjöld stamps went from being worth thousands of dollars back to exactly what they paid for them, 4¢ each.

Sherman petitioned federal court to issue a restraining order to block the sale of the deliberate inverts, but the order came too late. Hundreds of thousands had already been purchased. Sherman ended up donating his "discovery pane" to the American Philatelic Society. The entire Hammarskjöld invert reissue has become known as "Day's Folly," for the postmaster general who created it.

Scott #1203, the non-error Dag Hammarskjöld stamp.

MARKET VALUES										
	1920	1930	1940	1950	1960	1970	1980	1990	2000	2007
MINT						$0.12	$0.18	$0.09	$0.15	$0.20
USED						$0.06	$0.08	$0.06	$0.15	$0.20

EXPERIMENTAL PAPER
1909 1¢ BLUISH PAPER
Scott #357 • Quantity Known: 1,480,000

Excessive and unequal paper shrinkage resulted in an enormous amount of waste for the Bureau of Engraving and Printing early in the 20th century. As many as 20% of the stamps printed by the bureau had to be destroyed because misplaced perforations made the stamps unsightly and virtually unusable.

To combat the loss, various components were added to the normal stamp paper. In a 1909 experiment, about 1/3 rag stock was added to the wood pulp in hopes of reducing the shrinkage. The rag stock changed the color of the paper. Stamps made with this experimental paper, Scott #357 through #366, are known as "bluish paper" stamps. A 2¢ Lincoln commemorative was also printed on the rag-stock paper.

Unfortunately for the Bureau of Engraving and Printing, the rag stock was not successful in stopping paper shrinkage and was discontinued after a very short time. As the United States Post Office Department didn't recognize the experimental stamps as a new issue, every stamp printed on bluish paper was sent to the Washington Post Office for sale as a regular stamp. The 4¢ and 8¢ denominations were never intentionally distributed, and only a few examples are known to collectors.

Most Scott #357 stamps were used on mail, where 1¢ satisfied the postcard rate. Collectors of the day failed to notice the difference between the short-lived experimental stamps and the normal issues, so few were saved.

The 1909 1¢ Franklin on bluish paper is an essential acquisition for those collectors who desire a complete Washington-Franklin collection. Due to the limited number saved and the failed attempt to control shrinkage, well-centered stamps printed on bluish paper are difficult to find. Examples with good centering command a premium price. An examination of the back of the stamp, where the grayish color of the paper can be seen through the gum, helps determine authenticity.

Stamps of 1909 on bluish paper.

MARKET VALUES										
	1920	1930	1940	1950	1960	1970	1980	1990	2000	2007
MINT	$0.20	$1.00	$5.00	$5.00	$8.00	$16.00	$70.00	$75.00	$95.00	$100.00
USED	$0.05	N/A	$5.00	$5.00	$8.00	$15.00	$50.00	$65.00	$100.00	$100.00

Stamps issued to commemorate the Olympic Games are fine additions to both United States and topical collections. The first U.S. Olympic Games stamp was issued in 1932 as athletes gathered in Lake Placid, New York, for the international sports competition. It was the third Winter Games, and the first time the event was held in the United States.

The Lake Placid Chamber of Commerce approached the postmaster of the tiny Adirondack village in 1929 to suggest a stamp to commemorate the upcoming Games. Although initially it was rejected as a suitable U.S. stamp topic, postal officials relented after pressure was brought by New York congressman Bertrand Snell.

Showcasing the most dramatic event of the Winter Olympics, promoters used images of a ski jumper in mid-air to advertise the games. Postal officials decided to follow suit and pictured a stocking-capped ski jumper on the 2¢ stamp. A true action photograph couldn't capture a skier and slope adequately for a stamp, so the designers worked from a sketch of a live model.

The 2¢ Winter Olympic Games stamp was issued on January 25, 1932, just days before the Olympic opening ceremonies. The stamp was sold only in Washington, DC, and Lake Placid, New York, a village of fewer than 3,000 year-round residents. Demand for the stamp was heavy from the moment the Lake Placid post office opened at 7 a.m. until mid-morning, when the entire supply of 400,000 stamps was exhausted. State police were called to control the crowd.

Although it passed the scrutiny of athletes and other dignitaries gathered for the First Day ceremony, postal officials were soon embarrassed to learn that the handsome red stamp design contained an error. Ski jumpers don't use poles, but the athlete pictured on the 2¢ Winter Olympic Games stamp is clearly grasping a pair as he flies mid-air.

The Winter Games returned to Lake Placid in 1980, where a U.S. men's hockey team composed of amateurs and college students defeated the mighty Soviet Union team in what is famously remembered as the "Miracle on Ice." The U.S. team went on to defeat Finland in the final game to win the gold medal.

In 1980 the Winter Games returned to Lake Placid. The U.S. men's hockey team defeated the Soviet Union in a famous match known as the "Miracle on Ice."

	MARKET VALUES									
	1920	1930	1940	1950	1960	1970	1980	1990	2000	2007
MINT			$0.05	$0.08	$0.14	$0.18	$0.35	$0.35	$0.40	$0.40
USED			$0.03	$0.05	$0.12	$0.15	$0.20	$0.16	$0.20	$0.20

INTERNATIONAL CIVIL AERONAUTICS
1903 2¢ 25TH ANNIVERSARY OF FLIGHT

Scott #649 • Quantity Issued: 51,342,273

Although the 1928 International Civil Aeronautics Conference is little more than a footnote in history today, the stamp that was issued to commemorate the event captures the spirit of aviation's "Golden Age."

The conference was held to promote the United States' role as a world leader in aviation. It was scheduled to coincide with the 25th anniversary of Orville and Wilbur Wright's historic first heavier-than-air manned flight, which took place on December 17, 1903. More than 440 delegates from 50 nations attended the Washington, DC, meeting.

One of the primary purposes of the conference was to introduce American aircraft manufacturers to foreign markets. Prior to the symposium, delegates were given the opportunity to attend an international aeronautics exhibition in Chicago. The show featured nearly every American plane currently in production, special exhibits, motors, and accessories.

The 2¢ International Civil Aeronautics Conference stamp was issued on the first day of the summit. A 5¢ stamp depicting a modern plane in the style of Charles Lindbergh's *Spirit of St. Louis* was also issued in conjunction with the conference.

Delegates were treated to a gathering of our nation's most outstanding aviators. In addition to Orville Wright, Amelia Earhart and Charles Lindbergh posed for photographs and mingled with the attendees.

Although the conference was not intended to result in international regulations or agreements, the topics discussed during the three-day event reflected the hurdles that had yet to be overcome: international air transport, airway development, meteorology, communications, aeronautical research and photography, and private piloting.

The 2¢ International Civil Aeronautics Conference stamp depicts the plane the Wright Brothers flew at Kitty Hawk. The name and dates of the conference are inscribed above and below the plane. To avoid overcrowding in the vignette, the U.S. Capitol and the Washington Monument are pictured in place of the words "Washington, DC."

At the close of the conference, guests were transported to the North Carolina site of the Wright brothers' groundbreaking flight, where the cornerstone of the Wright Brothers National Monument was laid.

Scott #650, the 5¢ International Civil Aeronautics Conference commemorative stamp.

	MARKET VALUES									
	1920	1930	1940	1950	1960	1970	1980	1990	2000	2007
MINT	N/A	$0.04	$0.10	$0.18	$0.35	$0.60	$1.00	$1.00	$1.00	$1.00
USED	N/A	$0.03	$0.06	$0.12	$0.30	$0.55	$1.00	$1.00	$1.00	$1.00

FIRST U.S. SE-TENANT
1964 5¢ CHRISTMAS ISSUE
Scott #1254–1257 • Quantity Issued: 351,940,000

Thanksgiving turkey, the Macy's parade, and new Christmas stamps are all harbingers of the holiday season—so much so that it is hard to believe the United States did not always have festive Christmas stamps for postal customers to use on their holiday greeting cards.

The U.S. Post Office Department issued its first Christmas stamp on November 1, 1962. Two years later, great new Christmas holiday designs by Thomas F. Naegele gave the Post Office Department a good reason to try something new.

Naegele came up with four designs—not one—illustrating flora associated with the Christmas holiday. These four designs were accepted, and the 1964 Christmas stamps were produced "se-tenant" (joined together) so that a two-by-two block of four stamps had one of each design. It was the first se-tenant stamp issue the Post Office Department had ever done. Holiday greeting cards sent during the 1964 season were decked with boughs of holly, poinsettia, mistletoe, and pine.

The stamps owed their crisp appearance not solely to great design work, but also to what was then a fairly new method of production using the Giori press. This allowed, in one pass through the press, multi-color printing from the same engraved plate. The United States stamps printed on Giori presses are acclaimed for their sharp detail and outstanding use of color.

In the early 1960s, many of the world's postal administrations began experimenting with methods to speed the processing of their escalating volume of mail. In 1963, the U.S. Post Office Department conducted experiments using automated sorting equipment that scanned letters fed into it. The equipment would seek stamps that had been coated with an ink that glowed when subjected to ultraviolet light. The glowing triggered the machine to turn the letter in the proper position to receive a cancel. The coating printed on the stamps, invisible until exposed to ultraviolet light, is called "taggant" or "tagging."

The 1964 Christmas stamps were released both tagged and without tagging. The tagging experiments proved so successful that today nearly all United States stamps are tagged, assisting high-speed machinery to position, cancel, and sort the mail.

MARKET VALUES										
	1920	1930	1940	1950	1960	1970	1980	1990	2000	2007
MINT						$0.40	$5.00	$1.00	$1.00	$1.00
USED						$0.15	$0.40	$1.00	$1.00	$1.00

FIRST GOVERNMENT-PRODUCED COIL
1908 1¢ BENJAMIN FRANKLIN

Scott #316 • Quantity Known: 25

The 1¢ Franklin sidewise coil stamp is one of philately's greatest prizes. The ornate green stamps are also a direct connection to early-20th-century American innovation. Similar to the Express Mail of today, Scott #316 represents the government's attempt to bolster United States commerce.

Prior to 1908, private stamp-vending companies in the United States had produced the world's first coil stamps. These were quickly placed on mail by means of a specially designed affixing machine. The practice allowed large companies to process heavy volumes of mail quickly. The private coil stamps were created from sheets of imperforate stamps produced specifically for this purpose.

In 1908, the U.S. Post Office Department issued the first government-produced coil stamps. Large sheets of 400 imperforate Series of 1902 stamps were perforated 12 in the horizontal gutters (area between the stamps). The sheets were then cut vertically to form strips of 20 stamps. The strips were pasted into rolls of 500 and 1,000 stamps. As a result of this process, these "endwise coil" stamps are perforated at the top and bottom and imperforate on each side.

The government production of coil stamps was considered to be an experiment, and the distribution was very limited. Most of the 1¢ Franklin coil stamps were used in machines created especially for endwise coils. The 1¢ denomination satisfied the postcard rate, which was an inexpensive method for companies to communicate with their customers.

One year later, the 1908 coil stamps were replaced by the Series of 1908–1909. Due to the limited distribution and short period of use, many collectors of the era were completely unaware of the 1¢ Franklin sidewise coil stamp. Today, only 25 examples are recorded—12 unused pairs and one unused single.

As with many coil stamps, collectors prefer to acquire Scott #316 in pairs as an assurance of the stamps' authenticity. Counterfeits of the rare 1¢ Franklin sidewise coil have been discovered. However, the provenance of the known examples is well established, and collectors interested in purchasing these philatelic gems should expect to see an accompanying certificate.

					MARKET VALUES					
	1920	1930	1940	1950	1960	1970	1980	1990	2000	2007
MINT	N/A	N/A	N/A	N/A	N/A	N/A	$16,000.00	$50,000.00	$100,000.00	$55,000.00
USED	N/A	N/A	N/A	N/A	N/A	N/A	N/A	N/A	N/A	N/A

At the beginning of 1917, much of the world had been at war for more than two years. Austria-Hungary had declared war on Serbia in 1914 after Gavrilo Princip (a Bosnian Serb and, incidentally, the son of a postman) assassinated Austrian archduke Franz Ferdinand and his wife, Sophie. Russia joined the fight on the side of Serbia. In return, Germany declared war on Russia and then invaded Belgium and declared war on France. Then Britain declared war on Germany because of treaty violations. The war expanded to colonial territories in Africa, Asia, and the Pacific. In short, the skirmish between Austria-Hungary and Serbia had escalated into a world war.

The United States had adopted an isolationist policy, but there was growing American sentiment that President Woodrow Wilson should "do something" about the German threat, especially after several American merchant ships were sunk by German U-boats. On April 6, 1917, the United States declared war on Germany and, later, on Austria-Hungary as well.

The first soldiers of the American Expeditionary Force (AEF) arrived in France in June 1917. Eventually the AEF would number four million, many of whom would be called to serve through the Selective Service Act. Efficient postal services needed to be established quickly to maintain good morale.

AEF troops did not get "free franking" privilege until October 1917. Free franking meant that letters inscribed "Soldier's mail" required no additional postage. Most soldiers' letters sent before October 1917 were stamped, and troops purchased those stamps from Army Post Offices (APOs).

The APOs that traveled with the troops as they mobilized needed a convenient method of carrying supplies of stamps. Panes of 100 stamps were too large and prone to damage in the field. The U.S. Post Office Department created AEF booklets of 1¢ and 2¢ stamps for use by the APOs. Each booklet contained 300 stamps. The stamps were produced in panes of 30, ten panes per booklet, with interleaving between each pane. The panes were positioned within green cardboard covers and stapled.

Until recently, it was believed the Post Office Department sent one shipment of booklets to the AEF. Now it is recognized that two shipments were sent, one in July or early August and the second in September. The earliest documented use of a stamp from the 1¢ booklet is on a censored picture postcard postmarked from Army Post Office No. 2 on August 8, 1917. The earliest documented use of a 2¢ booklet stamp is on an envelope postmarked from APO No. 2 on August 7, 1917. The booklet stamps, complete panes from the booklets, and the stamps used on postcards or envelopes are scarce.

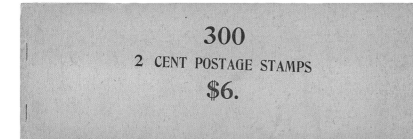

AEF stamp booklet cover.

The earliest documented use of #499f was August 7, 1917.

		MARKET VALUES								
	1920	1930	1940	1950	1960	1970	1980	1990	2000	2007
MINT	N/A	N/A	$225.00	$350.00	$350.00	$1,000.00	$5,500.00	$600.00	$27,500.00	$28,000.00
USED	N/A	N/A	N/A	N/A	N/A	N/A	N/A	N/A	N/A	N/A

COLOR CHANGE CREATES A CLASSIC
1887 3¢ GEORGE WASHINGTON
Scott #214 • Quantity Issued: 20,167,850

As with so many United States stamps within the classic period, it is impossible to talk about one stamp without delving backwards and discussing from whence it evolved. The beautiful 1887 3¢ vermilion Washington is a good case in point.

The *Scott Catalogue* has eight primary catalog numbers for stamps with this design, seven of which are in varying shades of green. There are many other sub-varieties.

The handsome profile of George Washington on a 3¢ stamp originated in 1870. That is when the National Bank Note Co. contracted with the U.S. Post Office Department to produce a new series of stamps. These stamps, commonly known as "large bank notes" because of their size, would replace the 1869 pictorial stamps that were unpopular in their time.

The Post Office Department contracted with three different bank-note printing companies over the course of the next 10 years. Each time the department awarded a contract to a different bank-note company, the stamp dies and plates were transferred to the new contractor. This "round robin" approach was supposed to engender uniformity in stamp design, but as stamp collectors who study this period know, uniformity was not achieved.

In 1873, the contract shifted from the National Bank Note Co. to the Continental Bank Note Co. and "secret marks" were engraved into the stamp dies used to produce printing plates. The secret marks made the stamps different from one another, and thus created collectible varieties.

In 1879, the Post Office Department gave the stamp-printing contract to the American Bank Note Co., who took custody of the stamp dies (which now had secret marks engraved into them) and made more stamps.

By 1880, the American Bank Note Co. observed that some of the plates used to print stamps were no longer making crisp, well-defined images. The engraved dies were re-engraved or retouched, and new printing plates made from them. The re-engraved American Bank Note Co. 3¢ Washington first made its appearance in

the usual blue-green color in 1881 (Scott #207). The shading on the bottom right of the oval that contains the vignette is much thinner than on earlier, similar-looking stamps, and there is a dash under the TS in CENTS.

In 1887, the American Bank Note Co. printed the re-engraved 3¢ Washington in a bright orange color known as vermilion. It is unclear why the drastic color change was made, but the modification created one of the loveliest stamps of the day.

	MARKET VALUES									
	1920	1930	1940	1950	1960	1970	1980	1990	2000	2007
MINT	$0.20	$0.60	$1.00	$2.00	$5.00	$9.00	$30.00	$45.00	$75.00	$80.00
USED	$0.02	$0.03	$0.03	$0.05	$4.00	$7.00	$23.00	$38.00	$55.00	$63.00

NATIONAL BANK NOTE CO.
1865 5¢ NEWSPAPER STAMP
Scott #PR1 • Quantity Issued: Unknown

"Nothing but a newspaper can drop the same thought into a thousand minds at the same moment. A newspaper is an adviser that does not require to be sought, but that comes of its own accord and talks to you briefly every day of the common weal, without distracting you from your private affairs."
Alexis de Tocqueville in Democracy in America, *1835*

In 1865, the United States Post Office Department released stamps that would be used to prove postage had been paid on bulk shipments of newspapers. These large stamps were beautifully designed and printed by the National Bank Note Co. The 5¢ denomination was the lowest of three values released that year. It was printed by typography in blue, and embossed and issued without gum. The overall cameo effect of George Washington in silhouette is very pleasing.

Their use on bundles of newspapers seems degrading, but that was what these stamps were meant to do. However, genuinely used examples are scarce. Cancels, which were painted in big black strokes, have been faked. It is wise to acquire a certificate of genuineness from a reputable expertizing service before making a purchase.

The base of the stamp has a tablet with the words "Sec. 38, Act of Congress Approved/ March 3d, 1863." This act stated in part:

"And be it further enacted that the Postmaster General may from time to time provide by order the rates and terms by which route agents may receive and deliver, at the mail car or steamer, packages of newspapers and periodicals delivered to them for that purpose by the publishers or news agents in charge thereof, and not received from or designated for delivery at any post office."

The 5¢ denomination was released with a colored border on white paper, and another version was made with a white border on yellowish paper. Official reprints were made by the National Bank Note Co. in 1875 of the 1865 5¢ newspaper stamp with a white border. Essays (preliminary, unapproved designs), die proofs, and trial color proofs exist.

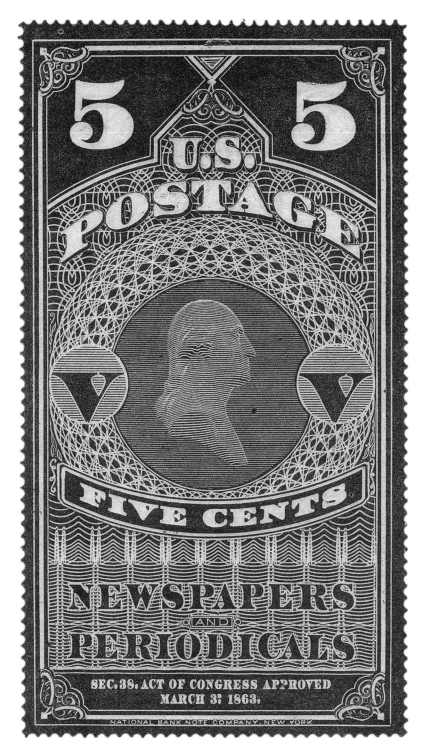

	MARKET VALUES									
	1920	1930	1940	1950	1960	1970	1980	1990	2000	2007
MINT	$20.00	$20.00	$20.00	$18.00	$20.00	$32.00	$90.00	$150.00	$350.00	$625.00
USED	N/A	N/A	N/A	N/A	N/A	N/A	N/A	N/A	N/A	$2,000.00

Each episode of the 1960s spy-thriller television program "Mission: Impossible" began with a scene-setting audio message and the phrase, "This tape will self-destruct in five seconds."

Although it took a little longer than five seconds for the first self-adhesive stamps of the United States to self-destruct, nevertheless, self-destruct they did.

Other countries had been issuing self-adhesive (sometimes called "pressure-sensitive") stamps. The earliest was Sierra Leone in 1964. The 1974 U.S. self-adhesive Christmas stamp showed an antique dove weathervane. The stamp was an experiment, not only in self-adhesives, but also in a new form of precancel. The stamps were die cut with rounded edges and given a security cross-cut in the center of the stamp. If anyone tried to remove and reuse the stamp, the cuts would (theoretically at least) make the stamp pull apart in pieces. Many stamps were reused anyway, causing lost revenue for the U.S. Postal Service. If that wasn't bad enough, the stamps were also considerably more expensive to produce.

These self-adhesive stamps were attached to a shiny-surfaced peelable backing paper before being delivered to postal customers. The self-adhesive stamps were easily removed from the shiny surface and required no moisture to affix them to an envelope. For stamp collectors who wanted to collect the stamps in Mint condition, the backing paper had to stay intact. Hinges would not stick properly, so mounts were needed. For those who wanted to collect the stamps postally used, soaking them off the envelopes in a water bath, as was usual for other stamps, was an exercise in futility.

The problem was the self-adhesive gum that was used. In a surprisingly short amount of time, the gum leaches into the stamp, discolors the paper, turns greasy, and eventually loses its adhesive properties. This is precisely what happened to the 1974 10¢ Christmas precancel. It took a little longer than five seconds for this self-destruction to happen, but nearly all of the Mint stamps whose gum was not removed by an application of naptha (lighter fluid) or some other solvent are stained and have greasy or non-functioning gum.

Nearly every stamp the U.S. Postal Service issues now is self-adhesive. The self-adhesive gum is more stable and collectors of used stamps can almost always soak them in warm water and have them float free of the attached paper. Apparently after the 1974 10¢ Christmas Dove precancel, perfecting self-adhesive stamps became "Mission: Possible."

	1920	1930	1940	1950	1960	1970	1980	1990	2000	2007
MINT							$0.25	$0.18	$0.20	$0.20
USED							$0.08	$0.08	$0.15	$0.20

MARKET VALUES

On April 18, 1906, a devastating earthquake struck San Francisco, California. That quake has now been estimated to have registered between 7 and 8 on the Richter scale. About a quarter of a million people were instantly rendered homeless, and the death toll from the quake was said to be 3,000. The subsequent fires left much of the "City by the Bay" in ruins. Yet, just nine years later, San Francisco hosted a gigantic fair and invited the whole world to come.

The Panama-Pacific Exposition was held from February 20 to December 4, 1915, as a celebration of the opening of the Panama Canal, the 400th anniversary of Balboa's discovery of the Pacific Ocean, and the discovery of San Francisco Bay. More than 18 million people attended the fair that was built on filled-in mud flats at the northern end of the city. Today, that area is known as the Marina District.

The United States Post Office Department issued a set of four commemorative stamps in 1913 to publicize the exposition and the Panama Canal that would be completed in 1914. These stamps were intaglio-printed (from engraving) on single-line-watermarked paper with perforations that gauge 12. They were designed by Clair Houston for the Bureau of Printing and Engraving.

The 10¢ denomination illustrates the discovery of San Francisco Bay in 1769 by Spanish soldier Gaspar de Portolo, who was governor of Baja and Alta California at that time. When first issued, the stamp was printed in a shade of orange-yellow that made the details of its design difficult, if not impossible, to discern. In August of 1913 the stamp was reissued in a darker shade of orange to enhance the design.

The 1¢, 2¢, and 5¢ Panama-Pacific Exposition stamps were released again just prior to the opening of the exposition. The 10¢ value arrived later, in July 1915. These stamps looked like the earlier stamps, but by the time they were printed the Bureau of Printing and Engraving had converted from perforating equipment that gauged 12 holes per 2 centimeters to 10 holes.

A popular way to collect these stamps and those issued for other expositions is on envelopes (covers) that were mailed at the event and have exposition cancellations.

The Panama-Pacific Exposition commemorated the 400th anniversary of Balboa's discovery and celebrated the opening of the Panama Canal. This half dollar (shown enlarged at 1.5x) was minted to commemorate the Exposition.

MARKET VALUES										
	1920	1930	1940	1950	1960	1970	1980	1990	2000	2007
MINT	$0.30	$1.00	$7.00	$10.00	$14.00	$33.00	$150.00	$90.00	$125.00	$135.00
USED	$0.06	$0.25	$1.00	$1.00	$2.00	$6.00	$20.00	$14.00	$20.00	$23.00

PRICE HISTORY OF THE 100 GREATEST

No.	DESCRIPTION	1920	1930	1940	1950	1960	1970	1980	1990	2000	2007
1	**1847 · 5¢ Benjamin Franklin**										
	Mint	$ 15.00	$ 35.00	$ 40.00	$ 63.00	$ 90.00	$ 285.00	$ 3,000.00	$ 4,000.00	$ 5,250.00	$ 6,500.00
	Used	$ 3.00	$ 8.00	$ 9.00	$ 28.00	$ 38.00	$ 60.00	$ 550.00	$ 500.00	$ 600.00	$ 650.00
2	**1847 · 10¢ George Washington**										
	Mint	$ 75.00	$ 150.00	$ 150.00	$ 175.00	$ 275.00	$ 1,300.00	$ 15,000.00	$ 17,500.00	$ 26,000.00	$ 32,500.00
	Used	$ 15.00	$ 35.00	$ 33.00	$ 80.00	$ 110.00	$ 190.00	$ 1,650.00	$ 1,400.00	$ 1,400.00	$ 1,500.00
3	**1918 · 24¢ Jenny Invert**										
	Mint	n/a	$2,000.00	$4,500.00	$4,000.00	$6,000.00	$25,000.00	$115,000.00	$135,000.00	$150,000.00	$ 450,000.00
	Used	n/a	n/a	n/a	n/a	n/a	n/a	n/a	n/a	n/a	n/a
4	**1893 · $5 Columbian Commemorative**										
	Mint	$ 9.00	$ 20.00	$ 65.00	$ 90.00	$ 125.00	$ 450.00	$ 3,100.00	$ 3,000.00	$ 3,750.00	$ 3,500.00
	Used	$ 9.00	$ 20.00	$ 45.00	$ 80.00	$ 110.00	$ 300.00	$ 1,000.00	$ 1,300.00	$ 1,600.00	$ 1,800.00
5	**1869 · 90¢ Abraham Lincoln**										
	Mint	$ 50.00	$ 125.00	$ 175.00	$ 200.00	$ 225.00	$ 700.00	$ 4,250.00	$ 7,000.00	$ 7,500.00	$ 12,000.00
	Used	$ 20.00	$ 50.00	$ 50.00	$ 95.00	$ 120.00	$ 235.00	$ 750.00	$ 1,200.00	$ 2,100.00	$ 2,250.00
6	**1898 · $1 Western Cattle in Storm**										
	Mint	$ 3.00	$ 9.00	$ 35.00	$ 65.00	$ 90.00	$ 265.00	$ 1,400.00	$ 1,325.00	$ 1,250.00	$ 1,800.00
	Used	$ 3.00	$ 9.00	$ 23.00	$ 48.00	$ 75.00	$ 170.00	$ 450.00	$ 475.00	$ 525.00	$ 600.00
7	**1869 · 30¢ Shield, Eagle, and Flag**										
	Mint	$ 15.00	$ 40.00	$ 50.00	$ 88.00	$ 95.00	$ 300.00	$ 1,300.00	$ 2,250.00	$ 5,500.00	$ 8,000.00
	Used	$ 4.00	$ 5.00	$ 9.00	$ 25.00	$ 25.00	$ 53.00	$ 160.00	$ 1,200.00	$ 550.00	$ 550.00
8	**1898 · $2 Mississippi River Bridge**										
	Mint	$ 6.00	$ 17.00	$ 50.00	$ 85.00	$ 115.00	$ 350.00	$ 2,250.00	$ 1,950.00	$ 2,100.00	$ 2,250.00
	Used	$ 6.00	$ 17.00	$ 35.00	$ 60.00	$ 85.00	$ 200.00	$ 650.00	$ 725.00	$ 900.00	$ 1,000.00
9	**1920s · $5 America**										
	Mint	n/a	$ 8.00	$ 8.00	$ 10.00	$ 17.00	$ 32.00	$ 425.00	$ 200.00	$ 150.00	$ 150.00
	Used	n/a	$ 2.00	$ 1.00	$ 1.00	$ 2.00	$ 4.00	$ 10.00	$ 13.00	$ 15.00	$ 15.00
10	**1860 · 90¢ George Washington**										
	Mint	$800.00	$1,000.00	$1,000.00	$ 80.00	$ 125.00	$ 300.00	$ 900.00	$ 1,250.00	$ 2,500.00	$ 3,500.00
	Used	n/a	n/a	n/a	$ 125.00	$ 175.00	$ 800.00	$ 2,000.00	$ 3,500.00	$ 5,500.00	$ 9,000.00
11	**1930 · $2.60 Graf Zeppelin**										
	Mint	n/a	n/a	$ 22.00	$ 63.00	$ 100.00	$ 300.00	$ 2,750.00	$ 1,050.00	$ 800.00	$ 775.00
	Used	n/a	n/a	$ 22.00	$ 55.00	$ 80.00	$ 190.00	$ 1,000.00	$ 550.00	$ 575.00	$ 575.00
12	**1845 · 20¢ St. Louis Bears**										
	Mint	n/a	n/a	n/a	n/a	n/a	n/a	n/a	n/a	n/a	n/a
	Used	n/a	n/a	$2,500.00	$2,500.00	$2,500.00	$11,000.00	$ 18,500.00	n/a	n/a	$ 85,000.00
13	**1845 · 5¢ New York Postmaster Provisional**										
	Mint	$ 50.00	n/a	$ 100.00	$ 100.00	$ 150.00	$ 225.00	$ 550.00	$ 800.00	$ 1,300.00	$ 1,500.00
	Used	$ 30.00	n/a	$ 50.00	$ 55.00	$ 75.00	$ 110.00	$ 300.00	$ 325.00	$ 500.00	$ 525.00
14	**1869 · 24¢ Declaration of Independence**										
	Mint	$ 15.00	$ 30.00	$ 50.00	$ 78.00	$ 80.00	$ 250.00	$ 1,400.00	$ 2,500.00	$ 5,500.00	$ 9,500.00
	Used	$ 7.00	$ 10.00	$ 15.00	$ 38.00	$ 38.00	$ 90.00	$ 375.00	$ 450.00	$ 700.00	$ 775.00
15	**1868 · 1¢ Z Grill**										
	Mint	n/a	n/a	n/a	n/a	n/a	n/a	n/a	n/a	n/a	n/a
	Used	n/a	n/a	n/a	n/a	n/a	$20,000.00	$ 90,000.00	$418,000.00	$935,000.00	$3,000,000.00
16	**1861 · $2 Wells Fargo Pony Express**										
	Mint	n/a	n/a	$ 7.00	$ 7.00	$ 23.00	$ 45.00	$ 125.00	$ 100.00	$ 150.00	$ 175.00
	Used	n/a	n/a	$ 50.00	$ 35.00	$ 50.00	$ 100.00	$ 250.00	$ 250.00	$ 500.00	$ 800.00
17	**1869 · Pictorial Inverts**										
	Mint	$ 50.00		$ 175.00		$ 225.00		$ 4,250.00		$ 7,500.00	$ 12,000.00
	Used	$ 20.00		$ 50.00		$ 120.00		$ 750.00		$ 2,100.00	$ 2,250.00
18	**1869 · 3¢ Locomotive**										
	Mint	$ 1.00	$ 2.00	$ 2.00	$ 4.00	$ 5.00	$ 17.00	$ 85.00	$ 135.00	$ 300.00	$ 350.00
	Used	n/a	$ 0.06	$ 0.15	$ 0.30	$ 1.00	$ 2.00	$ 4.00	$ 6.00	$ 20.00	$ 20.00
19	**1863 · 2¢ Andrew Jackson**										
	Mint	$ 1.00	$ 3.00	$ 3.00	$ 5.00	$ 9.00	$ 27.00	$ 85.00	$ 110.00	$ 325.00	$ 400.00
	Used	$ 0.20	$ 0.35	$ 1.00	$ 2.00	$ 3.00	$ 6.00	$ 14.00	$ 23.00	$ 50.00	$ 65.00
20	**1857 · 1¢ Benjamin Franklin**										
	Mint	n/a	$ 14.00	n/a	$ 16.00	$ 35.00	$ 90.00	$ 300.00	$ 425.00	$ 850.00	$ 1,250.00
	Used	n/a	$ 5.00	n/a	$ 13.00	$ 19.00	$ 35.00	$ 75.00	$ 150.00	$ 240.00	$ 275.00
21	**1901 · 10¢ Fast Ocean Navigation**										
	Mint	$ 0.30	$ 1.00	$ 4.00	$ 8.00	$ 11.00	$ 30.00	$ 175.00	$ 150.00	$ 170.00	$ 175.00
	Used	$ 0.12	$ 0.45	$ 2.00	$ 3.00	$ 4.00	$ 9.00	$ 20.00	$ 22.50	$ 25.00	$ 30.00
22	**1871 · $500 Documentary Revenue Stamp**										
	Mint	n/a	n/a	n/a	$1,250.00	n/a	$ 2,350.00	n/a	n/a	n/a	n/a
	Used	$500.00	$ 700.00	$1,250.00	n/a	$1,500.00	n/a	$ 6,000.00	n/a	$ 5,000.00	$ 13,000.00

No.	DESCRIPTION	1920	1930	1940	1950	1960	1970	1980	1990	2000	2007
23	**1901 · 4¢ Automobile**										
	Mint	$ 0.15	$ 0.35	$ 3.00	$ 4.00	$ 8.00	$ 17.00	$ 95.00	$ 70.00	$ 80.00	$ 100.00
	Used	$ 0.10	$ 0.20	$ 1.00	$ 1.00	$ 3.00	$ 6.00	$ 12.00	$ 13.00	$ 15.00	$ 18.00
24	**1893 · $1 Columbian Commemorative**										
	Mint	$ 3.00	$ 9.00	$ 22.00	$ 45.00	$ 58.00	$ 200.00	$ 1,000.00	$ 1,050.00	$ 1,500.00	$ 1,200.00
	Used	$ 3.00	$ 9.00	$ 20.00	$ 38.00	$ 45.00	$ 130.00	$ 400.00	$ 475.00	$ 650.00	$ 650.00
25	**1869 · 2¢ Post Horse and Rider**										
	Mint	$ 2.00	$ 3.00	$ 3.00	$ 6.00	$ 11.00	$ 33.00	$ 110.00	$ 160.00	$ 600.00	$ 800.00
	Used	$ 0.35	$ 1.00	$ 1.00	$ 2.00	$ 3.00	$ 8.00	$ 20.00	$ 25.00	$ 50.00	$ 100.00
26	**1866 · 15¢ Abraham Lincoln**										
	Mint	$ 13.00	$ 23.00	$ 30.00	$ 30.00	$ 38.00	$ 90.00	$ 325.00	$ 500.00	$ 1,200.00	$ 4,000.00
	Used	$ 2.00	$ 4.00	$ 5.00	$ 9.00	$ 10.00	$ 16.00	$ 40.00	$ 68.00	$ 130.00	$ 200.00
27	**1918 · 24¢ Curtiss Jenny**										
	Mint	n/a	$ 0.85	$ 3.00	$ 5.00	$ 9.00	$ 27.00	$ 200.00	$ 100.00	$ 105.00	$ 120.00
	Used	n/a	$ 0.60	$ 2.00	$ 4.00	$ 7.00	$ 18.00	$ 40.00	$ 35.00	$ 35.00	$ 45.00
28	**1901 · 5¢ Bridge at Niagara Falls**										
	Mint	$ 0.20	$ 0.50	$ 3.00	$ 4.00	$ 8.00	$ 17.00	$ 95.00	$ 82.50	$ 95.00	$ 95.00
	Used	$ 0.15	$ 0.50	$ 2.00	$ 2.00	$ 3.00	$ 7.00	$ 13.00	$ 12.50	$ 14.00	$ 15.00
29	**1962 · 4¢ Project Mercury**										
	Mint						$ 0.08	$ 0.20	$ 0.08	$ 0.15	$ 0.20
	Used						$ 0.04	$ 0.10	$ 0.05	$ 0.15	$ 0.20
30	**1901 · 4¢ Automobile Invert**										
	Mint	n/a	$ 850.00	$1,350.00	$1,000.00	$1,100.00	$ 4,750.00	$ 10,000.00	$ 13,000.00	$21,000.00	$ 35,000.00
	Used	n/a	n/a	n/a	n/a	n/a	n/a	n/a	n/a	n/a	n/a
31	**1901 · 2¢ Fast Express**										
	Mint	$ 0.06	$ 0.10	$ 0.40	$ 0.50	$ 1.00	$ 4.00	$ 18.00	$ 14.00	$ 18.00	$ 20.00
	Used	$ 0.01	$ 0.04	$ 0.05	$ 0.04	$ 0.15	$ 0.35	$ 1.00	$ 1.00	$ 1.00	$ 1.00
32	**1903 · $5 John Marshall**										
	Mint	$ 10.00	$ 28.00	$ 50.00	$ 95.00	$ 135.00	$ 300.00	$ 1,750.00	$ 1,650.00	$ 2,900.00	$ 3,000.00
	Used	$ 7.00	$ 17.00	$ 30.00	$ 60.00	$ 80.00	$ 160.00	$ 500.00	$ 450.00	$ 675.00	$ 750.00
33	**1901 · 1¢ Fast Lake Navigation**										
	Mint	$ 0.05	$ 0.08	$ 0.40	$ 0.45	$ 1.00	$ 4.00	$ 18.00	$ 14.00	$ 18.00	$ 25.00
	Used	$ 0.02	$ 0.06	$ 0.12	$ 0.20	$ 0.40	$ 1.00	$ 4.00	$ 3.00	$ 3.00	$ 3.00
34	**1885 · 10¢ Special Delivery**										
	Mint	n/a	$ 2.00	$ 4.00	$ 5.00	$ 11.00	$ 35.00	$ 200.00	$ 175.00	$ 300.00	$ 500.00
	Used	n/a	$ 0.60	$ 2.00	$ 3.00	$ 5.00	$ 10.00	$ 25.00	$ 20.00	$ 45.00	$ 70.00
35	**1918 · $5 Benjamin Franklin**										
	Mint	$ 8.00	$ 10.00	$ 10.00	$ 15.00	$ 23.00	$ 45.00	$ 400.00	$ 275.00	$ 220.00	$ 250.00
	Used	$ 1.00	$ 4.00	$ 2.00	$ 3.00	$ 4.00	$ 8.00	$ 20.00	$ 20.00	$ 35.00	$ 40.00
36	**1893 · $3 Columbian Commemorative**										
	Mint	$ 6.00	$ 15.00	$ 45.00	$ 70.00	$ 95.00	$ 325.00	$ 1,850.00	$ 1,950.00	$ 2,400.00	$ 1,900.00
	Used	$ 6.00	$ 15.00	$ 33.00	$ 63.00	$ 85.00	$ 225.00	$ 650.00	$ 700.00	$ 1,000.00	$ 1,000.00
37	**1938 · $5 Calvin Coolidge**										
	Mint			$ 8.00	$ 8.00	$ 10.00	$ 18.00	$ 225.00	$ 105.00	$ 95.00	$ 90.00
	Used			$ 1.00	$ 0.60	$ 1.00	$ 1.00	$ 5.00	$ 4.00	$ 3.00	$ 3.00
38	**1920s · 14¢ American Indian**										
	Mint		$ 0.24	$ 0.40	$ 0.45	$ 1.00	$ 1.00	$ 5.00	$ 3.00	$ 4.00	$ 4.00
	Used		$ 0.05	$ 0.10	$ 0.08	$ 0.20	$ 0.30	$ 0.45	$ 1.00	$ 1.00	$ 1.00
39	**1969 · 10¢ Moon Landing**										
	Mint						$ 0.20	$ 0.35	$ 0.20	$ 0.25	$ 0.25
	Used						$ 0.10	$ 0.10	$ 0.15	$ 0.15	$ 0.20
40	**1893 · $4 Columbian Commemorative**										
	Mint	$ 8.00	$ 18.00	$ 50.00	$ 80.00	$ 110.00	$ 400.00	$ 2,850.00	$ 2,750.00	$ 3,250.00	$ 2,600.00
	Used	$ 8.00	$ 18.00	$ 40.00	$ 73.00	$ 90.00	$ 265.00	$ 900.00	$ 1,000.00	$ 1,350.00	$ 1,300.00
41	**1901 · 2¢ Fast Express Invert Error**										
	Mint	$750.00	$1,750.00	$3,500.00	$2,500.00	$3,250.00	$15,000.00	$ 35,000.00	$ 45,000.00	$37,500.00	$ 45,000.00
	Used	n/a	n/a	$2,500.00	$2,500.00	$2,600.00	$ 5,500.00	$ 8,000.00	$ 13,500.00	$15,000.00	$ 55,000.00
42	**1896 · 1¢ Benjamin Franklin**										
	Mint	$ 2.00	$ 6.00	$ 7.00	$ 10.00	$ 18.00	$ 58.00	$ 165.00	$ 225.00	$ 650.00	$ 850.00
	Used	$ 1.00	$ 3.00	$ 4.00	$ 7.00	$ 10.00	$ 20.00	$ 45.00	$ 60.00	$ 140.00	$ 175.00
43	**1873 · 90¢ Perry With Secret Marks**										
	Mint	$ 6.00	$ 12.00	$ 20.00	$ 50.00	$ 70.00	$ 185.00	$ 775.00	$ 1,350.00	$ 2,750.00	$ 2,750.00
	Used	$ 3.00	$ 7.00	$ 9.00	$ 15.00	$ 19.00	$ 40.00	$ 100.00	$ 185.00	$ 250.00	$ 275.00
44	**1901 · 8¢ Canal at Sault Ste. Marie**										
	Mint	$ 0.30	$ 1.00	$ 4.00	$ 5.00	$ 8.00	$ 20.00	$ 125.00	$ 100.00	$ 120.00	$ 130.00
	Used	$ 0.18	$ 1.00	$ 3.00	$ 4.00	$ 6.00	$ 13.00	$ 40.00	$ 50.00	$ 50.00	$ 50.00

No.	DESCRIPTION	1920	1930	1940	1950	1960	1970	1980	1990	2000	2007
45	1869 · 12¢ SS Adriatic										
	Mint	$ 5.00	$ 8.00	$ 12.00	$ 23.00	$ 30.00	$ 90.00	$ 475.00	$ 750.00	$ 1,750.00	$ 2,600.00
	Used	$ 3.00	$ 5.00	$ 5.00	$ 9.00	$ 9.00	$ 19.00	$ 65.00	$ 90.00	$ 150.00	$ 160.00
46	1893 · 1¢ Columbian Commemorative										
	Mint	$ 0.05	$ 0.06	$ 0.30	$ 0.60	$ 1.00	$ 4.00	$ 24.00	$ 17.50	$ 25.00	$ 23.00
	Used	$ 0.01	$ 0.02	$ 0.03	$ 0.03	$ 0.10	$ 0.18	$ 0.25	$ 0.25	$ 0.40	$ 0.40
47	1869 · 15¢ Landing of Columbus (Type II)										
	Mint	$ 8.00	$ 15.00	$ 20.00	$ 28.00	$ 33.00	$ 110.00	$ 550.00	$ 850.00	$ 2,500.00	$ 4,000.00
	Used	$ 2.00	$ 4.00	$ 6.00	$ 9.00	$ 10.00	$ 24.00	$ 80.00	$ 150.00	$ 250.00	$ 275.00
48	1893 · $2 Columbian Commemorative										
	Mint	$ 4.00	$ 8.00	$ 25.00	$ 48.00	$ 65.00	$ 230.00	$ 1,100.00	$ 1,150.00	$ 1,550.00	$ 1,250.00
	Used	$ 4.00	$ 6.00	$ 14.00	$ 32.00	$ 45.00	$ 120.00	$ 350.00	$ 400.00	$ 600.00	$ 600.00
49	1918 · $2 Benjamin Franklin										
	Mint	$ 4.00	$ 9.00	$ 25.00	$ 48.00	$ 75.00	$ 110.00	$ 1,150.00	$ 675.00	$ 625.00	$ 625.00
	Used	$ 1.00	$ 4.00	$ 12.00	$ 24.00	$ 40.00	$ 55.00	$ 140.00	$ 250.00	$ 230.00	$ 240.00
50	1895 · $1 Oliver Hazard Perry (Type I)										
	Mint	$ 3.00	$ 8.00	$ 18.00	$ 70.00	$ 38.00	$ 90.00	$ 450.00	$ 375.00	$ 600.00	$ 700.00
	Used	$ 1.00	$ 1.00	$ 4.00	$ 14.00	$ 9.00	$ 15.00	$ 40.00	$ 45.00	$ 65.00	$ 95.00
51	1934 · 1¢–10¢ National Parks Issue										
	Mint			$ 1.00	$ 2.00	$ 3.00	$ 6.00	$ 12.00	$ 9.00	$ 9.00	$ 10.00
	Used			$ 0.48	$ 1.00	$ 2.00	$ 3.00	$ 6.00	$ 6.00	$ 7.00	$ 7.00
52	1852 · 13¢ Hawaii and United States										
	Mint				$9,000.00	$9,000.00	$16,000.00	$ 30,000.00	$ 45,000.00	$40,000.00	$ 55,000.00
	Used				$4,000.00	$4,000.00	$ 7,500.00	$ 17,500.00	$ 21,000.00	$ 27,500.00	$ 32,500.00
53	1869 · 5¢ George Washington										
	Mint	$ 6.00	$ 10.00	$ 12.00	$ 22.00	$ 29.00	$ 90.00	$ 525.00	$ 775.00		$ 3,250.00
	Used	$ 2.00	$ 4.00	$ 5.00	$ 9.00	$ 9.00	$ 19.00	$ 65.00	$ 100.00	$ 180.00	$ 250.00
54	1861 · 5¢ Jefferson Davis										
	Mint	$ 3.00	$ 12.00	$ 6.00	$ 6.00	$ 13.00	$ 14.00	$ 65.00	$ 140.00	$ 225.00	$ 275.00
	Used	$ 2.00	$ 6.00	$ 8.00	$ 8.00	$ 8.00	$ 14.00	$ 30.00	$ 100.00	$ 150.00	$ 175.00
55	1869 · 10¢ Shield and Eagle										
	Mint	$ 8.00	$ 10.00	$ 14.00	$ 25.00	$ 33.00	$ 98.00	$ 550.00	$ 850.00	$ 1,600.00	$ 2,500.00
	Used	$ 2.00	$ 4.00	$ 5.00	$ 9.00	$ 9.00	$ 19.00	$ 70.00	$ 95.00	$ 140.00	$ 150.00
56	1926 · 2¢ White Plains										
	Mint		n/a	$ 7.00	$ 24.00	$ 60.00	$ 115.00	$ 650.00	$ 350.00	$ 400.00	$ 375.00
	Used		n/a	$ 7.00	$ 23.00	$ 58.00	$ 90.00	$ 400.00	$ 300.00	$ 450.00	$ 450.00
57	1873 · $20 State Department Official										
	Mint	$ 65.00	$ 150.00	$ 150.00	$ 150.00	$ 150.00	$ 225.00	$ 1,350.00	$ 2,250.00	$ 3,250.00	$ 4,500.00
	Used	$ 65.00	$ 150.00	$ 150.00	$ 150.00	$ 150.00	$ 225.00	$ 850.00	$ 1,100.00	$ 1,700.00	$ 3,250.00
58	1967 · 5¢ Accomplishments in Space										
	Mint						$ 0.20	$ 6.00	$ 2.00	$ 1.00	$ 1.00
	Used						$ 0.08	$ 2.00	$ 1.00	$ 1.00	$ 1.00
59	1895 · $5 John Marshall										
	Mint	$ 14.00	$ 28.00	$ 50.00	$ 88.00	$ 110.00	$ 260.00	$ 1,350.00	$ 2,000.00	$ 2,250.00	$ 2,400.00
	Used	$ 7.00	$ 14.00	$ 15.00	$ 33.00	$ 45.00	$ 75.00	$ 225.00	$ 425.00	$ 425.00	$ 650.00
60	1766 · British Revenue Stamp										
	Mint			n/a	n/a	n/a	n/a	n/a	n/a	n/a	n/a
	Used			n/a	n/a	n/a	$ 400.00	$ 1,750.00	n/a	$ 2,000.00	$ 2,000.00
61	1847 · 5¢ Alexandria Blue Boy										
	Mint	n/a	n/a	n/a	n/a	n/a	n/a	n/a	n/a	n/a	n/a
	Used	n/a	n/a	$15,000.00	$15,000.00	$15,000.00	$32,000.00	$ 85,000.00	n/a	n/a	$3,000,000.00
62	1851 · 1¢ Carrier Stamp										
	Mint	$ 1.00	$ 2.00	$ 2.00	$ 2.00	$ 4.00	$ 7.00	$ 15.00	$ 20.00	$ 25.00	$ 25.00
	Used	$ 3.00	$ 5.00	$ 5.00	$ 5.00	$ 7.00	$ 10.00	$ 20.00	$ 20.00	$ 50.00	$ 60.00
63	1842 · 3¢ City Despatch Post										
	Mint	n/a	n/a	$ 25.00	$ 38.00	$ 63.00	$ 110.00	$ 175.00	$ 350.00	$ 400.00	$ 375.00
	Used	n/a	n/a	$ 75.00	$ 75.00	$ 75.00	$ 110.00	$ 125.00	$ 250.00	$ 250.00	$ 275.00
64	1911 · 10¢ Registration Stamp										
	Mint	n/a	$ 0.25	$ 2.00	$ 4.00	$ 5.00	$ 11.00	$ 100.00	$ 55.00	$ 75.00	$ 70.00
	Used	n/a	$ 0.06	$ 0.25	$ 0.40	$ 1.00	$ 1.00	$ 4.00	$ 2.00	$ 8.00	$ 9.00
65	1925 · 5¢ Norse-American Commemorative										
	Mint	n/a	$ 0.40	$ 2.00	$ 4.00	$ 7.00	$ 10.00	$ 33.00	$ 14.00	$ 15.00	$ 12.00
	Used	n/a	$ 0.30	$ 2.00	$ 3.00	$ 5.00	$ 9.00	$ 20.00	$ 11.00	$ 11.00	$ 11.00
66	1986 · $1 Rush Lamp Error										
	Mint	n/a	n/a	n/a	n/a	n/a	n/a	n/a	$ 15,000.00	$15,000.00	$ 22,500.00
	Used	n/a	n/a	n/a	n/a	n/a	n/a	n/a	n/a	n/a	n/a

No.	DESCRIPTION	1920	1930	1940	1950	1960	1970	1980	1990	2000	2007
67	**1895 · $100 Newspaper and Periodical**										
	Mint	$ 40.00	$ 40.00	$ 45.00	$ 27.00	$ 33.00	$ 55.00	$ 300.00	$ 775.00	$ 1,600.00	$ 3,500.00
	Used	$ 10.00	$ 10.00	$ 10.00	$ 13.00	$ 19.00	$ 43.00	$ 150.00	$ 350.00	$ 525.00	$ 2,500.00
68	**1904 · 10¢ Map of Louisiana Purchase**										
	Mint	$ 0.15	$ 2.00	$ 10.00	$ 14.00	$ 25.00	$ 58.00	$ 225.00	$ 115.00	$ 180.00	$ 175.00
	Used	$ 0.01	$ 0.65	$ 3.00	$ 5.00	$ 8.00	$ 12.00	$ 25.00	$ 20.00	$ 28.00	$ 30.00
69	**1879 · 1¢ Postage Due**										
	Mint	n/a	$ 0.20	$ 0.40	$ 0.40	$ 1.00	$ 2.00	$ 12.00	$ 30.00	$ 50.00	$ 90.00
	Used	n/a	$ 0.12	$ 0.30	$ 0.35	$ 1.00	$ 1.00	$ 3.00	$ 5.00	$ 9.00	$ 14.00
70	**1920 · $2 Benjamin Franklin**										
	Mint	n/a	$ 4.00	$ 7.00	$ 14.00	$ 5.00	$ 38.00	$ 400.00	$ 225.00	$ 190.00	$ 160.00
	Used	n/a	$ 0.60	$ 2.00	$ 2.00	$ 5.00	$ 9.00	$ 20.00	$ 25.00	$ 40.00	$ 40.00
71	**1983 · $9.35 Express Mail**										
	Mint								$ 26.00	$ 21.00	$ 23.00
	Used								$ 8.00	$ 14.00	$ 15.00
72	**1907 · 5¢ Pocahontas**										
	Mint	$ 0.30	$ 0.50	$ 5.00	$ 7.00	$ 12.00	$ 30.00	$ 110.00	$ 67.50	$ 135.00	$ 150.00
	Used	$ 0.01	$ 0.25	$ 2.00	$ 4.00	$ 5.00	$ 9.00	$ 24.00	$ 15.00	$ 28.00	$ 30.00
73	**1942 · 3¢ Win the War**										
	Mint				$ 0.08	$ 0.08	$ 0.08	$ 0.10	$ 0.08	$ 0.15	$ 0.30
	Used				$ 0.02	$ 0.02	$ 0.02	$ 0.03	$ 0.05	$ 0.15	$ 0.20
74	**1917 · $5 John Marshall**										
	Mint	$ 8.00	$ 10.00	$ 11.00	$ 16.00	$ 25.00	$ 50.00	$ 375.00	$ 250.00	$ 240.00	$ 220.00
	Used	$ 2.00	$ 2.00	$ 2.00	$ 4.00	$ 7.00	$ 13.00	$ 25.00	$ 32.50	$ 43.00	$ 40.00
75	**1945 · 3¢ Iwo Jima**										
	Mint				$ 0.06	$ 0.09	$ 0.10	$ 0.10	$ 0.08	$ 0.15	$ 0.30
	Used				$ 0.02	$ 0.05	$ 0.05	$ 0.05	$ 0.05	$ 0.15	$ 0.20
76	**1913 · $1 Parcel Post**										
	Mint	$ 2.00	$ 5.00	$ 15.00	$ 25.00	$ 33.00	$ 68.00	$ 275.00	$ 300.00	$ 350.00	$ 375.00
	Used	$ 0.25	$ 1.00	$ 1.00	$ 2.00	$ 3.00	$ 7.00	$ 15.00	$ 20.00	$ 30.00	$ 45.00
77	**1965 · 5¢ Winston Churchill**										
	Mint						$ 0.10	$ 0.12	$ 0.10	$ 0.15	$ 0.20
	Used						$ 0.04	$ 0.05	$ 0.05	$ 0.15	$ 0.20
78	**1933 · 3¢ Byrd Expedition**										
	Mint			$ 0.08	$ 0.30	$ 1.00	$ 0.65	$ 1.00	$ 0.40	$ 1.00	$ 1.00
	Used			$ 0.06	$ 0.20	$ 1.00	$ 0.60	$ 1.00	$ 0.40	$ 1.00	$ 1.00
79	**1875 · 5¢ Zachary Taylor**										
	Mint	$ 4.00	$ 7.00	$ 8.00	$ 9.00	$ 10.00	$ 28.00	$ 110.00	$ 175.00	$ 475.00	$ 850.00
	Used	$ 0.15	$ 0.45	$ 1.00	$ 1.00	$ 1.00	$ 3.00	$ 5.00	$ 9.00	$ 18.00	$ 25.00
80	**1903 · $2 James Madison**										
	Mint	$ 5.00	$ 13.00	$ 25.00	$ 50.00	$ 70.00	$ 150.00	$ 900.00	$ 600.00	$ 1,100.00	$ 1,200.00
	Used	$ 2.00	$ 7.00	$ 10.00	$ 23.00	$ 25.00	$ 50.00	$ 135.00	$ 125.00	$ 170.00	$ 200.00
81	**1993 · 29¢ Elvis Presley**										
	Mint									$ 0.50	$ 1.00
	Used									$ 0.12	$ 0.20
82	**1919 · 3¢ Victory**										
	Mint	$ 0.06	$ 0.12	$ 1.00	$ 1.00	$ 2.00	$ 4.00	$ 11.00	$ 6.00	$ 10.00	$ 10.00
	Used	$ 0.02	$ 0.08	$ 0.25	$ 0.60	$ 1.00	$ 2.00	$ 4.00	$ 3.00	$ 3.00	$ 3.00
83	**1909 · $1 George Washington**										
	Mint	$ 0.12	$ 7.00	$ 15.00	$ 23.00	$ 35.00	$ 75.00	$ 325.00	$ 300.00	$ 500.00	$ 550.00
	Used	$ 0.01	$ 1.00	$ 5.00	$ 8.00	$ 13.00	$ 20.00	$ 45.00	$ 50.00	$ 75.00	$ 100.00
84	**1902 · 4¢ With Schermack Coil**										
	Mint	n/a	n/a	$1,500.00	$1,250.00	$1,500.00	$ 4,350.00	$ 12,000.00	$ 17,500.00	$ 27,500.00	$ 75,000.00
	Used	n/a	n/a	$1,500.00	$ 750.00	$ 850.00	$ 2,350.00	$ 6,000.00	$ 9,000.00	$ 22,500.00	$ 45,000.00
85	**1877 · 5¢ Buffalo Balloon**										
	Mint	n/a	n/a	n/a	n/a	n/a	n/a	$ 4,000.00	n/a	$ 6,500.00	$ 7,500.00
	Used	n/a	n/a	n/a	n/a	n/a	n/a	n/a	n/a	n/a	n/a
86	**1902 · 8¢ Martha Washington**										
	Mint	$ 0.20	$ 0.45	$ 1.00	$ 1.00	$ 2.00	$ 4.00	$ 25.00	$ 25.00	$ 40.00	$ 45.00
	Used	$ 0.02	$ 0.05	$ 0.10	$ 0.12	$ 0.25	$ 0.50	$ 2.00	$ 1.00	$ 2.00	$ 3.00
87	**1908 · 5¢ Abraham Lincoln Imperforate**										
	Mint	$ 0.05	$ 10.00	$ 28.00	$ 73.00	$ 100.00	$ 140.00	$ 525.00	$ 375.00	$ 290.00	$ 240.00
	Used	$ 0.02	n/a	n/a	$ 48.00	$ 65.00	$ 120.00	$ 250.00	$ 150.00	$ 475.00	$ 1,000.00
88	**1959 · $3 Dog and Mallard Duck**										
	Mint					$ 6.00	$ 6.00	$ 55.00	$ 65.00	$ 93.00	$ 120.00
	Used					$ 1.00	$ 1.00	$ 4.00	$ 5.00	$ 10.00	$ 11.00

No.	DESCRIPTION	1920	1930	1940	1950	1960	1970	1980	1990	2000	2007
89	1894 · 50¢ Thomas Jefferson										
	Mint	$ 2.00	$ 4.00	$ 9.00	$ 15.00	$ 18.00	$ 34.00	$ 175.00	$ 160.00	$ 275.00	$ 325.00
	Used	$ 0.30	$ 0.65	$ 1.00	$ 2.00	$ 3.00	$ 5.00	$ 12.00	$ 14.00	$ 20.00	$ 35.00
90	1962 · 4¢ Dag Hammarskjöld Invert										
	Mint						$ 0.12	$ 0.18	$ 0.09	$ 0.15	$ 0.20
	Used						$ 0.06	$ 0.08	$ 0.06	$ 0.15	$ 0.20
91	1909 · 1¢ Bluish Paper										
	Mint	$ 0.20	$ 1.00	$ 5.00	$ 5.00	$ 8.00	$ 16.00	$ 70.00	$ 75.00	$ 95.00	$ 100.00
	Used	$ 0.05	n/a	$ 5.00	$ 5.00	$ 8.00	$ 15.00	$ 50.00	$ 65.00	$ 100.00	$ 100.00
92	1932 · 2¢ Winter Olympic Games										
	Mint			$ 0.05	$ 0.08	$ 0.14	$ 0.18	$ 0.35	$ 0.35	$ 0.40	$ 0.40
	Used			$ 0.03	$ 0.05	$ 0.12	$ 0.15	$ 0.20	$ 0.16	$ 0.20	$ 0.20
93	1903 · 2¢ 25th Anniversary of Flight										
	Mint	n/a	$ 0.04	$ 0.10	$ 0.18	$ 0.35	$ 0.60	$ 1.00	$ 1.00	$ 1.00	$ 1.00
	Used	n/a	$ 0.03	$ 0.06	$ 0.12	$ 0.30	$ 0.55	$ 1.00	$ 1.00	$ 1.00	$ 1.00
94	1964 · 5¢ Christmas Issue										
	Mint						$ 0.40	$ 5.00	$ 1.00	$ 1.00	$ 1.00
	Used						$ 0.15	$ 0.40	$ 1.00	$ 1.00	$ 1.00
95	1908 · 1¢ Benjamin Franklin										
	Mint	n/a	n/a	n/a	n/a	n/a	n/a	$ 16,000.00	$ 50,000.00	$100,000.00	$ 55,000.00
	Used	n/a	n/a	n/a	n/a	n/a	n/a	n/a	n/a	n/a	n/a
96	1917 · AEF Booklet Pane										
	Mint	n/a	n/a	$ 225.00	$ 350.00	$ 350.00	$ 1,000.00	$ 5,500.00	$ 600.00	$ 27,500.00	$ 28,000.00
	Used	n/a	n/a	n/a	n/a	n/a	n/a	n/a	n/a	n/a	n/a
97	1887 · 3¢ George Washington										
	Mint	$ 0.20	$ 0.60	$ 1.00	$ 2.00	$ 5.00	$ 9.00	$ 30.00	$ 45.00	$ 75.00	$ 80.00
	Used	$ 0.02	$ 0.03	$ 0.03	$ 0.05	$ 4.00	$ 7.00	$ 23.00	$ 38.00	$ 55.00	$ 63.00
98	1865 · 5¢ Newspaper Stamp										
	Mint	$ 20.00	$ 20.00	$ 20.00	$ 18.00	$ 20.00	$ 32.00	$ 90.00	$ 150.00	$ 350.00	$ 625.00
	Used	n/a	n/a	n/a	n/a	n/a	n/a	n/a	n/a	n/a	$ 2,000.00
99	1974 · 10¢ Dove Weathervane										
	Mint	n/a	n/a	n/a	n/a	n/a	n/a	$ 0.25	$ 0.18	$ 0.20	$ 0.20
	Used	n/a	n/a	n/a	n/a	n/a	n/a	$ 0.08	$ 0.08	$ 0.15	$ 0.20
100	1913 · 10¢ Panama-Pacific Commemorative										
	Mint	$ 0.30	$ 1.00	$ 7.00	$ 10.00	$ 14.00	$ 33.00	$ 150.00	$ 90.00	$ 125.00	$ 135.00
	Used	$ 0.06	$ 0.25	$ 1.00	$ 1.00	$ 2.00	$ 6.00	$ 20.00	$ 14.00	$ 20.00	$ 23.00
Totals*		$4,778.75	$9,670.19	$39,457.14	$50,066.28	$55,321.25	$162,945.88	$542,663.42	$872,908.86	$1,571,382.87	$7,194,552.25

* Total cost to purchase one of each available stamp in Mint and Used conditions.

Many wonderful stamps deserve to be considered among the greatest of all American stamps. They might be prized because of their great rarity, their historical significance, an intriguing story behind their issuance, or a host of other equally interesting reasons. A few of the most outstanding of these desirable stamps—ones which were ranked high by our voters, but not among the 100 Greatest—are showcased here, and given our honorable mention.

The First United States Postal Card

Postal cards are government-issued rectangular pieces of thick paper or cardboard with postage preprinted on one side. Postal cards are mailed without an envelope and at a lower rate than letters, providing businesses with an affordable means to send brief messages and advertising through the mail. The United States issued its first postal card in 1873, when domestic-letter postage was 3¢. The 1¢ Liberty postal card was distributed in Boston, New York City, and Washington, DC. Printed in brown ink, the buff card features a large United States Post Office Department watermark in its monogram.

The World's First Airplane Stamp

The 25¢ Vin Fiz Flyer, listed as a semiofficial airmail, is the first stamp in the world to depict an airplane. Only 13 of these rare stamps are known. The private and local stamp was produced for letters flown aboard Calbraith Perry Rodger's historic 1911 flight. Flying in a plane named for a new grape-flavored soft drink called Vin Fiz, Rodgers departed from Sheepshead Bay, New York, on September 17, 1911. The inexperienced pilot hoped to win a $50,000 prize offered by William Randolph Hearst, to be awarded to the first person who could complete the first flight across the United States in 30 days or less. Rodger's brother organized the printing of stamps bearing the likeness of a biplane and the inscriptions RODGERS AERIAL POST and VIN FIZ FLYER. The 25¢ denomination paid for a card or letter flown aboard one leg of Rodger's flight. A U.S. postage stamp was also required for delivery via conventional post. Rodgers crashed at least 16 times during his 49-day flight, and lost out on the cash prize. However, he had successfully carried the first transcontinental mail pouch and was met by a crowd of 20,000 people. Rodgers, who had received a mere 90 minutes of flight instruction from Orville Wright and was licensed for only five weeks before his historic flight, was killed in a 1912 plane crash.

The "Lost" Continental Bank Note?

The 24¢ General Winfield Scott is one of the most unique—and controversial—of all U.S. stamp issues. Its very existence was in question for a century, until the Philatelic Foundation certified the only known example. Like the rest of the Bank Note issues, plates for the 24¢ Scott stamp were passed from the National Bank Note Company to the Continental Bank Note Company when the printing contract changed hands. While Continental placed secret marks on the other denominations to distinguish their stamp from National's, they did not do so on the 24¢ and 90¢ stamps. Experts theorized that a sufficient inventory of 24¢ stamps existed at the time, and that Continental didn't print more. In the 1960s, a single example was discovered printed on ribbed paper, indicative of a Continental Bank Note issue. It is the only 24¢ Continental stamp known.

Certified Mail Introduced to Track Important Documents

Certified Mail was introduced on June 6, 1955. It provides the sender with proof of mailing and proof of delivery for First Class mail sent within the United States. The service, which does not offer indemnity for lost mail, is an affordable alternative to Registered Mail. The Certified Mail fee is in addition to the regular First Class rate, whether sent by surface mail, air mail, or special delivery. Certified Mail receipts are kept on file by the United States Postal Service for six months, offering customers a secure record of transactions involving important documents such as legal notices, tax records, and official public notices.

Civil War Coin Hoarding Leads to Postal Currency Stamp

In 1862, the Union's fate seemed uncertain following the Confederate victory in the Battle of Bull Run. The public began hoarding silver and gold coins, fearing that the metal in them would be worth more than the coins' face value. Purchasing everyday items costing less than $1 became nearly impossible. Congress authorized the use of postage stamps to fill the void. Sticky gum on the postage stamps proved impractical, and Postal Currency was approved on July 17, 1862. The gumless stamps were used until October 10, 1863, when the Union began to print Fractional Currency—miniature banknotes with denominations ranging from 3¢ to 50¢.

Stamp Collectors Lead Battle for Lincoln Commemorative

When the Series of 1908–1909 was introduced, officials were flooded with complaints. Fallen president Abraham Lincoln, who had appeared on every ordinary issue since 1866, was excluded from the new series. Congressman and stamp collector Ernest J. Ackerman led a delegation to request a commemorative stamp in honor of the upcoming 100th anniversary of Lincoln's birth. A joint resolution was passed on January 22, 1909, less than one month before the February 12th anniversary. The memorial commemorative was the first of its type to be issued in both perforate and imperforate form. The design, which is based on Augustus Saint-Gaudens's sculpture of Lincoln, is also found on experimental bluish paper.

The First Triangular U.S. Stamp

Although the 1853 triangle stamps issued by the Cape of Good Hope inspired many other nations to follow suit, the United States waited until 1997 to utilize the popular shape. The Pacific '97 Triangle stamps were issued to give publicity for an upcoming international stamp show held in San Francisco. The commemorative stamps picture a sailing ship and a mail stagecoach, which were important 19th-century forms of transportation to and from San Francisco. Panes were printed with 16 stamps (eight of each design), arranged in four blocks of four stamps each. The layout, which resembles a stained glass window, offers a variety of combinations for collectors.

The First U.S. Semi-Postal Stamp

Although semi-postal stamps have been a tradition in other countries for more than a century, the United States issued its first semi-postal stamp in 1998. The non-denominated stamp sold for 40¢, with 32¢ paying the first-class letter rate. The remaining 8¢ helped fund breast-cancer research. Diane Sackett Nannery, a U.S. Postal Service employee and breast cancer survivor, led the battle for Congressional approval of the stamp. Sadly, Nannery lost her personal battle with the deadly disease in 2003. However, the Breast Cancer Awareness semi-postal stamp raised more than $6 million for research in a single year, offering hope to others.

The Orangeburg Coil

The "Orangeburg Coil" is the rarest U.S. coil stamp. It was created exclusively for the Bell Company of Orangeburg, New York, which is how Scott #389 got its name. An unknown number were issued, and to date only 154 genuine examples are known. The Orangeburg coil stamp can be distinguished by its distinctive wavy-line machine cancellation, its unusual deep color, its size, and its single-line watermark paper.

"Most Desirable Non-Error Commemorative Stamp of the 20th Century"

Approximately nine million 10¢ Discovery of San Francisco Bay stamps were issued in 1915 and 1916 with gauge-10 perforations. However, collectors almost completely overlooked the issue and Scott #404 is scarce today. There were a number of factors that led to the collector apathy. The 10¢ Panama-Pacific commemorative had been issued in a pale shade of orange yellow, perforated 12, in 1913, before being quickly reissued in a deeper, more appealing shade of orange. In 1915 the complete set of Panama-Pacific commemoratives was reissued with gauge-10 perforations to strengthen the stamp sheets. Collectors at the time were largely uninterested in adding this third lookalike stamp to their collections, which led renowned philatelic author Max Johl to later call Scott #404 "the most desirable 'non-error' commemorative stamp of the 20th century."

Scarce and Controversial "Legends of the West" Error Sheet

The Legends of the West pane of 20 stamps honors people and concepts associated with the American West. It was the first of the popular Classic Collection series, which features panes of 20 different stamps depicting American subjects topped with a decorative selvage. Shortly after the Legends of the West panes were distributed, authorities learned that the stamp honoring Bill Pickett actually depicted his brother, Ben. The USPS announced that all of the panes would be recalled and destroyed—only to learn that 183 panes had been sold before the official first day of issue, a procedural error that created precious rarities. Soon after, the Postal Service made the controversial decision to sell 150,000 Legends of the West error sheets by mail-order lottery to recoup the printing costs. A historically accurate Legends of the West pane was also released, picturing the real Bill Pickett.

Ultramarine 4¢ Columbian: A Memorable Stamp

The handsome 4¢ Columbian commemorative stamp, Scott #233a, was printed in ultramarine. At least two sheets of 100 stamps each were printed in error in a lively shade of rich blue. Some collectors believe the blue ink used for the 1¢ denomination was mistakenly used for the 4¢ denominations. Others discount the idea. Nearly all who have seen this great rarity agree that the dramatic design, executed in the vivid ink color, is very hard to forget.

Experimental Stamp Deemed Environmentally Toxic

A trio of engineers developed the first automatic teller machine and patented their creation in 1973. Less than 20 years later, ATMs were an important part of American life. In 1990, the Postal Service experimented with a special plastic stamp designed to be conveniently vended from ATMs. The plastic stamp, which featured a stylized American flag printed in panes of 12, was later declared to be toxic to the environment.

America's First Christmas Stamp

The Post Office Department issued its first Christmas stamp in 1962, and a modern holiday tradition was born. The stamp, which pictured a candle and wreath, was well received by the public. In 1964, the popular Christmas stamps were issued as a se-tenant, becoming the first U.S. stamps to be issued in that format. In 1966, the first "Madonna" stamp was issued. To avoid controversy over the separation of Church and State, the Madonna stamps are always based on great works of art that are displayed or owned by entities in the United States. The Madonna stamps were replaced by George Washington praying at Valley Forge in 1977. An uproar followed, and the Madonna stamps resumed in 1978.

The Century of Progress Souvenir Sheet

Shortly after President Franklin D. Roosevelt was sworn in, the avid stamp collector approved two designs to commemorate the upcoming Century of Progress World's Fair. The event was to be held in Chicago. Accordingly, the stamp designs featured historic Fort Dearborn and the expo's Federal Building. The stamps went on sale on May 25, 1933. On July 8, Postmaster General Farley announced that imperforate, ungummed sheets of the Century of Progress commemoratives would be issued in honor of the upcoming American Philatelic Society's annual convention. The Bureau of Engraving and Printing produced the souvenir sheets at its exhibition site in the Century of Progress's Federal Building. Only 456,704 1¢ Fort Dearborn sheets of 25 stamps each were issued, compared to 348 million individual commemorative stamps. In spite of the relatively low number issued, the 1¢ Fort Dearborn souvenir sheet remains moderately priced today.

The Shanghai Overprint

In 1844, the United States was granted rights to conduct business in several bustling Chinese ports. U.S. citizens established settlements on the foreign soil, and a postal agency was opened to meet their needs. At the close of World War I, the American dollar was worth nearly twice that of the local currency. To accommodate patrons who wished to pay with the Maria Theresa thaler (a popular international-trade silver dollar), a surcharge of twice the face value was added to each stamp. The Series of 1917–1919 stamps were overprinted with the word SHANGHAI and the surcharge amount. The Shanghai overprints were sold only at three U.S. postal agencies, and sales ended in 1922.

A Message of Hope for Overrun Nations

As dawn broke on September 1, 1939, Nazi Germany invaded Poland. Acting in concert under secret terms contained in a non-aggression pact of 1939, Germany attacked Poland from the west as Russia invaded from the east. Nazi land, sea, and air forces quickly disabled Poland's air force. Air raids on the capital city of Warsaw began at 9 o'clock. 1.5 million troops swarmed over the border as German planes bombarded Poland's major cities. Nearly 100,000 Poles mounted a stiff resistance for more than a month before they were forced to flee. Poland, the first of many countries overrun by Germany, would remain under Nazi occupation throughout World War II. In 1943, President Franklin Roosevelt authorized a stamp series designed to show support for the 13 countries overrun by Germany. The stamp honoring Poland was issued on June 23, with ceremonies held in Chicago—home to the world's second-largest community of Poles, after Warsaw.

Crime Buster or Cost Cutter?

The 1929 Kansas Overprints are souvenirs of the final days of America's Wild West. Determined to thwart the theft of postage stamps from small, unprotected rural post offices, officials devised a plan to overprint regular-issue stamps to prevent their resale in Eastern markets. Critics charged that this was just a story the bureaucrats wanted the public to believe. Skeptics pointed out that small post offices were required to purchase an entire year's supply of stamps at once under the plan, which cut government distribution costs by more than half. These critics claimed that the overprints were a method to discourage would-be thieves from stealing the huge stockpiles of stamps that would be stored in poorly defended small towns as a result of the cost-cutting program. Postmasters were also confused by the overprints. The experiment was abandoned within one year.

Puerto Rico Overprints Aid American Expansion Efforts

Although it lasted less than six months, the Spanish-American War marked the emergence of the United States as a world power. On December 10, 1898, Spain signed the Treaty of Paris, granting Cuba its freedom and ceding Guam, Puerto Rico, and the Philippines to the United States. After the signing of the treaty,

the use of U.S. money and postage was made official. In 1899, overprinted U.S. stamps replaced the provisional issues that had been used previously. The first Puerto Rico overprints carried the inscription "Porto Rico."

The First U.S. Hologram Stamp

The United States Postal Service sponsored its second international stamp show in 2000. The agency introduced a set of five souvenir panes containing several innovations to commemorate World Stamp Expo 2000, which was held at the Anaheim, California, Convention Center. The series includes the first U.S. hologram stamps, featuring pictures that appear to display iridescent colors and to be three-dimensional when viewed from a certain angle. The $11.75 Space Achievement and Exploration souvenir pane also features the first circular U.S. stamp. Although it satisfied the Express Mail rate in effect at the time, most of the 1.695 million souvenir panes sold likely remain in stamp collections.

The Legendary Marijuana Revenue Stamp

As a valuable crop with a variety of uses, marijuana was excluded from America's earliest drug laws. In 1937, a revenue tax of $100 per ounce was applied to recreational marijuana usage. In addition to the prohibitive tax, applicants were required to provide personal information. Failure to comply could lead to charges of tax evasion. Three decades later, the practice was deemed unconstitutional by the Supreme Court. The $100 Marijuana revenue stamp was virtually unknown in private stamp collections until 2005, when the National Postal Museum sold part of its revenue stamp holdings.

London Prints

In the earliest days of the Civil War, the Confederate government contracted with Thomas De La Rue & Co. of London to acquire the plates and stamps to fill its need until a local printing house could begin production. Known as the "London Prints," the 5¢ Jefferson Davis typography stamp satisfied the 5¢-per-half-ounce rate for letters sent less than 500 miles. The earliest known use of CSA #6 is April 16, 1862. On July 1, 1862, a uniform rate of 10¢ per half ounce was applied, regardless of distance. De La Rue & Co. produced 12 million 1862 5¢ Jefferson Davis stamps.

Mystic Will Buy Your Entire Stamp Collection...

And Pay <u>You</u> More!

We want to buy your entire stamp collection and we'll pay you today's high market prices.

Mystic Stamp Company is America's leading stamp retailer. Every day, thousands of active stamp collectors look to Mystic to supply their collecting needs. So we need a vast supply of stamps to satisfy our customers. And that's why we're willing to pay the highest prices the market will allow for your stamp collection.

Simply put, Mystic has the financial resources to buy all the stamps you have for sale. We'll even write you a check "on the spot" when you accept our offer.

Mystic Stays On Top By Paying More for Your Stamps!

To stay on top in the competitive business of buying stamps, we know you expect top dollar. And Mystic delivers. In fact, we spent over $15 million on stamps last year. I believe this approach to stamp buying has been one of the keys to our success.

We'll Come to You!

Our expert stamp buyers will come directly to you to evaluate a high-value collection. If you're not sure of the value of your stamps, call today for honest advice on the best way to proceed. Because our buyers are always traveling, it can be very easy to set up a visit. Call today.

We Pay More For Your High-Value Stamps!

Call Today
1-800-835-3609

or e-mail us at:
StampBuyer@MysticStamp.com

Mystic Stamp Company
9700 Mill Street
Camden, NY 13316

Mystic
We Pay More For Your Stamps

Jenny
Invert
Plate
Block
World's Greatest Stamp Rarity

100 GREATEST
AMERICAN CURRENCY NOTES

THE "GRAND WATERMELON" NOTE
WORLD'S FIRST MILLION-DOLLAR CURRENCY NOTE

Q. David Bowers and David M. Sundman
Foreword by Chester L. Krause and Clifford Mishler

Hundreds of Full-Color Illustrations
•
Detailed Market Values
•
Fascinating Stories

100 Greatest American Currency Notes is a beautifully illustrated, full-color coffee-table book that explores one of the hobby's hottest collectible fields. Expert dealers, collectors, researchers, and historians have all weighed in on their opinions of the 100 all-time greatest examples of American paper money, including colonial, Confederate, private, and federal pieces. All of the rarities, the classics, and the great works of art are here—and some interesting surprises, too. With an engaging introduction and fascinating essays; plus intricately detailed, high-resolution photos; and historical and current market values, *100 Greatest American Currency Notes* will delight collectors and non-collectors alike.

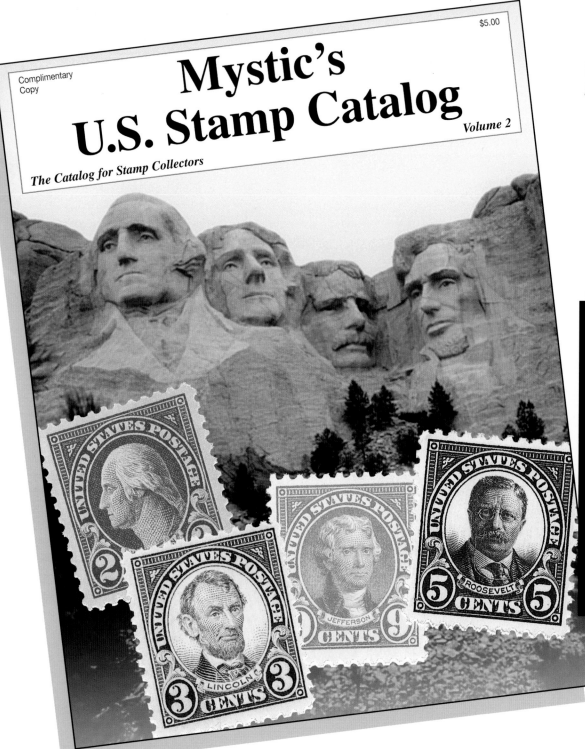

Yours Free – Mystic's Latest United States Stamp Catalog

If you enjoyed the history, romance, and artistry of the *100 Greatest American Stamps*...

...you'll also enjoy these interesting books from Whitman Publishing, available wherever books are sold.

Milestone Coins is a collection of interesting stories and beautiful photographs of 100-plus popular coins and tokens. Your tour guide is Kenneth Bressett, longtime editor of the *Guide Book of United States Coins* (the famous "Red Book") and a legend in coin collecting. The book features ten chapters covering all time periods and geographical areas: The Ancient World; Biblical Coins; The Roman World; Medieval Europe; The World of Islam; Merry Olde England; The Reign in Spain; Cathay and the Orient; Emerging Concepts in Coinage; and Money in America.

Features include full-color, high-detail enlarged and actual-size photographs of each coin; smaller photos of varieties and related issues; market conditions; collecting tips; prices you can expect to pay; a comparative gallery of actual-size images; a bibliography; and an index with more than 800 entries.

Enjoy the art of coinage as never before, and learn some fascinating history along the way, in *Milestone Coins: A Pageant of the World's Most Significant and Popular Money.*

Editors Ira and Larry Goldberg have gathered six of the best numismatic historians to tell the story of Western Civilization, as seen through (and influenced by) some of the greatest coins in the world.

Money of the World: Coins That Made History features nearly 200 magnificent coins in both actual size and grand, full-color enlargement. Every detail is showcased: the totemic animals of ancient Greece; the dramatic portraits of the Renaissance; the defiant emblems of the United States' hard-won freedom. The coins reflect empire and colony, conquest and defiance, revolution and decline, godly splendor and human power. They tell their stories with unique voices. Look and listen, and you will learn the course of human history with a fresh new perspective.

Whitman Publishing, LLC
PUBLISHING SINCE 1934

www.whitman**books**.com